# The Future of Law and eTechnologies

Tanel Kerikmäe • Addi Rull
Editors

# The Future of Law and eTechnologies

Springer

*Editors*
Tanel Kerikmäe
Tallinn Law School
Tallinn University of Technology
Tallinn, Estonia

Addi Rull
Tallinn Law School
Tallinn University of Technology
Tallinn, Estonia

ISBN 978-3-319-26894-1 ISBN 978-3-319-26896-5 (eBook)
DOI 10.1007/978-3-319-26896-5

Library of Congress Control Number: 2016931858

Springer Cham Heidelberg New York Dordrecht London


Printed on acid-free paper

Springer International Publishing AG Switzerland is part of Springer Science+Business Media (www.springer.com)

# Foreword

The rise and rise of the Internet and the digital economy that it enabled had a profound and as yet not fully mapped out impact on our understanding of law and the limits of regulation. Its borderless nature (seemingly) undermined the central regulatory role that the nation-state had since early modernity. The disintermediation that it facilitated subverted existing hierarchies and disrupted well-established business models. We see this tension when the EU tries to subject Google to its data protection regime, when Uber and the sharing economy get into conflict with regulation aimed at traditional services or when peer-to peer file servers call into question the business model of the film industry, especially the practice to release films for specific geographic areas at a time. Information technology did, however, not only create novel legal problems; it also created novel ways of finding out about them. Historically, the World Wide Web was conceived as a communication tool between research institutions worldwide, and without any doubt cross-border, collaborative research benefited greatly from the sharing of data and ideas that the new technology facilitated. Academic knowledge production changed dramatically as a consequence. The ethos of the academy had always been one of disinterested search for the truth. The open sharing of results and ideas, the cooperation across national borders in pursuit of universal truths and allegiance to one's discipline rather than country, creed or race come naturally to such a world view. The new technology proved an ideal environment for such an ethos to flourish, often to the dismay of national governments which did not appreciate their researchers sharing such sensitive knowledge as, e.g., optimal encryption methods with the entire globe. While the eventual pushback was significant, it cannot be doubted that the mode of academic knowledge production changes dramatically through the WWW, making research more open, less parochial and more truly international.

If the Internet thus poses challenges to the international legal order that transcend the capacity of nation-states to regulate them, and if in turn research communities have formed through international collaboration that address the international nature of these problems by forming globally distributed research networks, where then is the place for collections such as the present book, which brings together research and researchers from a specific geographical region? Surely, the legal and technological problems that Estonia faces through the global information revolution cannot be substantially different from those encountered in the US, the UK, China or India? Surely, the geolocation of an academic is much less relevant than the issues s/he studies? In short, is there still a place for books like this that organise around a shared tradition, research culture and national experience rather than, thematically, around topics and questions? Anyone reading through this collection will answer this question with an emphatic yes. It is a display of a rich and varied research culture, substantially connected and interlinked with international debates and informed by international research efforts, sure, but it is also responsive to the particular intellectual traditions and local problems, ideas and solutions of Estonia.

The importance of these distinctive, local research cultures is difficult to overestimate. Technological monocultures are a main reason behind the vulnerability of the Internet to crime and attacks. When almost everyone is using a Windows machine, a virus that attacks this operating system has devastating effect. Similarly, when everybody, everywhere, thinks like Silicon Valley, every flaw in the model, any angle of attack, is multiplied in its effects. Legal systems and legal cultures, as Pierre Legrande observed in the context of the debate on European legal integration, are breeding grounds and test beds for new solutions, regulatory experiments and problem-solving strategies. If they are replaced by (legal, intellectual) monocultures, the diversity, and with that the robustness of the system against attacks, suffers. Only if we maintain the ability to develop and test new ideas in a competitive and diversified environment can we hope to find the answers to the pressing challenges of tomorrow.

In this collection, we can find excellent examples of the dialectic between global problems and discourses and local, specific and particularistic solutions. The paper by Sandra Särav and Tanel Kerikmäe on E-Residency and the Digital Identity Card is an example in point. Estonia is not only a country with an excellent IT infrastructure, where successive governments have pursued aggressively and successfully an agenda of digital growth; it also came up with a unique solution to open up this infrastructure to the world. From this, a new concept was born, the Estonian digital identity or an e-residency that grants its holder a number of rights and privileges unknown, in this form, anywhere else in the world. The intended result will be a massive migration of electronic services to Estonia, where people from all over the globe will be able to store, access and process their documents. At a time when concerns over large-scale migration in the physical world hits the news headlines in Europe once again, e-migration, if the pun is excused, is a novel and radical approach to share local infrastructure globally and to put counties that are geographically at the periphery of Europe at the very centre of its digital agenda. While there is much to be applauded and to learn form this novel approach to grant access to non-citizens to government-funded IT infrastructures, Särav and Kerikmäe's paper is far from self-congratulatory. Rather, it reminds the reader of the various ways Estonia is integrated into an international legal regime, in particular EU data protection law, and how despite the technological soundness of the approach there remain serious legal concerns if this solution as implemented is compliant with these international legal obligations. Lehte Roots and Costica Dumbrava, in their contribution on e-citizenship opportunities in the changing technological environment, take up this theme in their analysis of the changing nature of citizenship and belonging in a digital world. In their analysis, the Estonian e-residency approach can serve as a blueprint for a much more ambitious endeavour, the creation of a European e-citizenship and with that a European e-demos. As a Scot by adoption, I have to mention at this place that Scotland's revolutionary e-petition already now allows all EU citizens (and indeed everybody in the world, including the considerable Scottish diaspora) to become active participants in our political process, by forcing, potentially, Parliament into a discussion. Developments like this in Scotland or the ones described by Roots and Dumbrava for Estonia show once again how small countries at the geographic fringes of Europe can build on their history of geo-migration to lead the way in defining a new form of European identity, where physical distance becomes irrelevant.

Another contribution that expresses particularly well the importance of the local in a time of global threats is the contribution by Norta, Nyman-Metcalf, Othman and Rull that investigates the role of software agents as a tool against Internet scams. We may all have been at one time or the other at the receiving end of a social engineering attack—the sudden and unexpected death of an African dictator who left billions of pounds behind for us to collect, the corrupt bank official who promises a share in the riches of a deceased client with similar name as us or the damsel in distress who needs quick financial support in exchange for undying gratitude are just a few of the cardboard characters that flood our email inboxes or approach us on social networking sites. Can we outsource the handling of this modern-day scourge to computer programs that handle the nuisance on our behalf? The paper shows that these attacks, designed to hit thousands of targets worldwide, are particularly susceptive to a bit of "local knowledge"—for everyone who understands local customs, habits, way of speaking and doing things, they raise immediately warning flags. Because they are premised on a "one size fits it all" approach, they cannot respond well to specific forms of common knowledge or socially shared expectations. The paper gives a fascinating account of how such local knowledge, for instance about typical dating cycles, could be rendered computational to allow software agents to identify and protect against these scams.

The other papers contribute to the rich tapestry of IT law research in Estonia, with often surprising new solutions to problems that capture at the moment worldwide attention. Sepp, Vedeshin and Dutt tackle the thorny issue of IP protection in the age of 3D printing, developing a new solution, secure streaming, that bypasses through technological means the intricate legal issues that the new technology raises while preventing stifling overregulation and overprotection. They do not make an explicit connection to the paper by Särav and Kerikmäe, but we can wonder if between the two a new type of business model could evolve—3D printer farms, located in countries that benefit from a strong IT infrastructure and flexible IT regulation, could become the places where designs from all over the world are printed out and assembled into shippable objects.

How would the German designer of a 3D pattern pay for having it printed, on the request of his Australian customer, in Estonia? Ideally, in a closed system, with a cryptocurrency using a "smart" or "self-fulfilling" contract, thus creating a fully digital value chain. Kõlvart, Poola and Rull in their paper give an overview of the challenges to contract law that self-fulfilling or "smart" contracts pose. Self-fulfilling contracts have recently taken centre stage in the discussion on the AI and law interface, though one could argue that some of the conceptual issues that they raise are as old as the classical vending machine, which would "execute" the contract of buying a bottle of Coke by measuring the weight of the coin and, if appropriate, through a mechanical contraption release the bottle without human interference. More recently, this idea gained renewed interest through the success of using automated agents in contract formation and online auctions. At the same time, digital rights management can also be seen as an early digital form of smart contracting, where the rights transferred through the copyright licence are "self-enforcing" But it was only with the emergence of blockchain technology and cryptocurrencies that all aspects of a contract could become "self-fulfilling". Where in the past humans were still needed to act on the required payment, we can now think of a transaction where all constituent parts are automated, automatic and digital: my CD player profiling my preferences, on that basis buying a music file from another machine, downloading the use rights of the cloud-based file and at the same time transferring the right amount of bitcoin to the seller. The blockchain technology that could one day soon enable these automated contract execution together with digital payment are discussed in the paper by Künnapas. He charters the new legal territory that we need to conquer and the radical challenges to contract law that this new technology poses. Comparing Estonian and UK responses to bitcoin, he reminds us also of the often overlooked issues in the debate, most importantly tax law. The ICT infrastructure that enables all this, after all, is also (partly) financed by our taxes, and global digital markets are particularly prone to separate the beneficiary from such an investment from the taxation that enabled it. The topic of smart contracts, arguably one of the most fascinating developments in recent years, is taken up; a final paper by Solarte-Vasquez, Järv and Nyman-Metcalf analyses the usability factors in smart contracting. As with many other papers in this collection, it shows the benefits of sustained and systematic cross-disciplinary research, collaboration between computer science and law. Their contribution centres around the "Proactive Law Movement", a way to think about the relation between law and technology that has in recent decades gained considerable traction, particularly in northern European countries. While law is often (mis)perceived as the "spoilsport at the party", the incessant raiser of objections, concerns and warnings that get in the way of exciting and beneficial new technologies, proactive law considers law as a beneficial and indeed creative force that increases value and opportunities for companies, individuals and wider societies.

Solarte-Vasquez, Järv and Nyman-Metcalf show how proactive law and transactional design can come together to assist technology-supported smart contracting and finish their analysis with a glimpse on a potential role for visualisation techniques, an avenue pursued, inter alia, by the multisensory law paradigm.

The blockchain technology and the inherent transparency that it brings should facilitate also issues of evidence and proof if a contract fails, or in the case of fraud. Yet for the time being at least, difficult issues of electronic evidence mean that the best substantive laws for the online world will be insufficient unless enforcement catches up. This in turn shifts out attention to the issue of evidence and proof, all to often the poor relation in the discussion on IT law and Internet regulation. Agnes Kasper and Eneli Laurits in their chapter give a broad overview of the various challenges that collecting on digital evidence still faces. They highlight in particular one of the perennial problems of all Internet law—how a private, commercial environment that is nonetheless based on a public infrastructure, and perceived by its inhabitants as a public space, can navigate the tension between private and public laws. This tension is normally discussed for substantive law issues: how can we regulate freedom of speech online when, from the perspective of the citizen, posting on a forum is an activity in a "public space" government by the constitution and its civil rights guarantees, yet from the perspective of the law it will be more often than not a private, commercial place governed by contract law, a shopping mall rather than Speaker's corner? Kasper and Laurits raise this issue in the context of the law of evidence and procedure. In the offline world, we give the police special powers to collect, curate and control physical pieces of evidence. In the online world by contrast, we (inadvertently, necessarily) give similar rights to system administrators and other private parties. What does this mean for the different forms of procedure, criminal, civil and administrative, and are existing legal frameworks that regulate the collection, analysis and admissibility of evidence that rely on a strict police/private dichotomy suitable for the Internet? While Kasper and Laurits give an overview of the issues that digital evidence and proof generate for the law, the contribution by Kristi Joamets focuses on one specific area, the question of digital marriages and divorces. Getting married or getting divorced are administrative actions that in the state of the twenty-first century, citizens expect increasingly to be supported, if not replaced, by online functionality. In 2007, there were predictions that two per cent of all marriages in the US would be conducted in virtual worlds by 2015, and while reality fell well short of this prediction, the concept of virtual marriage took hold. Less adventurous, even traditional marriages officiated by civil servants in brick-and-mortar registry offices increasingly rely on digital licences and certificates. This raises issues about data quality, security and robustness against fraud.

Throughout this introduction, we have seen the extraordinary range of topics that are addressed in this collection, from electronic evidence and the law of civil and criminal procedure to contract law, criminal law, tax law and intellectual property law. We have also seen how each of them is located in the intersection between different discourses, negotiating the tension between the global and the local, international and national, the technological and the legal. It is from these creative tensions that genuinely new solutions and approaches emerge. The papers give an account of the richness and interconnectedness of contemporary debates on cyber governance and technology regulation, and in a microcosm of a national research tradition also of the diversity of voices that need to be heard to find sustainable regulatory solutions for our digital future.

Burkhard Schafer
Professor of Computational Legal Theory
University of Edinburgh
Old College, South Bridge
Edinburgh, UK

Director, SCRIPT Centre for IT and IP Law
School of Law, University of Edinburgh
Old College, South Bridge
Edinburgh, UK

# Contents

# Theorising on Digital Legal (Outer)Space

**Tanel Kerikmäe and Addi Rull**

*Computers are unreliable, but humans are even more unreliable. Any system which depends on human reliability is unreliable.*[1]

**Abstract** Although we tend to agree that innovation makes us smarter, happier and more skilful, securing the process of developing and exploiting technology remains an essential issue. The authors analyse somewhat controversial developments through the viewpoint of legal theorists to find out how to balance the rule of law with the rapidly growing world of tech. What are the guiding principles that have to be followed in the context of unpredictable and socially untested advancements? What are the constitutional dogmas and doctrines that cannot be damaged when adopting the new inventions? Kerikmäe and Rull are convinced that creating a legal principle cannot be rooted in a specific technological advancement and the new technology is not assumed to change the common values. Customer's rights and "dehumanisation" perspectives are discussed in the light of "surveillance state" and "service state" policies. The chapter gives conceptual overview of the contributions in the book and concludes with the statement that "user-centricity" and the common values should be prioritised as once when space law suddenly emerged.

## 1 Who Determines the Principles of eRegulation?

New technologies are making us all smarter—thus, should we worry about combining the existing values to all-embracing dominance of tech? Despite of the prediction of one of the leading priests of technological singularity, Kurzweil, namely that "by 2045, we will multiply our intelligence a billion fold by linking wirelessly from our neocortex to a synthetic neocortex in the

[1] Myrphy/anonymous author at: http://www.murphys-laws.com/murphy/murphy-technology.html.

T. Kerikmäe (✉) • A. Rull
Tallinn Law School, Tallinn University of Technology, Akadeemia tee 3, 12618 Tallinn, Estonia
e-mail: tanel.kerikmae@ttu.ee; addi.rull@ttu.ee



T. Kerikmäe, A. Rull (eds.), *The Future of Law and eTechnologies*,
DOI 10.1007/978-3-319-26896-5_1

cloud",[2] the questions related to reaching this nirvana status for mankind, i.e. securing the process of developing and exploiting technological hype, remain. These questions are mainly related to the question of citizens to become e-citizens (willingness), digital divide, clashes between stakeholders in the market and political arena and—the most intriguing—who decides what is wrong and what is right, i.e. what is legal and why.

In the previous book, "Regulating eTechnologies in the European Union",[3] edited by one of the authors and published last year (2014), the researchers had to admit that various EU agendas and initiatives are still shadowing the unshaped legal framework, proposed methodological approach for better regulation and emphasised the key element in this process—electronic identity for all stakeholders[4] that should rely on legally binding principles.

We may try to find hints from philosophers who have been worried of the nature of law in the context of changing society. However, it might even confuse Hobbs what kind of "new social contract" or "new deal" would be preferred by ePersonalities. The beautiful idea of having a legal system where a regulation is supported and screened by principles needs renaissance in the context of presumed unbalance between law and tech. Before discussing the institutional source of the principles, i.e. *pouvoir constitué*, the collisions behind "right and best" doctrines may arise. Thus, the ultimate distinction between policy and law as suggested by Kelsen in his *Reine Rechtslehre* is not possible anymore as technology develops so much faster than legislator can ever admit and Bentham's utilitarianism should be revisited.

The current collection of articles is Europe oriented and seeks the premature answer to the question: how should the EU legislator represent the interests of EU (e)citizen when regulating e-technologies, assuming that Steve Saxby might be right when saying that "we are in the middle of a global identity crisis"?[5]

As Semmelmann stresses, "different legal principles import different sorts of content into the EU legal system".[6] The author refers to different driving forces, prioritising

(a) rule of law (proportionality and legitimate expectation);
(b) governance (subsidiarity);
(c) fundamental rights (equality, dignity, privacy);
(d) economic policy (free competition).

The most relevant general approach is the rule of law. But what if we have to reconsider even the borders of our current understandings? A good colleague from Folke Bernadotte Academy (FBA) working group, prof. Krygier, suggests that—

[2] Ray Kurzweil's Mind-Boggling Predictions for the Next 25 Years, available at http://singularityhub.com/2015/01/26/ray-kurzweils-mind-boggling-predictions-for-the-next-25-years/ (accessed 15.09.2015).

[3] Kerikmäe (2014).

[4] Kerikmäe and Dutt (2014), pp. 28–29.

[5] Steve (2013).

[6] Simmelmann (2014), p. 321.

before putting the bridle for lawmakers—we should discuss "what we might want the rule of law for".[7] The editors of the current book believe that "the EU's legal framework has been based on economic rationalities rather that were only gradually and selectively replaced by a fully-fledged constitutional approach".[8] It is true that the principles as such, frequently politically highlighted, are mostly not systematically positioned in the EU legal space. Often derived from the so-called primary treaty law and then specified by the CJEU, we may only assume the teleological nature of this process of interpretation—taking account also certain contradictions when mapping the development in case law.

However, the legitimacy of principles in the field of law and technology is something desirable when looking forward to strengthen the legal culture that may face unexpected technological challenges without fear of losing its normative character. Martin, explaining the scholarship of philosopher Raz, emphasises that for legitimacy, the rules (being in the form of norm or principle) must "be identifiable in a content-independent way".[9] It means that the reason for interpreting or creating a legal principle cannot be rooted from a specific technological advancement but should embrace various aspects described above. Totally new and distinct principles, even if they meet new challenges in e-technologies, cannot be justified as the new technology is not assumed to change the common values but should rather be seen as a tool for applying these values. Legitimacy is secured when the rule of law and human rights are prioritised already in the beginning of the process of an initiative that elaborates a set of legal norms.[10]

Austin once determined the law as a tool for the sovereign and expects the citizens to follow the rules habitually. In case we admit that innovators are leading the process, they can be considered the new Leviathan. This is why many IT architects also suppose digital by default! Sometimes the aforementioned slogan is justified by the idea of distributive or social justice—which can also explain citizen–State (EU) relationship as a compensatory or trade-like phenomenon, i.e. individuals lose some privacy but get compensated by other means. For example, by Rudder, Facebook and Google are free services and can be seen as the recompense for taking away some privacy, although he also admits, it would be complicated to find a fair balance[11] between the power line of governments and citizens' rights and obligations.

This approach would be opposed by the theorists who suggest that a coercive role of law ("sanctions" by Hart, the "minimum of liberty" by Kelsen) should derive not from interest groups but from the legislator. At the same time, the so-called technological neutrality principle, as an idealistic justification, means that despite of the type of technology, the principle can be applied to all of them and legal intervention is needed only if the stakeholder is abusing his/her rights.

[7] Martin (2008).

[8] Ibid., p. 322.

[9] Martin (2014), p. 16.

[10] Kerikmäe and Dutt (2014), p. 24.

[11] Rudder (2014), pp. 235–237.

Would "after-adjustment" be a reverse *grundnorm* in the context of a tech regulation? Can it be seen as a self-regulation of the digital world? Martin, analysing the positivism, claims that law has relative autonomy and there are moral values leading the decision-making process of those who apply the law.[12] She asks two relevant questions: "Are we able to conceptualize law without contestable value-laden assumptions? Does an account of the nature of law inevitably rely on assumptions about the human condition?"[13]

Thinking about the history of law—the establishment of the first democratic state or the adoption of the first constitution by *populi* was, at this time, most likely severe violations of *de lege lata*, existing law. These acts were contrary to the beliefs of most of the legal scholars and rather seen as temporary outbursts caused by mismanaged kingdoms. However, the new order was justified only if *demos* agreed upon and obeyed the rules. Social need is a prerequisite of efficient technology and legalisation of new advancements depends on crucial stakeholders: eCitizen, eCustomer.

## 2 Two Colliding Perspectives: Customer's Rights or Dehumanisation?

Leading authors in the field, Hoikkanen et al., are suggesting EU-wide regulatory infrastructure, mapping the multi-level potential policy responses to regulatory challenges.[14] The authors present several relevant choices to be examined when modelling the renewed, "technofriendly" legal space,[15] namely whether

(a) to opt out of general rules or from specific transactions;
(b) to identify "new legal categories" (such as eIdentity) that require special attention;
(c) to recognise that distinction of tech regulation derives primarily from stakeholder's interests (citizens, customers, software developers, etc.), although there can be intersections of layers such as personal, group, space and infrastructure profiles;
(d) to admit the (changing) borderline between the eIdentity allocated by the State and so-called user-chosen identity, indicating clearly the need for a separate level of regulation.

Lips is further developing the concept of citizen (customer)–State/EU relationship as a crucial element in the era of ICT-enabled development and a wide range of public service environments.[16] She unlocks the eIdentity from the perspective of

[12] Martin (2014), p. 51.

[13] Ibid.

[14] Hoikkanen et al. (2010), pp. 2–3.

[15] Ibid.

[16] Lips (2010), pp. 273–289.

(a) what you are (DNA, fingerprints),
(b) what you do (click-behaviour),
(c) what you know (passwords), etc.[17]

Lips also compares the doctrines "surveillance state" versus "service state" with examples: in the case of the first doctrine, the approach of monitoring and social sorting is preferred; in the case of the other, the approach is based on holistic needs of service provision—and ends up with "fair state perspective" with emphasis on client focus and citizens' rights implications.[18] This fits with the theory of Gallings, who, trying to elaborate the minimum requirements of eIdentity management, proposes several safeguards to control state power and secure citizens' rights (authorised personnel, secured storage and handling of data, monitored process, etc.). The sample test question, for example, could here be the following: can the electronic trackers rather be developed to reduce police brutality or discover attempts for possible criminal activities by the citizens?

The EU has certain advantages and disadvantages when it comes to legal history. In the current context, the fact that it is derived from international public law and constitutional law of Member States and it is still a rather young legal system would be an advantage to regulate technological developments in combination with Digital Market and Citizens Europe, contrary to what the United States leading theorists are predicting on eRegulation and eIdentity management issues. Namely, Smedinghoff is quite convinced that the "federated approach" is possible with a focus on private legal framework due to jurisdictional varieties and conflicts and that public law in the field, being "unclear, ambiguous" (and that's why "inappropriate"), can only have supportive role in regulating the area.[19] This angle of view seems to be adopted by the US federal government, which seeks for contractual relationships when solving legal issues related to technologies.[20]

However, even if a fear that technophiles would replace our (offline) rights with digital rights is perhaps even overestimated, the question of endless interpretation of *de lege lata* vs. new digital legal space still exists. Law is a conservative phenomenon, and its developments should be grounded. The "dehumanisation of law"[21] is, a general problem, related to unexpected and unforeseen technological developments directly embracing ourselves. There have been attempts to create principles that are higher than the will of sovereigns in public international law (*ius cogens* or peremptory norms) such as the principle of *hostis humani generis* and universal jurisdiction when fighting against piracy. D'Amato, disappointed of attempts to create such

[17] Ibid., p. 276.

[18] Ibid., pp. 277–279, 285.

[19] Smedinghoff (2012), p. 537.

[20] See, e.g., Warren, Zach. White House to Seek Comment for Government Contractor Cybersecurity Regulations. Legaltech News available at: http://www.legaltechnews.com/id=1202733514159/White-House-to-Seek-Comment-for-Government-Contractor-Cybersecurity-Regulations#ixzz3hZVSK4Na (accessed 15.09.2015).

[21] Gervassis (2012).

supernorms in international law, states: … there are competitive, politically associated, heartless governments who may interpret peremptory norms as they wish (and as the international law is based on consensualism, others have at least consider any of this interpretations of non-democratic international society of States).

The search for neutral and objective legislator in the era of technological triumph is somewhat similar to the *ius cogens* phenomenon. The creator of a discipline named social physics,[22] Alex Pentland from MIT, warns us that the revolutionary technology may also feed "the development of a "big brother" model, with government using the data but denying the public the ability to investigate or critique its conclusions".[23] To avoid cataclysms, he proposes "new deal on data" composing of three rights:

(a) right to possess data;
(b) data owner's control over the use of data;
(c) right to dispose or distribute your data.[24]

The author of the theory is convinced that securing these rights is not complicated. But one should not become worried about the technicalities and price of creating the enforcement mechanisms of these safeguards. The editors rather tend to agree with Haukamäki that "the aspect of social interaction must be on the agenda of social research" and "to practice Social Physics alone means dehumanization …".[25] In other words, legal theorists may get worried about anarchism, which gives the rights to people from an individualist point of view not from the angle of community, legal society or, more precisely, e-legal society composed of eRegulation.

There is a temptation to take both approaches and combine, balance them. Actually, it has been done already. The most comprehensive theory that combines different angles and approaches of law and technology is written almost 10 years ago by Cockfield and Pridmore representing the idea of "Synthetic Theory".[26] The authors claim that instrumental theories are idealistically focusing on technology as a "neutral tool" without taking account of social impacts.[27] The authors refer to the

---

[22] An Interview with Alex "Sandy" Pentland about Social Physics available at: https://idcubed.org/home_page_feature/an-interview-with-alex-sandy-pentland-about-social-physics/ (accessed 15.09.2015).

"Social physics is a new, quantitative science of human society that can accurately predict patterns of human behavior and influence those patterns. Social physics helps us understand how ideas flow from person to person through the mechanism of social learning and ends up shaping the norms, productivity, and creative output of our companies, cities, and societies. Importantly, social physics also tells us how to deal with the privacy concerns raised by big data: by giving individuals more control over data that is about them."

[23] Pentland (2008–2009), p. 79.

[24] Ibid.

[25] Huhtamaki, Antti. Social Physics studies idea flow by big data. A critique of Alex Pentland's new book, p. 5. Available at: http://www.academia.edu/6508962/Social_Physics_studies_idea_flow_by_big_data._A_Critique_of_Pentlands_new_book (accessed 16.09.2015).

[26] Cockfield and Pridmore (2007).

[27] Ibid., p. 476.

idea that traditional approaches should be revisited time to time as technology changes the world and also the mentality of appliers. The authors indicate that new technologies are so different that they can be referred to as post-modernity phenomena.[28]

Authors in this book provide the insight to the discourse of cutting-edge technologies and law from several different angles. Topics discussed here are hotspots in the world of e-technologies. Novel concepts such as e-residency, smart contracting, use of secured streaming in 3D printing, smart agents and others offer opportunities that were difficult to imagine a few years ago, but they also pose challenges to regulators around the world. This is about taking the reader to unregulated territories.

Norta, together with his co-authors, explores the possibilities to use software agents to tackle Internet scams. The scenario of scam described in this chapter is a real-life case study experienced by Katrin Nyman-Metcalf. Scammers around the world have reached out to most of us. In most cases, people recognise a scammer, but many fall for a scam. As scams become more sophisticated, the risk of falling for a scam is rising. Authors suggest that a scam-filtering individual software agent able to recognise a fraud is a solution to the problem.

Särav and Kerikmäe discuss the implications of the concept of e-residency developed in Estonia. Several other countries consider similar developments while closely monitoring how Estonia handles the novel concept of attracting people around the world to benefit from Estonian e-services. We believe that this is just the beginning and soon we will see several countries advancing in the field of e-governance competing against each other in the offering of e-services to the world outside. This is part of a bigger phenomenon where blockchain technologies underlying cryptocurrencies are able to support decentralised autonomous organisations such as Bitnation (www.bitnation.co). These platforms demonstrate the power of social networks, peer-to-peer information production and crowd sourcing.[29] Multinational software companies and governments are investigating possibilities to use the blockchain technologies for governing purposes in the future.[30]

We are moving towards new governing ecosystems, and any new service or functionality developed contributes to the paradigm shift in many traditional practices. Joamets discusses the possibilities of digital marriage and divorce. She points to different legal issues that need to be solved before the digital solution can be legally ascertained. Kasper and Laurits cover the topic of digital evidence. This is an emerging field with many technological and legal challenges. States are increasingly in the need to secure the efficient collection of digital evidence as the use of digital technologies grows exponentially. Roots and Dumbrava discuss the possibility of the model of e-citizenship for Europe.

---

[28] Ibid., pp. 478–479.

[29] See, e.g., Benkler (2002a), pp. 81–107; Benkler (2002b).

[30] See, e.g., The Blockchain is a New Model of Governance. http://www.coindesk.com/consensus-algorithm-and-a-new-model-of-governance/ (accessed 13.09.2015).

Several chapters discuss smart contracting and smart property. Kõlvart, together with co-authors, brings out different understandings of smart contracting and outlines what is necessary for a smart contract to become a legal contract. Künnapas approaches the topic from the Bitcoin perspective, which has become highly controversial, because it is breaking the understandings of how monetary systems should function. There is a lot of legal uncertainty about cryptocurrencies. The blockchain technology may have proven already that a digital monetary system without a centralised state supervision is possible. Solarte-Vasquez et al. propose the concept of transactional design for conflict management and dispute resolution.

Sepp and Dutt have written a chapter together with Anton Vedeshin, who is one of the founders of 3DPrinterOS. This innovative start-up company originating from Estonia develops the operating system for easy and secured 3D-printing. In the future, it may be comparable to what operating systems such as Windows, Mac OS and Android have done with computers and smartphones in terms of functionality and usability. 3DPrinterOS operating system is definitely a frontrunner amongst its peers, but this topic enters into the field of complex legal issues ranging from digital rights management to trademark, copyright and design laws. This chapter is by far one of the few to cover these topics comprehensively.

Today, e-technology and its legal regulation are often unbalanced. So-called e-regulation is left behind as "digital by default" is not really guided by overwhelming concepts that attempt to adjust the (soon)-to-be-true realities with the structural and systematic, sometimes idealistic, world of lawyers. At the same time, in few fields, the legislation is very detailed and does not reach the addressee, especially taking into account the digital divide in the world and in Europe. Seeking for principles, new social contract, *grundnorm*, utilitarism and trying to shape a somewhat conservative legal world with the digital world is a natural attempt to secure rule of law in the changing environment. This is what the current book is made for: the group of researchers, supporting e-development and innovation, remaining critical and analytical. We are trying to avoid the situation that was evident when the space law emerged. There is a certain similarity—unknown scope of issues to be regulated, fragmented and abstract legal acts (sometimes controversial in national level). Now, although the definition of outer space is still not uniformly agreed within international society, it has been concluded by Lafferranderie almost two decades ago that "the space law is no longer the sole prerogative of States".[31] For digital world, the whole development should also follow the ideal of "user-centricity" and the common values. We hope that the current book will wake up the spirit and mind of many, interested in the new era of regulation of e-technology.

[31] Lafferanderie (1997), p. 7.

## References

Benkler Y (2002a) Intellectual property and the organization of information production. Int Rev Law Econ 22:81–107

Benkler Y (2002b) Coase's Penguin, or, Linux and the nature of the firm. Yale Law J 112(3)

Cockfield A, Pridmore J (2007) A synthetic theory of law and technology. Minn J Law Sci Technol 8(2):475–513

Gervassis NJ (2012) The dehumanisation of law: digital reflections. Eur J Law Technol 3(3)

Hoikkanen A, Bacigalupo M, Compano R, Lusoli W, Maghiros I (2010) New challenges and possible policy options for the regulation of electronic identity. J Int Commer Law Technol 5 (1):1–10

Kerikmäe T (2014) Regulating eTechnologies in the European Union. Normative realities and trends. Springer Verlag

Kerikmäe T, Dutt P (2014) Conceptualization of emerging legal framework of E-Regulation in the European Union. In: Kerikmäe T (ed) Regulating eTechnologies in the European Union. Normative realities and trends. Springer Verlag, pp 28–29

Lafferanderie G (1997) Introduction. In: Lafferaderie G, Crowther D (eds) Outlook on space law over the next 30 years. Kluwer Law International, p 7

Lips M (2010) Rethinking citizen – government relationships in the age of digital identity: insights from research. J Inf Polity 15(4):273–289

Martin K (2008) The rule of law: legality, teleology, sociology. In: Gianluigi P, Neil W (eds) Re-locating the rule of law. Hart Publishers, Oxford

Martin M (2014) Judging positivism. Hart Publishing, p 16

Pentland A (2008–2009) Reality mining of mobile communications: toward a new deal on data. In: Dutta S, Mia I (eds) The Global Information Technological Report 2008–2009. Mobility in a Networked World, p 79

Rudder C (2014) Dataclysm: Who We Are (When We Think No One's Looking). Crown Publishers, pp 235–237

Simmelmann C (2014) Legal principles in EU law as an expression of a European legal culture between unity and diversity. In: Helleringer G, Purnhagen K (eds) Towards a European legal culture. Nomos, p 321

Smedinghoff TJ (2012) Solving the legal challenges of trustworthy online identity. Comput Law Secur Rev 28:537

Steve S (2013) The CLSR-LSPI seminar on electronic identity: the global challenges. Presented at the 8th International Conference on Legal, Security and Privacy issues in IT Law (LSPI) November 11–15, 2013. Tilleke & Gibbins International Ltd., Bangkok

# "My Agent Will Not Let Me Talk to the General": Software Agents as a Tool Against Internet Scams

**Alexander Norta, Katrin Nyman-Metcalf, Anis Ben Othman, and Addi Rull**

**Abstract** This chapter takes as its basis an attempted so-called romance scam to evaluate a common modern communications phenomenon: the difficulty in evaluating human interaction online. Without having access to the kind of well-established, largely subconscious physical signals that we use to assess a situation in the offline world, extra vigilance is needed. The option of avoiding online communications is becoming increasingly unrealistic in personal as well as professional situations. The chapter examines whether, in addition to experience, training or personal characteristics, technology can help to avoid risks of misuse of personal data, fraud, extortion and so on.

We argue that the elements that arose suspicions in a sceptical and above-average vigilant Internet user can be generalised and instrumentalised through software agents. This would allow such agents to assist the user and raise the red flags where appropriate, even when the user herself may not detect the danger. Such software agents can be made required companions on cyber journeys, becoming an integral part of communication networks.

## 1 Introduction

The West African scammer who targeted a Professor of Law and Technology in his romantic scam may not have made the most appropriate choice for his purposes but inadvertently provided an excellent case study of a common modern communications phenomenon: the difficulty in evaluating human interaction online. The story of an attempted romance scam can provide a good illustration to a problem that is

A. Norta (✉) • A.B. Othman
Department of Informatics, Tallinn University of Technology, Akadeemia tee 15a, 12618 Tallinn, Estonia
e-mail: alex.norta.phd@ieee.org; anis.ben@gmail.com, http://www.smarpshare.com

K. Nyman-Metcalf • A. Rull
Tallinn Law School, Tallinn University of Technology, Akadeemia tee 3, 12618 Tallinn, Estonia
e-mail: katrin.nyman-metcalf@ttu.ee; addi.rull@ttu.ee

 
T. Kerikmäe, A. Rull (eds.), *The Future of Law and eTechnologies*,
DOI 10.1007/978-3-319-26896-5_2

more and more important in today's Internet-dependent society, where so much interaction is done virtually. Many of us who frequently use electronic communication are aware of the risks of misuse of our personal data that we may be exposed to through virtual communication, social networks and other websites. We also know that being present in the cyberworld is essential for professional and personal reasons. Thus, an assessment has to be made of the risks and benefits. A factor to consider in this context is whether the technology can help us: if IT can mitigate the risks that using this same technology causes.

In the technology environment, traditional social norms and inherent tools to evaluate trust cannot work. Trust is, however, an important commodity for all kinds of interactions. Trust exists in different forms and contexts, like social trust, cultural trust, professional trust and so on.[1] The creation of online trust is of key importance. There are different possibilities to create such trust if technology is properly applied to assist with this. If the problem of scams due to insufficient trust mechanisms is solved on a meta level, this will lead to a positive chain reaction with the whole industry benefitting. Authorities would not need to ask for information from ICT firms—which has negative privacy implications—since the problem would not reach that far.

A sceptical cyberspace user, with good skills and awareness of threats, navigates the treacherous waters of the cyberworld in a cautious and careful manner. He or she notices warning flags that are raised by strange behaviour even without meeting or seeing the person in real life. For a less-skilled person or any person in a setting in which one is less likely to be suspicious, it can be problematic to estimate risks. We are used to noticing what someone looks and sounds like, how they make eye contact, how they answer to our questions and so on. When we interact through a computer, we lack that direct contact and do not even know if the picture we are looking at is the person we are talking to. There is thus a need for different signals to make us wary, but these should be reasonable so as not to hinder all normal interaction in cyberspace. In this article, we examine how technology can help to provide such signals. More specifically, we examine the use of agent technology.[2]

With the increasing role of the Internet for social interaction, there has been for several years an interest in technology to help match people and prevent scams. However, many of the algorithms used to establish characteristics for matching (people with other people or people with goods and services) are rather crude and do not really "understand" people. They can quite easily be manipulated. Collaborative filtering is a popular method used both by, e.g., Netflix for movies and by different dating sites. Constant development refines the algorithms, but what is

[1] The description of trust is inspired by the concept of economic, social and cultural capital discussed by Bourdieu (1986), pp. 241–258. The authors do not attempt to define the concept of trust in this chapter.

[2] The notion "agent" was first used in 1973, Hewitt et al. (1973), pp. 234–245. It is used, e.g., to predict the perception of consumers before the launch of new consumer goods. Gowda (2008), pp. 246–251.

much more difficult is to use technology not just to filter contacts but also to help against the various threats that online interaction may entail.

Given the potential grave impact of scams in cyberspace, the matter is of major legal importance. However, the law has proven to be an ineffective tool in cyberspace. The jurisdictional issue is one major reason for this, as actions and their consequences can be in totally different parts of the world.[3] This means that even if some behaviour is illegal, the chances of taking effective action may be so small that in reality it is the same as if there were no legal consequences imposed at all. This does not mean that there is no room for law. If it is possible to use IT to combat harmful behaviour, the law may be needed to ensure that such IT tools are actually used, obligating relevant websites to apply them. However, if and how legal obligation is the best way to do this should be examined—self-regulation or a business interest from the websites may be a more effective method.[4] If a climate of self-regulation can be created so that the different sites that enable communication as a matter of cause apply certain functions to prevent fraud, this can repair the negative effects of the feeling of impunity that is created by the inefficiency of the traditional legal system.

The importance of privacy and data protection law is growing with the increased use of the Internet in all kinds of situations. The Internet of Things will only exacerbate this, as the many location-based services have already done. Social networks add to the complexity as they rely on the responsible behaviour of users but with few tools to encourage such behaviour. New approaches are needed, and technology can provide important assistance in this respect.

## 2 Setting the Scene

The case on which this study is based took place during about 10 days in November 2014. The initial contact was made on LinkedIn. Whether this was a conscious choice or just a coincidence is not clear. On the one hand, it appears less suitable to use a professional network rather than a dating one for a romance scam. On the other hand, it is normal to connect with strangers on professional networks and many users may be less vigilant, as they are not looking for any intensive personal interaction and only post such information that they want to be in the public sphere. In this case, the intended target indeed presumed that the scammer was a connection of a connection or someone she briefly met in some professional context. After having accepted the contact request, the supposed US General wrote and said he had looked for a contact with the same last name, found the profile and "been swept away by the beauty". This was somewhat unexpected on LinkedIn but amusing more than anything else. However, it already raised a small warning flag because

[3] Chawki et al. (2015), pp. 7–9, 20.

[4] Examples related to Nigeria in Chawki et al. (2015), p. 143.

the type of exchange did not fit with the nature of the network. ***This can be warning flag number 1.*** In this case, the decision to continue communicating was a very conscious one, out of curiosity what would come next, with the targeted victim being aware and interested in Internet-based scams.

Later, the fact that the only common contact was a Latvian female lawyer appeared a bit strange, when it came out that the General had never been to the Baltic States and had no connection with this part of the world. This ***second possible warning sign*** was, however, not strong, for the mentioned reason: that LinkedIn is a network where it is possible to connect freely (and Baltic women are popular also with "real" men looking for contacts!). ***A stronger (third) warning sign*** was that it appeared after 2 or 3 days that the General had deleted his LinkedIn profile. When asked about it, he said that active military personnel are not allowed to be on social networks; he had joined only to look for a friend with a name similar to the target. This was not credible, as he did have a network of about 6–7 people, including the Latvian lawyer acquaintance with a completely different name.

As an intended target of a scam, it is easy with hindsight to claim to have known it was a scam from the very beginning, but this would be an after-construction. In this particular case, the extra vigilance due to personal characteristics as well as professional background may to some extent have been compensated by the fact that having never been on any dating websites or had social Internet chats with unknown people, there were no special expectations. Probably, had the General been a bit more restrained, some of his story would have appeared credible even to a sceptical user. However, with undying love being declared after 2 days, this was definitely a ***strong warning flag (number four)***. Admittedly, not at first being sure it was a scam, but thinking it may be that or a person looking for contact but being a bit weird—most probably not a successful General but an insecure and socially inept person. ***The main warning sign was the intensity of the exchange after such short time***. It is possible that on a dating site, this would not be a warning. After all, if both parties are there to make acquaintances it may make sense to be very direct.[5]

One evaluation that less analytical Internet users may not make was that when deciding to answer the mails of the General, this intended victim did consider whether it was wise to give out personal information and even pictures. However, as for many professional people today, a simple Google search on the last name gives about 77 200 initial results, including in excess of 50 pictures and about 10 videos. A full CV can be found, reports from a number of conferences and projects, academic articles and opinion pieces. This is despite the fact of having activated privacy settings on Facebook, not keeping a blog or actively uploading personal material to other sites. It is a conscious attitude that it is difficult to maintain a high degree of privacy in the current environment, and as it is possible to find interesting

---

[5] There are a number of websites (and Facebook pages) directed at helping detect scams, like http://askville.amazon.com/major-patterns-online-dating-scammer/AnswerViewer.do?requestId=58411519 and http://www.stop-scammers.com/. The problem with such sites is that people will often only consult them after they have already been scammed or possibly when things have gone so far that they are truly suspicious.

professional contacts and opportunities through different Internet-based information, information availability is more as an asset. ***A warning sign (number five)*** was that the General appeared *not* to have Googled his intended victim even if that is today the normal start of any interaction, as he asked about things that easily could have been found out and any legitimate contact would have known. Similarly, ***warning sign number six*** was the lack of information when Googling the General. It was possible to find his father who died in Vietnam but no mention of any of the decorations he received or anything else. One omission was to not do a Google image search early on: when this was later done, several of the photos sent came up with links to scam sites. This tool is, however, not always very useful, as it only shows reliable results for exactly the same or very similar photos, with many false positives. It rather speaks to the amateurism of my scammer that he chose a much-used and much-flagged image.

So the happy relationship developed quickly! We were clearly made for one another. It remained unclear how much analysis had gone into selecting the victim. There are most probably certain criteria used like age, civil status and so on, with more professional scammers most likely putting more effort into finding suitable victims. Presumably, dating sites are prime targets as people on them are actually looking for someone and will not find it strange to be approached in the first place. Also, in a dating context it is normal to gradually find out more and more personal details about one another. Having befriended the actual scammer later, he admitted that he had realised that the targeted profile was not too suitable. The very hasty and rather unprofessional way he tried to conduct the actual scam showed that by this time he was just looking for an end, having accelerated the process too much to make it even remotely credible. He became unsettled by his victim pushing things, which was ***another warning sign (number seven)***: After declaring his love in a few days, he later pulled back a bit when the object of this love started making concrete plans for where and how to meet. This cannot be said to be a very strong warning though, as it could be a completely normal reaction in a genuine dating situation.

Although there were several means to "test" the General, this presupposed that there already were some suspicions (and/or were related to the professional background). As any professor will understand, the copy-pasted love letters were not too difficult to spot! The text was different than his normal style of writing; there were phrases that did not fit at all as they alluded to having spent time together, etc.—***warning sign number eight.*** It took a few seconds by simple Google search to find the texts at a web page supporting people wanting to write love letters. ***Another warning flag (number nine)*** was that the General did not respond to specific questions, for example about Afghanistan where he was posted, where it happened that his intended victim had been. Otherwise, as opposed to what is warned about on the scam-busting sites, the General was quite responsive and did not just spin his same story.

A few other things appeared suspicious early on. They were all connected with facts that did not add up, ***warning sign number ten.*** To spot this, some knowledge, as well as probably awareness to detail, is needed. For example, the General mentioned his daughter who was just about to turn 18 and was studying medicine at Oxford University. At that age, one cannot yet be a medical student apart from in exceptional circumstances, which presumably then would be mentioned. The General also told the sweet story how he met his—now deceased—wife at a Dutch airport and after 2 months of exchanging e-mails, they married. Given that this was the mother of the 18-year-old daughter (plus the two sons killed in the same accident as the wife), it meant this would have been at least nearly 20 years ago. At that time, e-mail was not at all as common as now.

After about 5 days came the first sex. To get nude pictures, for titillation or as some kind of revenge or leverage, may be one reason for a scam, especially targeting young people. Any request for nude pictures or similar should be a ***warning sign in itself (number eleven),*** although there are also bona fide websites where people voluntarily engage in cybersex, so also here the right setting may mean it is not suspicious. In this particular case, the sex episode was a bit out of character with the rest of the conversation and not credible. The General by now felt things were a bit out of hand, so things were going off-script in more than one way: just after the hot sex came the most worrying messages about the sick daughter, which was not very appropriate. The strange order and context of very different interactions was a ***warning sign (number twelve).***

A request for money to help pay for a transport so the General could fly home with a special NATO plane and attend to his daughter's kidney transplant came rather out of the blue and was in no way credible, even to a much less suspicious user. For example, if normally the chat was written in small sentences or even a few words, with attached emoticons, the request for money with the explanation what it was for was in larger text segments, apparently pasted into the Skype chat or at least prepared separately. Style and even layout can be a ***warning sign (number 13).*** However, as mentioned, the scammer had by now given up and just went through the motions. Even if contact was established with him later, he would not divulge all details. It is probable that it was not a spur of the moment initiative by an inexperienced and not-too-expert scammer (as he claimed) but that the person was part of a gang or was running a major operation with many parallel contacts, which in both cases would mean he just decided to go through the motions to "close the case" while pursuing other more promising ones with more care. Normally, much more time is devoted to building up a relationship, sometimes even sending gifts or flowers in the process. This would make most users considerably less suspicious, and it would need to be emphasised clearly that this can actually be a warning sign rather than the other way around, ***warning sign number 14.***

The proof sent by the General to his genuine feelings and honest intentions to pay back the money was very inadequate ***(warning sign number 15)***: to prove that he was military, he sent the public web address of the US Army, and to introduce his superior to whom the money should be forwarded he sent a Wikipedia link to a US General. When asked for different evidence, to talk to him on Skype, to get the mail to his superior or even to get the bank account to where the money should be sent, he immediately detracted and said forget about the money, forget that he asked, etc. Actual requests for money are likely ***warning flags (number 16)*** for many people, although the amount of people who fall for scams indicates that even that is not always the case.

## 3 The Regulatory Situation

A scam such as the one detailed above is possible because the scammer has a possibility to get some basic information about a person, often located in a different country and most likely without there being any personal, physical contact. The more information that is available, the better targeted can a scam be—and thus the more likely to succeed. Many forms of scams and tricks are prevented more through social norms than directly by the legal system. What is different in the cyberworld as compared to the pre-Internet world is that the field of activities for both scammers and legitimate Internet communicators is so vast. Social norms need a small closed homogenous society to function.[6]

### *3.1 Identity Theft and Privacy Violations*

In the scenario described, the only illegal activity actually carried out fully was the scammer pretending to be someone else.[7] He used photographs of a real person but made up the rest of the personality. Whether this is personality theft that would be punishable under the laws of any country depends on many factors. Most likely, it would be very hard to find a punishable offence even without adding the additional complications of jurisdiction. Just lying may be morally wrong, but this does not translate easily to an offence that the legal system can deal with. If the scam succeeds and money is sent, it is a different matter as fraud is a crime in most jurisdictions. In such a situation, the reasons why the matter cannot be effectively dealt with are mainly due to problems of detection and jurisdiction than to any deficiencies in the law. As the difficulties in pursuing Internet scammers are so big and the damage that can be caused so important, there is a great interest in preventing the "final chapter"—the actual scam.

If the scammer has accessed personal data in other ways that just asking and getting information directly from the subject, there may be a privacy violation. However, any such privacy violation is likely to be so small that it is not reasonable to take legal measures because of it and especially it is not reasonable or feasible to create new institutions for the purpose.

[6] See, e.g., Moore (1984).

[7] We are presuming the actions of a human scammer in this chapter. It is unfortunately now technologically possible to have artificial agents fake to be humans in social-media platforms.

It is in the nature of the Internet that it is open and much of the material available on it can be used by anyone. So much information is uploaded that even a person who would try to keep strict control over what personal data is revealed would have a hard time doing this, as there are so many potential ways in which personal information reaches the Internet and very few guarantees against it being used in a different fashion or by different users than what it was intended for.[8] This includes not only personal data that people enter on social networks but also CVs or similar documents entered for work purposes, company websites with pictures and contact details, news items and so on.

There is a lot of case law from different countries as well as from the European Court of Human Rights (ECtHR)[9] on what it is that infringes privacy,[10] for example as concerns taking and using photographs of people. The case law is not consistent, or at least it shows that the actual situation can lead to similar situations being judged differently. A well-known case is *Von Hannover v. Germany*,[11] concerning Princess Caroline of Monaco and the publication of pictures of her in German tabloid press. The German courts focused on whether pictures of her were taken in public places and found that if this was the case, she would normally not have legitimate expectations of privacy. The ECtHR came to a different conclusion and felt her privacy had been infringed, partly as she was not exercising official functions when the pictures had been taken and there was no public importance to the pictures.[12] This differs from other cases where the ECtHR has denied a legitimate expectation of privacy to individuals.

Thus, even using someone else's picture without permission may be difficult to act against through any legal action.

Dealing with the prerequisites of such a scam occurring is at least as important (and potentially more rewarding) as dealing with the aftermath of an already perpetrated scam. To regulate away the problem appears impossible or at least very unlikely. Even if it is possible to identify what elements of a certain behaviour

---

[8] Poullet and Dinant (2010), pp. 60–90.

[9] Case of *Peck v. The United Kingdom* (2003) Application 00044647/98, judgement of 28 Jan. 2003, paragraph 57: "... include activities of a professional or business nature."; Case of *Niemietz v. Germany* (1992) Application 72/1991/324/396, judgement of 16 Dec. 1992, especially paragraph 29; Case of *Halford v. the United Kingdom* (1997) Application 73/1996/692/884, judgement of 25 June 1997, paragraph 44: "... a zone of interaction of a person with others, even in a public context ... ."; Case of *Rotaru v. Romania* (2000) Application 28341/95, judgement of 4 May 2000, paragraph 43; Case of *P.G. and J.H. v. The United Kingdom* (2001) Application 44787/98, judgement of 25 Sep 2001.

[10] As the ECtHR states, e.g., in *Peck*: *The Court has already held that elements such as gender identification, name, sexual orientation and sexual life are important elements of the personal sphere protected by Article 8. The Article also protects a right to identity and personal development, and the right to establish and develop relationships with other human beings and the outside world and it may include activities of a professional or business nature. There is, therefore, a zone of interaction of a person with others, even in a public context, which may fall within the scope of 'private life'.*

[11] *Von Hannover v. Germany* (2005) Application 59320/00, judgement of 24 June 2004.

[12] Barendt (2010), pp. 11–31.

that are or should be illegal and to make rules against this, enforcing these would be very difficult. More regulation is thus not a solution in this situation.

## 3.2 *Dealing with Data*

This brings us back to the question of data. In the interconnected and to a large extent virtual world, data is of great importance and value. This has led to questions of ownership of data. Combinations of huge amounts of data create new data. The better electronic information handling gets, the more value there is to data, as it is possible to make sense of what prior to IT was just white noise. This has led to the discussion about big data and whether governments are the holders and owners of big data or every owner of a component of big data—each individual—has the right to self-determination of information.[13] This expression is still to be filled with relevant content from a legal and philosophical viewpoint.

Clearly, there is a lot of data about individuals that is held by different entities. The responsibility for public entities is of a special nature, as they may require people to provide data,[14] while giving data to private entities is normally voluntary. Admittedly, such voluntariness is sometimes fictional, as it may be necessary to give data to give an essential service, but at least theoretically we can refrain from using a private service while many public ones are obligatory. There is a responsibility for many different organisations that require and deal with information to ensure secure and responsible data handling. This is achieved through the data protection legislation that exists in many countries. It varies if there is specific legislation on data protection or it is seen only as an element of general privacy protection (as protected by instruments such as the 1949 UN Universal Declaration on Human Rights and the 1950 European Convention on Human Rights and Fundamental Freedoms, as well as other regional human rights instruments).

The importance of developments in several European countries, like the first national data protection law in Sweden in 1973, should not be disregarded as the basis for the initiative that led to the enactment of the Convention 108[15] in January 1981 on the European level, pursuing two prime objectives:

> ... [(a)] to protect the privacy rights of individuals in circumstances where information about them is processed automatically. ... [(b) to] facilitate a common international standard of protection for individuals, with the aim that the free flow of information across international boundaries could proceed without disruption.[16]

---

[13] Robbers (2002), pp. 98–105, translated definition of the right to informational self-determination is available at https://www.datenschutz.de/privo/recht/grundlagen/ (accessed 9.07.2015).

[14] See, e.g., Rull et al. (2014), pp. 73–94.

[15] *Convention for the Protection of Individuals with regard to Automatic Processing of Personal Data*, Strasbourg, 28.I.1981, ETS No. 108, entry into force 1.X.1985 (hereinafter as *Convention 108*), available at http://conventions.coe.int/treaty/en/Treaties/Html/108.htm.

[16] Edwards and Waelde (2000), p. 85.

Privacy is protected by many constitutions, and case law has shown that this includes the right to family life, secrecy of correspondence, protection against libel and slander and many other elements of private life, also including data protection. The first international convention to specifically mention data protection is the EU Charter on Fundamental Rights, adopted in 2000 and made legally binding and part of the EU treaties in 2009 through the Lisbon Agreement.[17]

Data protection legislation dates from about the same time as electronic data handling became more common. There is a link between these phenomena, but it does not mean that data protection legislation is linked to only electronic data: it is the content of the data and not its form that should determine if and how it is protected. However, electronic data handling has meant that there are many more ways to make sense of vast amounts of data and new ways to find out things about people.[18] Data protection legislation aims at creating secure ways to handle data so that private information does not get into the wrong hands and can be abused. It is not a question of banning the use of data or imposing secrecy, as it is acknowledged in most societies and especially in democratic rule of law states that information is important and should be available. The first data protection legislation was in Germany, in the state of Hessen in 1970.[19] As mentioned, Sweden was the first country with data protection legislation, enacted in 1973. Following this, in a few years many countries had adopted similar laws.[20] The first international document to make specific mention of data protection was the OECD *Guidelines on the Protection of Privacy and Transborder Flows of Personal Data* of 1980.[21] In December 1983, the German Constitutional Court took a decision in which certain data collection (in the context of a census) was deemed unconstitutional because of privacy violations.[22]

Technology changes the ways data move and is dealt with, but perhaps even more important is the development of the culture of communications and perceptions of what a private and what a public sphere is that has come about in the past decade or so (the post-Facebook era). The interpretation of the right to privacy is in a process of change, even in cases where legislation may not have changed.[23] Indeed, it may be better to deal with new situations caused by new technology through interpretation as any detailed legislation would become obsolete soon after technology changes in any case. Some support for this thinking can be found from

[17] Nyman-Metcalf (2014), pp. 21–35.

[18] Gonzales Fuster et al. (2010), pp. 105–117.

[19] Engel and Keller (2000), pp. 44–52.

[20] Fraunhofer Fokus (2012), pp. 11–12.

[21] Amended in 2013. http://www.oecd.org/sti/ieconomy/oecdguidelinesontheprotectionofprivacyandtransborderflowsofpersonaldata.htm.

[22] Fraunhofer Fokus (2012), p. 12.

[23] Nyman-Metcalf (2014), p. 27.

the ECtHR,[24] which found that a concrete—in the case spatial—criterion for privacy was unsuitable and the criteria should be functional.[25]

What our example illustrates is the problem when a person herself divulges information that may then be abused.[26] Data protection rules seek to deal with cases where others (institutions, authorities) have access to information about persons, whereas more risky situations are created by people themselves voluntarily—but under false pretences—giving information to third persons. It is very difficult to imagine to legally restrict what a person can say about herself.[27] This is not to say that data protection is irrelevant but that it is not the most important remedy to many problems created by modern ways of communicating.

### 3.3 Technology-Assisting Regulation

Anandarajan et al. focus in their research of US data breach notification theory on the routine activity theory developed by Cohen and Felson in 1979. This theory examined the occurrence of crime by looking at the circumstances around incidences of crime instead of focusing on the perpetrators of crime, as was otherwise more common. Cohen and Felson stipulated that there are three necessary elements for a crime to occur: a motivated offender, a suitable target for victimisation and the absence of capable guardians against some violation.[28] Our example is suitable for the routine activities theory as what cyberspace has provided is that if there are people who are motivated to commit crime, they have many more ways of encountering suitable victims in an environment devoid of guardians.[29] Agent technology can provide such guardians.

An agent is an intelligent system that perceives its environment and takes actions that maximise its chances of success. This technology is described below. From a legal viewpoint, the purpose of the agent is to provide the functionality for solving a legal issue like limiting access to personal information in order to achieve better

[24] Case *von Hannover v. Germany* (2004).

[25] Grimm (2009), pp. 11–22.

[26] There is also a link between data theft through hacking or other means and the kind of situations we describe here as people who have their details stolen from various networks are likely to be the subject of scams, have their identities stolen to perpetrate scams and so on. Anandarajan et al. (2013), pp. 51–61.

[27] See, e.g., Westin (1970), pp. 32–37. Four basic criteria necessary for the development of personhood are (1) providing an individual autonomy to control disclosing one's self; (2) giving an individual opportunity for emotional release; (3) permitting an individual to conduct self-evaluation, engaging in moral and creative activities; (4) allowing an individual to share confidences and intimacies in the course of limited and protected communication.

[28] Anandarajan et al. (2013), p. 52.

[29] *Ibid.*

privacy protection.[30] The agent operates in a model in an environment that depicts the living world. In order to be successful, autonomous agents must be able to navigate in an environment that is not just complicated and rapidly changing but also may be hostile. A web-hosting provider might unscrupulously specifically locate all instances of a certain service and replace them with nodes that cheat in some fashion; an autonomous agent must be able to detect such cheating and remove or at least neutralise cheating nodes from the system.

A sociotechnical agent comprises different components with different functions. The sensor gathers events as input that occur in the context of an agent. Those events are split inside the agent between the knowledge base and the controller. The knowledge base comprises entities and facts of the agent's context, together with ontological repositories for allowing a correct interpretation of the stored data. The controller uses the knowledge base for algorithmic processing to perform pseudo-anthropomorphic reasoning that copy humans in a machine-learning way.[31]

The main encompassing control-flow element is a while loop that performs as long as the agent is unfulfilled. Inside the while loop, the agent senses events from the environment and uses that input for updating the knowledge base if needed. These events also serve for the reasoning in the controller in a way that the agent's machine-learning algorithm displays the pseudo-anthropomorphic properties in an artificial intelligence sense. Consequently, the sociotechnical agent projects events through the actuator component onto its contextual environment. The latter reacts to that projection, and the loops start again from the beginning unless a satisfaction occurs of the condition statement in the while loop.

Agents are just one technical tool to deal with problems in the cyberworld. Anandarajan et al. state that technology may guard against crime by increasing the effort which offenders need to expend to reach their victims and carry out the crime. They mention firewalls, filtering technology and similar technology and also point out the possibility of human guardians in the cyberworld, like chat room monitors.[32] There are many technology tools that can mitigate risks.

## 4 An Online-Dating Cycle and Related Metadata Model

The legal deliberations about dating-scam scenarios illustrated above describe a larger trend towards sociotechnical cybersecurity issues that emerge in open heterogeneous social media ecosystems. Note that sociotechnical systems are complex

---

[30] Rull et al. (2014), p. 85.

[31] This is a branch of artificial intelligence and focuses on the construction and study of systems that learn from data. See, e.g., Pak et al. (2012), pp. 1059–1072.

[32] Anandarajan et al. (2013), p. 53.

organisational collaboration designs that recognise the interaction between people and technology for achieving intersecting objectives.[33] Here, a focus is the interaction between complex technical infrastructures and human behaviour. Given the increased complexity of sociotechnical systems, individual users may be overwhelmed and more prone to multi-staged scam attacks. A possible solution to this problem is to design machine-learning-based[34] recommendation systems that warn users with the support of a multi-agent system[35] in time before becoming scam victims.[36]

Machine learning is a specialisation of computer science comprising pattern recognition and computational learning theory in artificial intelligence. Learning algorithms predict events based on large datasets that stem from diverse sources. A multi-agent system (MAS) is a computerised system composed of multiple interacting intelligent agents for solving difficult problems that an individual agent or a monolithic system cannot solve. An agent is an autonomous entity that observes via sensors its environment and projects actions via actuators for achieving goals. Besides sensors and actuators, an intelligent and self-learning agent also comprises a knowledge and a controller component. Note that the conventionally formulated laws and regulations of earlier sections are enforceable by programming them into the controller components of intelligent agents in the form of event-condition-action rules.[37] The latter take into account events from sensors and use the agent-inherent knowledge base to apply the controllers for machine-readable law enforcement that culminate in projections of actions to an agent's context.

With machine learning being a feasible option for a scam-warning system, we must establish a stepwise formalisation approach for enabling the ability of machine processing. Accordingly, Sect. 4.1 puts forward a conceptual dating lifecycle that serves as a taxonomy for organising related cybersecurity patterns. Section 4.2 shows an initial set of patterns for online dating scams that are inspired by Sect. 2 and that we map into the lifecycle taxonomy. Section 4.3 gives an overview of the ontological facts to be considered for pattern-related knowledge capturing. Ontologies describe formally taxonomies and classification networks that capture the structure of knowledge-specific domains where nouns represent classes of objects and verbs represent relations between these objects. Finally, Sect. 4.4 presents selected subsets of the ontological metamodel and we equip them with respective examples.

---

[33] Long (2013).

[34] Huang et al. (2008).

[35] Sterling and Taveter (2009).

[36] Swapneel et al. (2010), pp. 461–472.

[37] Isazadeh et al. (2014), pp. 7847–7857.

## 4.1 Dating Pattern Taxonomy

A pattern is a discernible regularity in a domain that keeps reoccurring in a predictable way and that can be human made. In architecture, a notable example for the development of pattern catalogues from the architecture domain comprises a language for pattern composition to build in a best-practice way towns and buildings to achieve higher quality of life for humans.[38] The idea of patterns is also a powerful concept for computer science where many catalogues exist for software engineering,[39] enterprise integration,[40] cloud computing,[41] different perspectives of workflows and so on. Consequently, we adopt a similar approach for this paper.

The depiction in Fig. 1 shows a lifecycle of engagement for individuals in an online-dating experience. The lifecycle is agnostic to the role of an individual, e.g., a sincere person dating or a scammer who engages in a fraud attack. Arcs denote transitions that lead between states, depicted as rectangles. Briefly, an account is created with an established profile being available to a more or less limited extent online and for appealing to a specific audience, such as mid-aged divorced women. Possible dating partners are either checked based on one criterion, or many criteria in the case of more elaborate evaluation.[42] Eventually, a potential date is chosen, either deliberately based on some criterion (or criteria) or entirely by random. The interaction between the parties commences being either rather well aware of the partner's background or merely limitedly aware, or the interaction starts without any awareness of the counterpart's background at all. While the online dating unfolds, the dating may be halted temporarily, because of a misconduct, shifting to a different dating partner, and so on. However, the interaction may resume again after a period of time.

A partner may eventually suggest to meet in person, and possibly the dating remains in this state. Alternatively, the parties resume online dating again. In both cases, the outcome is either a "successful" completion of the dating process or a failure that has specific semantics in the case of the role a person slips into. For a dating scammer, success means that a targeted malicious outcome has been reached, e.g., transfer of money, extraction of specific information. A failure means that the scam attempt did not unfold as planned, maybe because a recommendation system warns the sincere dater in time. Thus, the dating lifecycle in Fig. 1 serves as a taxonomy for organising and relating honest dating patterns and also so-called anti-dating patterns that represent cybersecurity attacks.

[38] Alexander et al. (1977).

[39] Gamma et al. (1994).

[40] Hohpe and Woolf (2004).

[41] Leymann et al. (2014).

[42] JingMin et al. (2015), pp. 216–236.

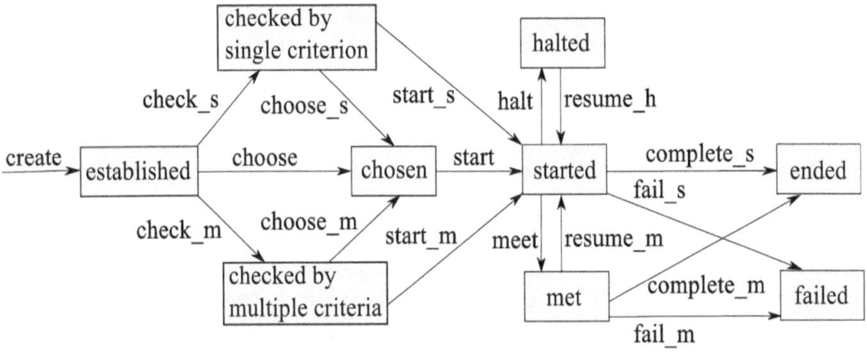


**Fig. 1** A lifecycle of online dating that forms a taxonomy for pattern sets of different perspectives, including cybersecurity

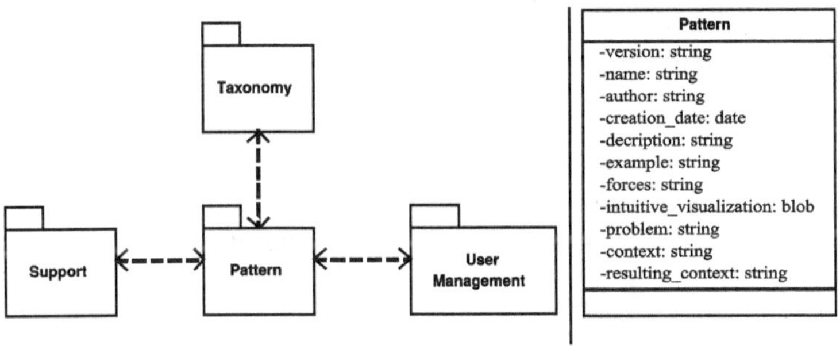


**Fig. 2** Packages with their dependencies and the Pattern-class attributes (*Ibid.*)

## 4.2 *Pattern Mapping*

The pattern examples from Sect. 2 we map into the taxonomy of Fig. 1. In order to do that, an extension[43] of the approach is necessary with respect to the relationship between the taxonomy, patterns and their context. Figure 2 shows to the left side a model of packages that are related to each other. These packages encapsulate classes that we explain in Sect. 4.2.1. After that, it is possible to specify in Sect. 4.2.2 a first set of pattern examples and, finally, to position the patterns in Sect. 4.2.3 in the logical taxonomy space.

### 4.2.1 The Pattern Context

The centre of the package model[44] is named *Pattern*, which contains classes to capture information for pattern specification. The *Taxonomy* package that relates to

[43] Norta et al. (2006), pp. 834–843.

[44] *Ibid.*

Fig. 2, contained classes are capture information online-dating perspectives, e.g., benevolent dating patterns versus anti-patterns in the realm of cybersecurity scams. Thus, this package contains classes that create a taxonomy into which patterns can be embedded. The *Support* package encapsulates classes for managing information about technologies that support patterns. Finally, the *User Management* package captures information of different users of the pattern repository, e.g., administrator, reviewer, pattern submitter and so on.

On the right side of Fig. 2, the core class of the *Pattern* package depicts the equally named *Pattern* class. The attributes of this class comprise the description template of a pattern specification. A pattern has a *version* and a meaningful *name*. Furthermore, a pattern has an *author* and a *creation date* for every *version*. The description of a pattern mentions the inherent pattern properties and describes their relationships for which the metadata elements of Sect. 4.3 are relevant. Furthermore, the *intuitive visualization* contains a model to support the comprehensibility of the pattern description. The *context* describes conflicting environmental objectives and their constraints. The idea is that a pattern application in a context yields in an alignment of objectives. The *forces* describe trade-offs, goals and constraints, motivating factors and concerns for pattern application that may prevent reaching a post-condition. Next, the *context* states a precondition that is the initial configuration of a system before pattern application. On the other hand, the *problem* of a pattern describes the scenario of pattern application. Finally, the *resulting context* describes the post-condition with possible side effects of pattern application.

#### 4.2.2 Pattern Specifications

The so-called set of warning flags in Sect. 2 we position into the taxonomy depicted in Fig. 2 and also translate them as far as possible to pattern specifications in adherence to the section above. The sequence of pattern specifications corresponds to the listing sequence of the Sect. 2 warning flags, while Patterns 17 till 19 are additions. In this initial specification of patterns, we omit giving intuitive visualisations.

**1. Pattern: (Name: Wrong social network) Version:** 0.1 **Author:** Alex Norta
**Date:**
**Description:** The purpose of an online communication platform does not match with the nature of interaction.
**Example:** On a professional networking website, one user indicates an intimate attraction towards another user.
**Forces:** A purpose mismatch is undetectable because the semantic vocabulary for a platform's purpose and inappropriate communication does not cover the most relevant terminology.
**Context:** Sincere users who network with professional objectives are caught off guard by interactions with a romantic intent. The profile information is input to develop a profile that allows for the development of a scam attack. A professional

social media gives the scam attack an unusual cover as users are expected to behave in a sincere and trustworthy way.
**Problem:** The semantic clarification of a communication platform's purpose and the content of user interaction must yield a mismatch.
**Resulting context:** A sincere user receives a warning that the content of an interaction is a mismatch with the platform purpose.

**2. Pattern: (Name: Geo-spatial connection) Version:** 0.1 **Author:** Alex Norta
**Date:**
**Description:** A scammer indicates in a communication either a direct or transitive location relationship with a sincere user.
**Example:** An Estonian user of a professional website who is sincere is connected with a Latvian user and a scammer unjustifiably claims to know the latter person.
**Forces:** It is technically not possible to check the validity of geo-spatial claims.
**Context:** The scammer uses pretended or real-location familiarity to create relatedness with a sincere user.
**Problem:** The establishment of relationships between elements that comprise geo-spatial information on a user profile fails to reveal false-related claims.
**Resulting context:** Invalid geo-spatial claims that do not match with the background of a scammer are established.

**3. Pattern (Name: Fresh accounts) Version:** 0.1 **Author:** Alex Norta & Anis Ben Othman
**Date:**
**Description:** Within a short period of establishing a connection between a sincere user and a scammer, the latter profile is deleted under which the initial communication establishment is accepted by the former.
**Example:** A LinkedIn scammer profile does not last long.
**Forces:** Either LinkedIn agents detect and delete the fake profiles or the scammer wants to erase clues that would allow detecting the identity, e.g., through tracking down the IP address.
**Context:** The scammer issues a profile with personal information that is either partially or completely fake.
**Problem:** The scammer profile can't be tracked back for a long period of time.
**Resulting context:** The profile deletion is performed, and it is not possible to trace back by any means to the scammer's information.

**4. Pattern (Name: Affection declaration) Version:** 0.1 **Author:** Alex Norta
**Date:**
**Description:** The scammer expresses in an untypically intense manner affection towards the sincere user only a short time after the first online encounter.
**Example:** An intense declaration of eternal love for a counterparty is communicated on a professional networking platform.
**Forces:** The scammer tries to emotionally capture the attacked potential victim.
**Context:** The connection between the sincere user and the scammer is established and the latter still trusts the former.

**Problem:** The emotional capture of the sincere user must happen without creating an irreconcilable breach of trust in the scammer.
**Resulting context:** The sincere user continues the interaction with the scammer, signalling that a critical level of trust is still intact.

**5. Pattern (Name: No digital-footprint check) Version:** 0.1 **Author:** Alex Norta
**Date:**
**Description:** A sincere user has a considerable digital footprint, while the scammer appears to have no awareness.
**Example:** The sincere user is a prolific researcher with a very active professional life that generates many online entries that are easily accessible.
**Forces:** The scammer is very time-pressed to carry out the attack since the low success rate results in a low return on effort investment. Thus, the trade-off is not feasible in terms of time budget investment for a deeper background check of the sincere user.
**Context:** The considerable digital footprint of the sincere user is accessible with no or very little effort.
**Problem:** The scammer must falsely pretend in the communication with the sincere user to have a coherent and consistent awareness of a user's digital footprint.
**Resulting context:** The sincere user does not perceive any mismatch of the claimed awareness the scammer has, compared to the actually existing digital footprint. The danger is that the scammer eventually fails to maintain this matching perception.
**6. Pattern (Name: Insufficient digital footprint found) Version:** 0.1 **Author:** Alex Norta
**Date:**
**Description:** The sincere user checks the covert attacker, who does not yield a sufficient online digital footprint about the latter party.
**Example:** An unassuming user of a professional networking site search engines a counterparty and there is a lack of results that matches with the profile information and occurred communication of the latter.
**Forces:** The sincere user has the goal to perform a larger background check with third-party information sources.
**Context:** The counterparty of the sincere user operates in an environment and carries out activities for which one can legitimately assume it generates a considerable digital footprint.
**Problem:** The found background information is not properly presented and disambiguated. Thus, even when a large digital footprint exists, the detected information drowns in noise, e.g., because the given name of the counterparty is very common.
**Resulting context:** The sincere user is able to filter through potential noise that an automatic background from third-party source check reveals and can perform an educated guess if the found information matches with the online profile and communication content of the counterparty.

**7. Pattern (Name: Personal meeting refusal) Version:** 0.1 **Author:** Alex Norta
**Date:**
**Description:** The scammer refuses a personal meeting following a period of online communication.
**Example:** After declaring his love in a few days, the scammer later pulls back when the sincere user starts making concrete plans for where and how to meet.
**Forces:** The sincere user wants to strengthen the bond and acquire more personal information, which the scammer cannot allow as the inconsistencies with the fake profile become apparent.
**Context:** The parties have communicated for a certain time and the sincere user considers a meeting in person appropriate.
**Problem:** There must be a sufficient proximity between the parties and/or a willingness to travel the distance for a personal meeting.
**Resulting context:** The scammer refuses the personal meeting without upsetting the sincere user to the point where the communication reaches a terminal end.

**8. Pattern (Name: Copy-pasted content) Version:** 0.1 **Author:** Alex Norta
**Date:**
**Description:** The scammer saves time by communicated text that is not original and taken from a third source.
**Example:** An affectionate letter is written in a style that does not match with the communication so far, and the content is incoherent with the context.
**Forces:** The scammer attempts to further emotionally capture the sincere user with additional effort without wanting to invest the time to produce coherent and original content.
**Context:** The communication between parties is established with a sufficient trust level.
**Problem:** The new target must capture the sincere user while the time budget for content generation is very limited.
**Resulting context:** The scammer successfully uses copy-pasted content in a communication without breaching a critical level of suspicion on the side of the sincere user.

**9. Pattern (Name: Lack of answer) Version:** 0.1 **Author:** Alex Norta
**Date:**
**Description:** Critical questions posed by the sincere user are not answered by the scammer.
**Example:** A counterparty claims to be a soldier who is posted in Afghanistan while refusing to reveal details in answers to questions.
**Forces:** While the sincere user wants to collect deeper information of interest, the scammer needs to cover up the inconsistencies between the profile and ongoing communication.

**Context:** Information gaps exist on the side of the sincere user that have not been filled yet by the profile and ongoing information.
**Problem:** The questions posed by the scammer must be ignored or circumvented by the scammer without creating suspicion.
**Resulting context:** The sincere user is distracted and led to other directions in the communication without raising sufficient suspicion to running the danger of halting the interaction permanently.

**10. Pattern (Name: Factual incoherence) Version:** 0.1 **Author:** Alex Norta
**Date:**
**Description:** The communicated facts contradict each other.
**Example:** A scammer mentions his daughter who turns 18 and studies medicine at Oxford University. At that age, one cannot yet be a medical student apart from exceptional circumstances, which presumably then would be mentioned.
**Forces:** The scammer must maintain many fake personalities as sincere users require respective attack strategies, which are complex to manage coherently.
**Context:** An elaborate profile with fake data is the foundation for elaborate communication.
**Problem:** With the assumption that many diverse fake profiles are managed, the resulting complexity poses a challenge for remaining without contradictions and inconsistencies.
**Resulting context:** The amount of contradictions and inconsistencies remain limited to the point where the sincere user maintains trust in the interaction.

**11. Pattern (Name: Indecent content communication) Version:** 0.1 **Author:** Alex Norta
**Date:**
**Description:** The scammer communicates content of compromising nature to, or from, the sincere user.
**Example:** The sincere user receives depictions of sexual nature per email.
**Forces:** The scammer attempts to harass or compromise the sincere user.
**Context:** The communication between the parties has been maintained for at least a short period of time.
**Problem:** The scammer considers the sincere user sufficiently receptive for indecent content.
**Resulting context:** The sincere user is receptive and/or not prudish enough to be put off by the communicated indecent content.

**12. Pattern (Name: Appeal to pity) Version:** 0.1 **Author:** Alex Norta
**Date:**
**Description:** A scammer appeals to feelings of pity from the sincere user.
**Example:** A scammer claims to have a sick relative who requires urgent help and action.
**Forces:** The scammer aims for enhanced emotional capture and blackmail.
**Context:** The sincere user has a sufficient degree of trust in the scammer.

**Problem:** The scammer considers the sincere user sufficiently receptive for an appeal to pity.
**Resulting context:** The sincere user feels sorry for the scammer.

**13. Pattern (Name: Style and layout inconsistencies) Version:** 0.1 **Author:** Alex Norta
**Date:**
**Description:** This is a narrower version of earlier specified Pattern 8 about copy-paste inconsistencies, limited to message style and layout.

**14. Pattern (Name: Lack of gift) Version:** 0.1 **Author:** Alex Norta
**Date:**
**Description:** The scammer fails to send a gift to the sincere user during the setup phase of communication.
**Example:** The sincere user expects with no avail the delivery of a bouquet of flowers.
**Forces:** The sincere user expects a reinforcement of the established affectionate trust relationship, while the scammer considers a gift an excessive investment given the low chance of return.
**Context:** The level of affectionate trust rises in the sincere user.
**Problem:** The scammer does not see evidence yet to successfully reach the goal of the attack and assumes there is no return on the extra investment.
**Resulting context:** The sincere user continues the interaction despite the disappointment of not receiving any gift.

**15. Pattern (Name: False compensation promise) Version:** 0.1 **Author:** Alex Norta
**Date:**
**Description:** The scammer puts forward a promise of compensation for loaning an artefact from the sincere user.
**Example:** The scammer requests money to be transferred to an offshore bank account with the promise to pay it back in the future.
**Forces:** There is a rush on the side of the scammer to reach the objective of the attack against the sincere user.
**Context:** The level of trust is estimated to be deep enough for the attacker to launch the final stage of the attack.
**Problem:** The sincere user must be emotionally captured and/or distracted to the point where the artefact is loaned to the scammer.
**Resulting context:** The sincere user is left in the belief that there will be a return and/or compensation for the loaned out artefact.

**16. Pattern (Name: Money transfer) Version:** 0.1 **Author:** Alex Norta
**Date:**
**Description:** This pattern is a specialised version of Pattern 15 limited to a money loan with or without the promise of return and/or compensation.

**17. Pattern (Name: Moving off-site) Version:** 0.1 **Author:** Anis Ben Othman
**Date:**
**Description:** After establishing contact with the sincere user, the scammer requests that the relationship move from the dating site to email and Instant Messenger.
**Example:** The fake relationship moves to including text messages and the telephone or voice-to-Internet protocol (VoIP).[45]
**Forces:** The scammer tries to avoid detection and deletion of his profile.
**Context:** The scammer makes sure to have a hold on the victim and no third party can terminate the connection.
**Problem:** It is not possible to monitor scammer activity and behaviour on-site.
**Resulting context:** The scammer safely continues interaction with the sincere user without the risk of being detected by the network agents.

**18. Pattern (Name: Geo-location mismatch) Version:** 0.1 **Author:** Anis Ben Othman
**Date:**
**Description:** The IP from where the scammer is connected a mismatch with the declared location.
**Example:** The American soldier serving in Afghanistan is connected from an African country.
**Forces:** The scammer is lying about his location to build a legitimate story.
**Context:** The scammer makes sure to hide his real location using a proxy or via the use of fast-flux service networks.[46]
**Problem:** It cannot be identified if the scammer is using proxy to hide his real network location.
**Resulting context:** The scammer safely continues interaction with the sincere user without the risk of being exposed.

**19. Pattern (Name: Native language) Version:** 0.1 **Author:** Anis Ben Othman
**Date:**
**Description:** The scammer claims to be from a native-born specific country but uses poor grammar indicative of a non-native speaker.
**Example:** The scammer claims to be a native-born American citizen but uses poor grammar indicative of a non-native English speaker.
**Forces:** The scammer aims to gain trust by falsely claiming to originate from a developed country.
**Context:** The scammer uses copy-pasted content and uses eloquent romantic language that is plagiarised from the Internet.
**Problem:** A lack of language skills reveals the scammer to make a false origination claim or the sincere user does not spot the poor grammar in messages.

[45] Whitty (2012).

[46] Konte et al. (2009), pp. 219–228.

**Resulting context:** The scammer successfully uses plagiarised content in a communication without breaching a critical level of suspicion on the side of the sincere user.

### 4.2.3 Taxonomy Positioning of Patterns

While the patterns listed above all fall into the Fig. 1 lifecycle category of *started* patterns, the remaining stages are not explored yet. Thus, there is a considerable scope for future work to expand the set of pattern specifications. Additionally, the patterns must be refined to the point where also suggestions for their detailed technical realisations are given. For example, a pattern of an experienced scammer during profile establishment may be to do so using a Tor Browser that anonymises the communication to a social networking site through a so-called Onion Router[47] that obscures a user's browsing location and also protects from network surveillance and traffic analysis.

Patterns pertaining to the amount of criteria taken into account are also not specified yet. As a rule of thumb, the more criteria a sincere user takes into account, the more likely it is that comparing their coherence yields a degree of suspicion when, for example, dates are out of the norm given the age of an individual that is indicated in an online profile.

Halted patterns that lead to a resume of interaction after a certain period of time are also not specified yet. We assume that such halts allow a scammer to assess the communicated information for inconsistencies. It also is an opportunity to adjust the attack strategy for achieving the goal of defrauding the sincere user more effectively.

There are patterns missing that fit into the meeting stage of the lifecycle in Fig. 1. For example, the body language used in a personal meeting may either enhance or diminish the trust of the sincere user in the scammer. The latter may be nervous and slip out incoherent information that conflicts with the online communication. However, these are patterns that are not automatically detectable with means of machine learning, unless in the very unlikely case at this point in time that the sincere user attends the personal meeting with wearing augmented-reality glasses that connect to highly sophisticated artificial intelligence software for the analysis of the scammer's body language.

Finally, also the ending and the failing of the dating-scam lifecycle requires coverage with pattern specifications. When a scammer achieves his objectives, either after intensified online communication or after a very successful personal meeting, the lifecycle ends successfully from the perspective of anti-patterns. If the sincere user becomes suspicious and the trust level in the counterparty collapses to the point where the scammer cannot reach a fraud goal, then the lifecycle is failed.

[47] Domingo-Pascual et al. (2011).

We next present a metamodel for capturing the knowledge required for machine-learning-based online-fraud pattern detection.

## 4.3 A Metadata Model for Security Measures

The metadata model we derive from the legal context given in earlier legal sections. A state-of-the-art formalisation means is to use the web ontology language OWL.[48] The latter is a representation language for specifying ontologies that are organised in class hierarchies. Note that ontologies represent constantly evolving information on the Internet originating from heterogeneous data sources.

The metamodel for this paper we design with the tool Protégé,[49] which is a free, open source ontology editor for systematic knowledge acquisition. The tools comprise a graphic user interface and many plug-ins for different types of ontology visualisation and correctness checks. For the latter, we employ the HermiT reasoner[50] to check the ontology consistency, identify subsumption relationships between classes and so on.

The OWL ontology that is the foundation for the metamodel is available for online download, and Fig. 3 shows the class hierarchy of the current version. In a technical sense, this HermiT-reasoner-checked ontology also serves as a script for a metadatabase since it is possible to store so-called individual instances that can be further read and updated. To do so, the simple protocol and RDF query language SPARQL[51] is available and reaching a suitable level of application maturity. The main idea is to use the metamodel as a pool into which diverse social media may share data for machine-learning-based automatic scam-detection systems.

Referring back to the class list in Fig. 3, the root of any OWL specification is class *Thing*. Due to space limitation, we split the class hierarchy into four columns and the descriptions of the respective classes follow next. An *Address* is a location of a *Role* or an *Agent* that we explain in the sequel. An *Address* has so-called data properties that are either *private* or *professional* of the range boolean. Thus, by setting *private* and *professional* to either *false* or *true*, the status of an address changes.

The class *Agent* with an online *Profile* is in commercial law a person with the authorisation to act on behalf of another principal to create a legal relationship with a third party. In software engineering, an agent[52] is a computer program that acts for a human user or other software program. Action on behalf of another human or artificial third party implies the authority to decide that a specific action is

[48] McGuinness and Van Harmelen (2004).

[49] Musen (2015), pp. 4–12.

[50] Horrocks et al. (2012).

[51] Buil-Aranda et al. (2013), pp. 277–293.

[52] Sterling and Taveter (2009).

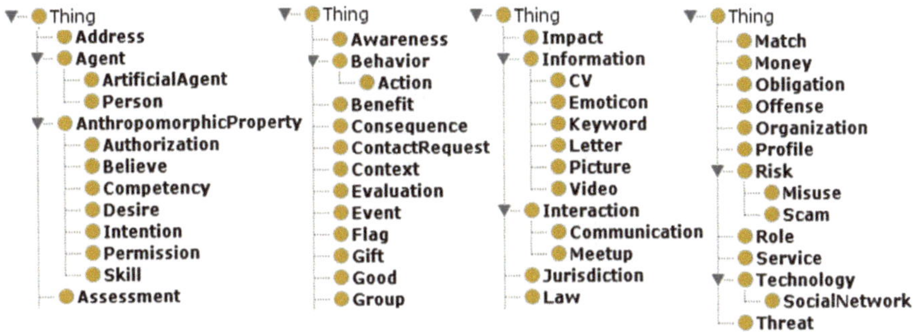


**Fig. 3** The class hierarchy of the dating-scam ontology

appropriate. This dual meaning of an agent being a natural person or an artificial artefact is reflected in the class hierarchy of the first column in Fig. 3.

The class *Anthropomorphic Property* gathers features of artificial agents that resemble or are made to resemble human characteristics. The listed characteristics cited as sub-classes in the first column of Fig. 3 are subsumed as BDI agents,[53] i.e., believe, desire intention. This concept provides a separation of the activity of selecting a plan from a library or an external planner application from the execution of active plans. Consequently, it is possible to develop artificial agents that behave as scammer bots[54] who act like real humans towards a sincere dater.

An *Assessment* is performed of *Benefit* and *Risk* sets that are compared against each other. Examples for *Risk* are *Misuse* or a *Scam* that links to *Behaviour* and *Information*. *Awareness* exists of a specific *Event* by an *Agent* to a certain degree. Class *Behaviour* has a sub-class *Action* that an *Agent* carries out. That *Behaviour* is of concern for the law and may involve a *Consequence* in reality. The *Context* is important for an *Interaction* and may involve some *Offence* that results from the use of *Information* that is part of an online-dating *Interaction*. An *Evaluation* is performed by an *Agent* and concerns an *Interaction* that unfolds. A *Flag* is raised by an *Agent* for an *Interaction* with a *Risk* suspicion.

A *Gift* is offered by an *Agent* to another one who might accept it, or not. A *Match* between a *Gift* and an *Agent* is established through *Technology*. The latter also facilitates a *Match* of a *Good*, *Money* or a *Service* with either another *Service* or *Agent*. A *Group* comprises an *Agent* set and may itself be part of a larger *Group* that is part of an *Organization*. An *Impact* captures how an *Agent* is affected by a *Threat* that leads to a *Consequence* that changes the *Context*.

The *Information* that flows between *Agents* can have sub-classes. Without claiming completeness, we list several in the third column of Fig. 3 that a scammer might consider for an attack. As a general rule, the more information from different sources can be combined about a potential victim, the higher the chance is that a

---

[53] Casali et al. (2011), pp. 1468–1478.

[54] Bose and Shin Kang (2013), pp. 1576–1589.

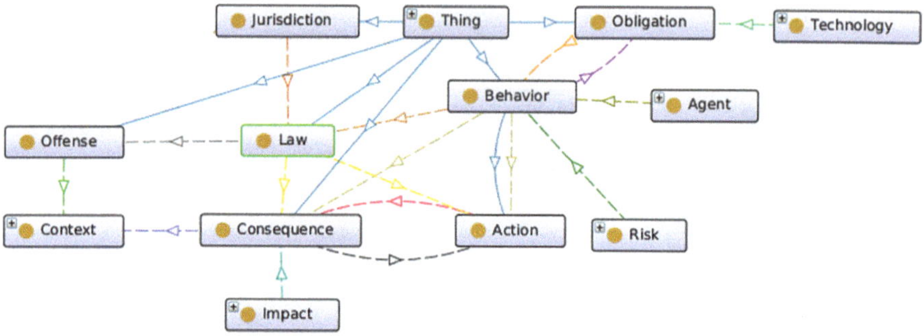


**Fig. 4** Law focus and neighbourhood of classes

scam attack succeeds. The *Interaction* in which *Information* exchange happens can be of variations that either remain online or there is an agreement for a *Meetup* in person. A *Jurisdiction* applies to a framework of specific *Law* that concerns the *Behaviour* that an *Agent* may have an *Obligation* to display or not to display.

## 4.4 Ontological Graphs

The following graphs show subsets of the overall metamodel. Next, we populate subsets of the metamodel with knowledge examples.

### 4.4.1 Class Law

Since the paper is about legal matters in online dating scams, Fig. 4 shows a graph with class *Law* in the centre. The latter class addresses an *Offence* that happens in a certain *Context*. Thus, preceding must be certain *Behaviour* that includes a set of *Action* carried out by a human or artificial *Agent*. A specific *Technology* that enforces an *Obligation* to enact *Behaviour* carries a *Risk* for scams, misuse and so on. The *Law* enactment entails a *Consequence* set that affects a *Context*.

Example: An interaction between a sincere user and a scammer as agents involves a sequence of behaviour with elementary sequences of actions that may also run in parallel branches. We assume the dating platform has minimalistic technological provisions for not permitting the use of certain indecent vocabulary. Thus, when an action of a message sending comprises a word that is part of the set of indecent vocabulary, a dedicated agent senses this incident and prompts a message to the scammer with a warning, i.e., an obligation to behave within certain limits is breached. Internally, the scam detection system increases the likelihood of the risk that this particular interaction is a scam case.

Next, we assume a sequence of actions that results in the sincere user sending money in good faith to a bank account under the control of the scammer. Thus, laws

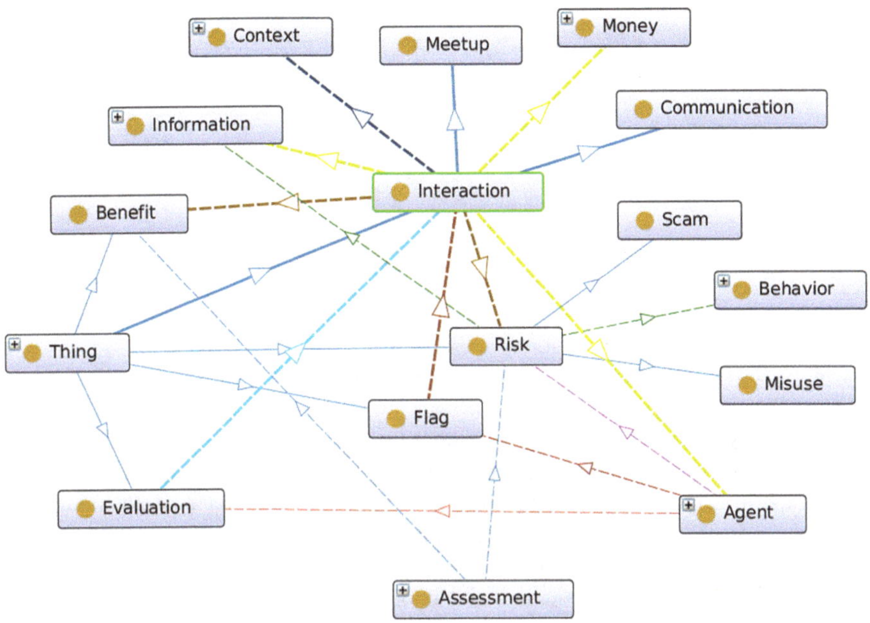


**Fig. 5** Interaction focus and neighbourhood of classes

pertaining to theft are violated, which is clearly an offence against the sincere user with the impact of a permanent monetary loss. We assume a different type of agent automatically detects the IP address and additional personal data of the scammer and automatically informs law enforcement in the detected location if the sincere user agrees with this action.

### 4.4.2 Class Interaction

The graph in Fig. 5 has a focus on class *Interaction* involving *Agent*s. A variation of *Interaction* is *Communication* where different types of *Information* are involved. Conforming to Fig. 1, *Interaction* can also be a personal *Meetup* or involve *Money* that a scammer aims to acquire fraudulently. The *Interaction* may be subjectively perceived as a *Benefit*, depending on an *Agent*'s requirements. However, an *Evaluation* may also yield a *Risk* for which a *Flag* is raised. Very common is also to perform an *Assessment* between a *Benefit* and *Risk* set.

Example: A sincere user interacts with a scammer on a dating site, and a lot of information exchange happens in the form of mostly text messages during an online communication. We assume the sincere user sends mostly truthful information, while the scammer faces the challenge that fake information in a communication must remain consistent with an equally fake profile. A communication listener

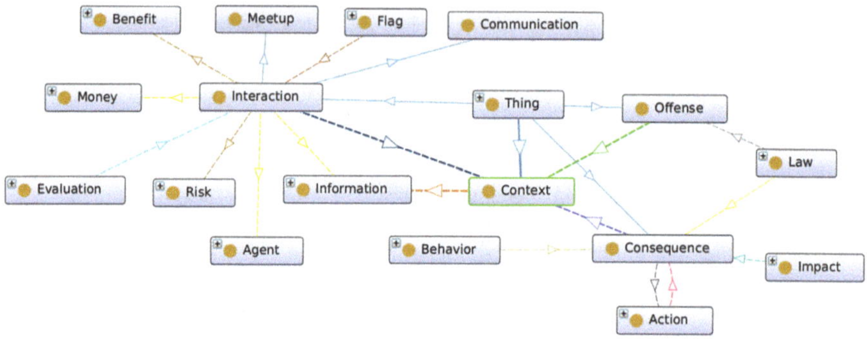


**Fig. 6** Context focus and neighbourhood of classes

agent employs techniques of computational linguistics[55] that is an interdisciplinary field concerned with the statistical or rule-based modelling of natural language from a computational perspective. Thus, the listener agent detects that a personal meeting suggestion is declined and also shortly after that, a request follows from the scammer to transfer money for covering the journey expenses. A second type of artificial agent evaluates the calculated benefits in an interaction based on some statistical machine-learning assumptions against the calculated risk and determines to flag the scammer while also sending a warning message to the sincere user.

### 4.4.3 Class Context

Class *Context* is the focus in Fig. 6. An *Interaction* falls into a *Context* that is driven by *Information*. An *Offence* happens in a *Context* that a specific *Law* addresses. The *Behaviour* of an *Agent* influences the *Consequence* the *Law* enforces. A *Consequence* is influenced by the *Behaviour*, task-oriented *Action* and *Impact* of threats.

Example: The interacting sincere user and scammer have their own respective contexts that expand based on information they communicate to multiple recipients. Thus, the context is the organised form of information that reveals a larger user profile. Since the interaction by individuals is governed in principle by a set of laws, the larger user profiles may reveal offences against the law and can be flagged accordingly. For example, it is universal that the law does not permit cases of theft or harming a person. Such actions by a scammer have an impact on a sincere user that trigger consequences. Since traditional law enforcement is a challenge in the case of online-dating scams, an option could be to employ a form of cyber-enforcement by configurable machine-learning-powered multi-agent systems.

[55] Paris et al. (2013).

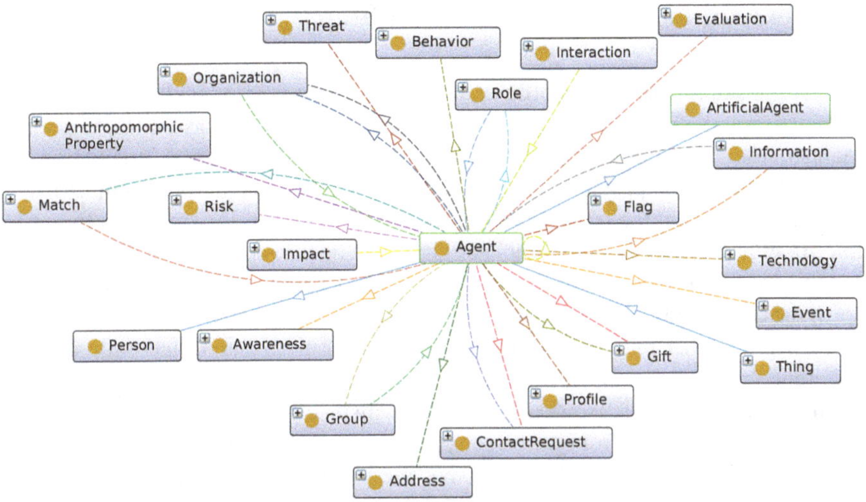


**Fig. 7** Agent focus and neighbourhood of classes

### 4.4.4 Class Agent

Finally, we depict the focus of class *Agent* in Fig. 7 that reveals a very elaborate context. Since we assume that a multi-agent system serves as a scam-warning system, this central position in the metadata model is a logical consequence. Note that an *Agent* individual may slip into multiple *Role* individuals and vice versa, at specific points in time. Since scammer bots spread in use and are in essence intelligent artificial agents posing as humans, they can adopt a set of so-called *Anthropomorphic Property* instances, i.e. human-like behaviour displays. That is certainly the case for earlier introduced BDI agents. The larger class context depicted in Fig. 7 suggests that a dating-scam warning system comprises rather diverse sets of agent flocks that are initiated and active every time an interaction establishment occurs, and we list an example below.

Example: Some types of agents we already mentioned above. There is a communication listener agent that checks messages with means of computational linguistics for indecent terminology to trigger the flagging of a scammer. Another agent type mentioned is for automatic location tracking of a scammer. We also mentioned a pattern-detection agent that recognises the decline for personal meetings and request for money transfer that leads to warning a sincere user and again flagging a user.

## 5 Concluding Remarks: The Next Steps

Law applies online as well as offline; this is true for national as well as international laws. However, the online world has provided so many opportunities to act in a manner where location does not matter. This leads to questions of jurisdiction and especially to major problems of enforcement. If effective enforcement is nearly enough impossible, the situation resembles that of no law existing. It is thus very important to examine how criminal activities can be prevented as much as possible, as the deterrent effect of criminals being afraid of getting caught is very small.

In the description of the scenario, we mentioned a large number of warning signs that a vigilant user may detect. It may be tempting to presume that with so many different "red flags", any user would notice at least some of them and not let themselves be trapped. However, the many instances of successful scams show that these flags are far from universally successful. Thus, an agent who raises the flags and will not permit himself to be overlooked or ignored may be what is needed. The agent should be able to detect the various issues that give raise to concern.

Even if the agent is automatic, it needs to be determined when he starts working. Does the agent enter into operation and begin checking right from the beginning when a new contact is made, or in an hour, or in a day? There may be many different possible settings, and it needs to be determined who decides which settings to use. The rules under which the agent operates are important so that it is clear when and how it should work. For example, it is possible that the agent also has the role to check the sites' privacy policy and that it complies with data protection law and policy. For this, it requires that the policy is formalised to the point of being machine readable. If this is the case, one needs to determine what the added value of the agent is in this context. It should be more than just to see if the site makes some references to certain policy or ticks some other boxes. To be useful, the agent should understand what is needed for any particular site, and if the policy is not adequate it should be able to inform people not to deal with the site in question. This must be human configured, e.g., by a cybersecurity expert. The agent autonomously evaluates the privacy policy.

We have explained above that it is difficult to imagine that the legal system can take very forceful measures with the problems of detection and jurisdiction that are typical for the cyberworld. At the same time, it is possible to obligate websites to pay more attention to risks and take measures, like installing suitable technology. It is known that companies are often neglecting to report data breaches and similar acts. In general, we support to let the society regulate itself. The most appropriate technology can be found by the various relevant sites. What is needed is a built-in trust assurance mechanism through a façade mechanism, using computational language.

We foresee a meta-level platform outside of the relevant website itself, like a façade, which shields or protects you from the "naked" site, like www.startpage.

com—"The World's most private search engine" which acts like a protective shield in front of other search engines.

Thus, what are needed are

(1) a meta platform with tailor-made interfaces to sites[56];
(2) agents to support you in your choices, helping to direct you to where you want to be;
(3) one agent per user that coordinates sub-agents, checks things and feeds back to the master agent (e.g., checking privacy policy; scanning interaction between parties; monitoring constantly for changes; like login, etc.; tracking key strokes; checking what goes on at someone's desktop; and so on). The agent will periodically verify the automated login: if credentials are changed a lot.

It will be an important question what to build in to the website, what the tasks and functions of the agent are. The system has to be easy with no or very few extra steps to enable the agent to work, or people will not accept it and will actively look for ways to disable the agent. To be effective, the agent needs to be tailor-made and not operate on one standardised XML-based protocol.

Websites may feel that they should not have any additional responsibility as they only offer the channel through which people can communicate as they wish. Against this can be argued that there are analogies based on which more responsibility can be put on the entity that provides the platform, which enables the public to access messages. In media like broadcasting or printed media, it is a well-established principle that the entity (and/or person) that is responsible for making a message available to the audience bears responsibility for the message regardless of whether it is created by that entity or by some other subject. This is shown in relation to, for example, letters to the editor in newspapers, statements made in direct broadcasting, phone-ins to radio or television, etc. It is expected of the media outlet that they have a policy and a system through which they can ensure that no illegal content is made available.

Relevant analogies can be found from the Internet area itself, on cases dealing with intellectual property. There are a number of cases over the years on illegal use of content protected by intellectual property, where the most interesting analogy is with the Napster case from 2000 as Napster—contrary to later file-sharing cases—kept the content on its server. As Napster knowingly hosted the service of uploads and downloads through its central file-exchange server, it facilitated copyright infringement.[57] Napster's mistake was to manage data centrally. With modern technology like BitTorrent, the data is replicated in a distributed way. Thus, once

[56] The OWL ontology would be part of a metadatabase into which several sites can channel data so that BDI agents can work with that metadata.

[57] *A&M Records, Inc. v. Napster, Inc.*, No. C99-05183 MHP, 2000 WL 573136 (W.D. Cal.); see also Smith (2003), p. 5. The Digital Millennium Copyright Act, 17 U.S.C. § 512 et seq., was enacted in response to concerns of online service providers, creating narrow safe harbours for copyright liability. See Zimmerman (2004).

the data is in the torrents, one would have to shut down the entire Internet to enforce copyright laws.

There are cases from different jurisdictions that stipulate that it is possible to take part in an action through omission. This could point to a responsibility for websites that open up the possibility to defraud—provided a causal link can be found between the website and the fraud. Although this may appear to be stretching matters a bit far, if e.g. a dating website actively encourages people to share a lot of information in order to meet suitable partners, the link may at least be strong enough to be used as a basis for requiring mitigation measures by the website. Cases about omission leading to, e.g., defamation that have been much quoted in Internet-related cases include *Byrne v. Deane* (1937, UK)[58] and *Urbanchich v Drummoyne Municipal Council* (1991, Australia).[59] These older offline cases have been quoted in cases about online defamation such as *Godfrey v. Demon Internet Ltd.* (1999, UK),[60] *Bunt v. Tilley* (2006, UK)[61] and *ACCC v Allergy Pathway Pty Ltd* (No 2) (2011, Australia).[62] What is essential is whether the website in question knew of the defamatory material (regarding Internet: the postings), had power to remove them and did not take any (or sufficient) steps to take them down.

In any event, it is essential to determine how and when the agent is activated. For the agent to be able to be effective, the checking should be a background that is automatically activated upon entering a certain website. A link between law and technology can be seen here as it is possible to regulate that agents must be activated on certain websites. The compulsory agent could be coupled with a function that makes it impossible to deactivate it. This is, however, impractical as well as excessively coercive. To have effective sanctions, there needs to be some form of monitoring of websites, which is not practical, given the general nature of Internet regulation, so it is better if the use of agents like of any other helpful technologies is done voluntarily by the websites or possibly monitored by a form of self-regulatory system. The use and intensity of the agent should be voluntary and the restrictiveness of the agent's warnings be dynamically configurable by the user. Otherwise, humans cease being in charge and become system slaves. As the agent may slow down interactions, add costs and some complexity to the websites, it is essential to consider what mechanisms are effective to make sure that agents are used. It thus needs to be carefully considered how it can be encouraged to use agents as the risk is that only the people with good awareness skills and an intellectual

[58] [1937] 1 KB 818.

[59] (1991) Aust. Tort Reports 81-127 (NSW SC).

[60] Godfrey v. Demon Internet Limited [1999] EWHC QB 244 (26th March, 1999) http://www.bailii.org/ew/cases/EWHC/QB/1999/244.html.

[61] John Bunt v. David Tilley [2006] EWHC 07 [QB] http://www.bailii.org/ew/cases/EWHC/QB/2006/407.html.

[62] [2011] FCA 74. See http://www.liv.asn.au/Practice-Resources/Law-Institute-Journal/Archived-Issues/LIJ-August-2011/Beware-the-social-network.

ability to be suspicious will use the agents—leaving the most vulnerable still just as vulnerable.

There may thus be a need for incentives for companies to install the required agents. One possibility is that the law stipulates that a company can avoid responsibility for any fraud committed via its website if they have the technology installed. This is not likely to be appreciated by service providers if the debate around the ACTA is an appropriate analogy. The service providers disliked this proposed legal act, as they did not want to be responsible for what people did using their service. There will always be question of some users' knowingly disabling technology and this giving rise to questions of the best place for responsibility. Most likely, a shared responsibility is the most appropriate.

In our modern communications space, new risks occur together with new possibilities. Technology, as well as law, needs to act in a manner that is suitable for the specific situations, neither over-complicating nor over-regulating.

## References


Alexander C, Ishikawa S, Silverstein M (1977) A pattern language: towns, buildings, construction. Oxford University Press, Oxford

Anandarajan M, D'Ovidio R, Jenkins A (2013) Safeguarding consumers against identity-related fraud: examining data breach notification legislation through the lens of routine activities theory. Int Data Priv Law 3(1):51–61

Barendt E (2010) Privacy and freedom of speech. In: Kenyon AT, Richardson M (eds) New dimensions in privacy law. Cambridge University Press, Cambridge, pp 11–31

Bose A, Shin Kang G (2013) Agent-based modeling of malware dynamics in heterogeneous environments. Secur Commun Netw 6(12):1576–1589

Bourdieu P (1986) The forms of capital. In: Richardson J (ed) Handbook of theory and research for the sociology of education. Greenwood, New York, pp 241–258

Buil-Aranda C, Hogan A, Umbrich J, Vandenbussche P-Y (2013) SPARQL web-querying infrastructure: ready for action? The Semantic Web–ISWC 2013. Springer, Berlin/Heidelberg, pp 277–293

Casali A, Godo L, Sierra C (2011) A graded BDI agent model to represent and reason about preferences. Artif Intell 175(7–8):1468–1478

Chawki M, Darwish A, Ayoub Khna M, Tyagi S (2015) Cybercrime, digital forensics and jurisdiction. Springer, Heidelberg

Domingo-Pascual J, Shavitt Y, Uhlig S (2011) Traffic Monitoring and Analysis: Third International Workshop, TMA 2011, Vienna, Austria, April 27, 2011, Proceedings, vol 6613. Springer Science & Business Media

Edwards L, Waelde C (2000) Law and the Internet. Hart Publishing, London

Engel C, Keller KH (2000) Governance of global networks in the light of differing local values. Nomos Verlagsgesellschaft, Baden-Baden

Fraunhofer Fokus (Hoepner, P., Strick, L., Löhe, M.) Historical Analysis on European Data Protection Legislation. Report March 2012, pp 11–12. www.fokus.fraunhofer.de

Gamma E, Helm R, Johnson R, Vlissides J (1994) Design patterns: elements of reusable object-oriented software. Addison-Wesley, Boston

Gonzales Fuster G, Gutwirth S, de Hert P (2010) From unsolicited communications to unsolicited adjustments. In: Gutwirth G, Poullet Y, de Hert P (eds) Data protection in a profiled world. Springer, Dordrecht/London, pp 105–117

Gowda RS (2008) Role of software agents in E-commerce. Int J Comput Eng 3(3):246–251
Grimm D (2009) Freedom of speech in a globalized world. In: Hare I, Weinstein J (eds) Extreme speech and democracy. Oxford University Press, Oxford, pp 11–22
Hewitt C et al (1973) A universal modular ACTOR formalism for artificial intelligence. In: Proceedings of the 3rd international joint conference on Artificial intelligence. Morgan Kaufmann Publishers Inc., Burlington, pp 234–245
Hohpe G, Woolf B (2004) Enterprise integration patterns: designing, building, and deploying messaging solutions. Addison-Wesley, Boston
Horrocks I, Motik B, Wang Z (2012) The HermiT OWL reasoned. OWL Reasoner Evaluation Workshop (ORE 2012). CEUR Workshop Proceedings, CEUR-WS.org
Huang K-Z, Yang H, Lyu MR (2008) Machine learning modeling data locally and globally. Springer, Heidelberg
Isazadeh A, Pedrycz W, Mahan F (2014) ECA rule learning in dynamic environments. Expert Syst Appl 41(17):7847–7857
JingMin H, Gianluca S, Peng Y (2015) Quit playing games with my heart: understanding online dating scams. Detection of intrusions and malware, and vulnerability assessment. Lect Notes Comp Sci 9148:216–236
Konte M, Feamster N, Jung J (2009) Dynamics of online scam hosting infrastructure. Passive and active network measurement. Lect Notes Comp Sci 5448:219–228
Leymann C, Fehling F, Retter R, Schupeck W, Arbitter P (2014) Cloud computing patterns. Springer, Heidelberg
Long S (2013) Socioanalytic methods: discovering the hidden in organisations and social systems. Karnac Books, London
McGuinness DL, Van Harmelen F (2004) OWL web ontology language overview. W3C recommendation 10, no. 10
Moore B (1984) Privacy studies in social and cultural history. M. E. Sharp Inc., New York
Musen MA (2015) The protégé project: a look back and a look forward. AI Matters 1(4):4–12
Norta A, Hendrix M, Grefen P (2006) A pattern-knowledge base supported establishment of inter-organizational business processes. On the move to meaningful internet systems. OTM 2006 Workshops. Springer, Heidelberg, pp 834–843
Nyman-Metcalf K (2014) The future of universality of rights. In: Kerikmäe T (ed) Protecting human rights in the EU. Springer, Heidelberg, pp 21–35
Pak R et al (2012) Decision support aids with anthropomorphic characteristics influence trust and performance in younger and older adults. Ergonomics 55(9):1059–1072
Paris C, Swartout WR, Mann WC (eds) (2013) Natural language generation in artificial intelligence and computational linguistics, vol 119. Springer Science & Business Media, Berlin/Heidelberg
Poullet Y, Dinant JM (2010) The internet and private life in Europe. In: Kenyon AT, Richardson M (eds) New dimensions in privacy law. Cambridge University Press, Cambridge, pp 60–90
Robbers G (2002) Informationelle Selbstbestimmung und allgemeine Informationsfreiheit in Deutschland. Juridica VII:98–105
Rull A, Täks E, Norta A (2014) Towards software-agent enhanced privacy protection. In: Kerikmäe T (ed) Regulating eTechnologies in the European Union. Springer, Heidelberg, pp 73–94
Smith S (2003) From Napster to Kazaa: the battle over peer-to-peer filesharing goes international. Duke Law Technol Rev
Sterling L, Taveter K (2009) The art of agent-oriented modeling. MIT Press, Boston
Swapneel S, Nipun A, Christian M, Gail K (2010) weHelp: a reference architecture for social recommender systems. IEEE/ACM Int Conf Autom Softw Eng Workshops; Pt-160:461–472
Westin A (1970) Privacy and freedom. The Bodley Head, London
Whitty TM (2012) Anatomy of the online dating romance scam. University of Leicester, Leicester
Zimmerman EM (2004) P2P file sharing: direct and indirect copyright infringement. Florida Bar J

# E-Citizenship Opportunities in the Changing Technological Environment

**Lehte Roots and Costica Dumbrava**

**Abstract** This chapter analyses the change that info technology has and will make to the concept of citizenship. E-citizenship can create new statuses, rights or privileges that we have not had before. Nevertheless, all this creates several challenges to be resolved: security and surveillance issues, residence and rights, tax collection and many more.

The article first explains the concepts of citizenship that might be under further pressure to be changed, the rethinking of rights and duties of the e-citizens and also the identity of the e-citizens. It also explains the benefits of this new type of citizenship that is emerging and developing. Finally, it is also shortly explained how Estonian e-residency can be used as a model to create the European e-citizenship model.

## 1 Introduction

The current chapter examines the implications of the Estonian e-residency initiative on the concept and practice of EU citizenship. The central claim is that the development of information and communications technologies (ICTs) changes some concepts and practices of citizenship. Some issues of citizenship, such as access to formal membership, the scope of rights or the link between citizenship and identity, have long been debated. Recent technological changes provide new impetus for revisiting key citizenship questions.

L. Roots (✉)
Tallinn Law School, Tallinn University of Technology, Akadeemia tee 3, 12618 Tallinn, Estonia
e-mail: lehte.roots@ttu.ee

C. Dumbrava
Faculty of Arts and Social Sciences (Politics), Maastricht University, Tongersestraat 6 Room 3.004, Maastricht, Netherlands

Maastricht Centre for Citizenship, Migration and Development (MACIMIDE), Tongersestraat 6 Room 3.004, Maastricht, Netherlands
e-mail: c.dumbrava@maastrichtuniversity.nl



T. Kerikmäe, A. Rull (eds.), *The Future of Law and eTechnologies*,
DOI 10.1007/978-3-319-26896-5_3

E-citizenship and e-residency schemes replicate or create certain statuses, rights and privileges and also transfer certain citizen practices from the physical space to the electronic realm. In doing so, these schemes seem to challenge at least two conventional assumptions about modern citizenship. Firstly, there is the assumption that citizenship describes membership in a territorial political community where access to rights and privileges depends heavily on physical residence. Secondly, modern citizenship is also built on the idea that membership in a political community is predefined by the existence of a shared national identity. It can be argued that e-citizenship and e-residency could provide genuine opportunities for expanding and enriching citizenship through widening access to rights, boosting citizen participation and increasing political accountability. On the other hand, e-citizenship and e-residency arrangements provide new tools for citizens' surveillance.[1]

The concept of citizenship is commonly perceived as a combination of three main elements: (1) a formal status of state membership, (2) a bundle of rights and duties and (3) a major form of identity.[2] To this should be added the key dimensions of political participation and citizenship practices.[3] This modern model of national citizenship prescribes that citizens possess the legal status of nationality, enjoy and make use of a set of rights, observe certain civic duties and develop and display a sense of national identity. The model of national citizenship is problematic because of its basic assumption of congruence between legal inclusion, political membership and national identity.[4]

There are a series of key factors that contributed to the reassertion of citizenship in recent decades. Firstly, the promises of social equality and welfare built into the post-war model of social citizenship[5] have been compromised by the neoliberal clamp down on the welfare state and by the economic realignment brought by globalisation.[6] Secondly, theorists and advocates of marginalised groups have denounced as deceitful and exclusionary a number of key assumptions of the liberal model of citizenship (e.g., about the separation between the public and the private sphere, about cultural neutrality and liberal assimilation).[7] Thirdly, new questions about citizenship and inclusion have been generated by the arrival of great numbers of international migrants in Western societies. E-citizenship at the EU level is one of the models that can be used as a further integration measure for international migrants.

EU citizenship has been criticized by scholars as being not effective enough. There is little inclusion and not much democracy or participation in the creation of

---

[1] Lips (2006).

[2] Joppke (2011), pp. 28–30.

[3] Bosniak (2006), p. 162.

[4] Dumbrava (2014), p. 131.

[5] Marshall (1965).

[6] Sassen (1996).

[7] See, for example, Kymlicka (1995) and Young (2000).

the European identity. EU citizenship is based on the state citizenship and has elements of legal inclusion, political membership and at the same time also national identity. It has a formal status, contains bundle of rights and obligations but is lacking form of identity that the general concept of citizenship includes. E-citizenship of the European Union can create more inclusion and identity feelings.

The chapter is organised as follows: firstly, the chapter discusses the concept of citizenship and the key links between citizenship, residence and identity; secondly, it considers the ways in which technological changes trigger changes in the conceptualisation and practices of citizenship; thirdly, the current Estonian scheme of e-residency is explained and analysed; fourthly and lastly, the chapter dwells on the implications of e-residency for the EU citizenship.

## 2 Citizenship and Technological Development

Technological development can develop the citizenship notion and also increase the control over personal life, exercise of rights and obligations. Information and communications technologies (ICTs) could provide new means for citizen engagement and deliberation, such as e-voting platforms, e-government services, online forums, focus groups, opinion polls, referendums and petitions.[8] ICTs can create "a new environment for public communication which is interactive, relatively cheap to enter, unconstrained by time or distance, and is inclusive".[9]

By providing new channels for the dissemination and exchange of information, the expression of opinions and preferences, the discussion of policy issues and values, ICTs could enable citizens to develop the civic skills and attitudes that are deemed essential for the well-functioning of democracy. The potentially inclusive character of e-democracy raises hopes not only about the deepening of (national) citizenship but also about the widening of citizenship in view of establishing global citizenship.[10] It is now conceivable that billions of people could be brought together in a common global electronic space, where they could discuss global policy issues and cast electronic votes if needed. Moreover, e-citizenship can also boost participation in the economic sphere by widening access to services, increasing the speed of interactions and reducing transaction costs (e.g., through opportunities for signing documents digitally).

Despite advantages, e-citizenship initiatives raise a number of concerns. Firstly is the unequal access to technology; e-initiatives may lead to distortions by deepening the existing digital divide between "technologically abled" and "technologically disabled" citizens.[11] There is also evidence that digital divide tends to draw

[8] Chadwick (2006).

[9] Coleman and Gotze (2001), p. 5.

[10] Bentivegna (2006).

[11] Van Dijk and Hacker (2003).

upon and repeat pre-existing similar divisions based on race, ethnicity and class.[12] Secondly, apart from enabling citizens to access public services and to engage in a potentially global public sphere, ICTs are used by states for increased and automatic control of citizens and borders and to regain control over public agenda.[13]

Technological development in the area of information and communication has created new opportunities and challenges for the ways in which citizens practise and experience democratic citizenship, and it provides states with additional means to bolster citizens' engagement, as well as to trace and control their electronic actions. But there is one more aspect of citizenship that has been profoundly affected by technological development, namely membership in the political community. The expanse of telecommunications, media and transportation technologies propelled increased cross-border flows of people, goods and ideas. The unprecedented growth of international migration led to the creation of significant populations of non-citizens within states and of emigrant diasporas abroad. E-citizenship and e-residency are practical technological tools that help to bridge between states and diasporas. The various opportunities for travel and the availability of accessible means of cross-border communication provided by technology enable people to stay connected across borders to overcome physical distance. This is also relevant in the case of intra-EU mobility, where technological development provides opportunities for exercising EU citizenship rights on free movement. ICT solutions may give further possibilities to feel EU citizens as part of the European Union and not only as citizens of a member state, to which EU citizenship contributes. It increases the membership possibilities. It enables to develop more cross-border services, including e-commerce, e-governance and other electronic services that can move cross borders without physical change of the place.

## 3 Migration, Residency and Citizenship

International migration and the development of transnational networks have resulted in the partial de-linking of citizenship from territorial membership.[14] This triggered a reassessment of traditional assumptions about citizenship as co-territorial membership, in which the scope of citizenship inclusion and the site of citizenship practices were strictly bound by territorial borders. ICT, e-citizenship, e-residency are the tools to maintain the membership without physical residence. Whereas, historically, the scope of citizenship has never been congruous with that of territory (i.e., there have always been groups of resident that were excluded from citizenship), physical presence in the territory has long been regarded as a basic prerequisite for membership in a state. E-citizenship and

[12] Mossberger et al. (2008).

[13] Karakaya Polat and Pratchett (2013).

[14] See, for example, Soysal (1994) and Bauböck (1994).

e-residency seem to provide access to membership without the condition of physical residence.

Residence plays a crucial role in political theories on admission to citizenship. Theorists of migration and citizenship have renewed their interest in membership issues in direct response to recent waves of international migration. The debate about who should be naturalised as citizen gravitates around the idea of a "genuine connection" with the country. The idea was consecrated by the International Court of Justice in the Nottebohm case, when the Court asserted that citizenship is "a legal bond having as its basis a social fact of attachment, a genuine connection of existence, interests, and sentiments, together with the existence of reciprocal rights and duties."[15] Whereas this definition of citizenship is notoriously vague, in legal discourse genuine connection is strongly associated with residence. For example, the European Convention on Nationality allows states to withdraw citizenship from citizens who habitually reside abroad and who lack a genuine link provided that they do not become stateless. A number of political theorists argue for the naturalisation of immigrants in virtue of their long-term residence and of the normative implications derived from residence. Scholars have claimed that immigrants should be granted access to citizenship in virtue of the fact that, as residents, they have become full members of the societies in which they live.[16] According to Bauböck's concept of stakeholder citizenship, residence plays a crucial role because having resided in the territory of the state is an indicator of immigrants' stake in the political community.[17] Residence in the country thus generates strong claims to legal and political inclusion that is one of the bases of citizenship.

In practice, residence alone has never been a sufficient condition for naturalisation. It could even be argued that the role of residency has been downgraded as countries have generally lowered the minimum period of residence required for naturalisation purpose[18] and, more recently, shifted the emphasis from physical presence towards conditions of civic-cultural integration, e.g. language requirements and citizenship tests.[19] New technology developments are changing this prerequisite requirement of residence in the country where citizenship is acquired.

The rapid expansion of transnational networks and technological development in recent decades and the accompanying diaspora policies adds a new challenge to the traditional link between residence and citizenship. An increasing number of states have launched special initiatives, policies, programmes aiming at reaching out to emigrant diasporas.[20] This includes the extension of formal entitlements to citizenship and political rights, as well as the symbolic incorporation of emigrants into the

[15] Liechtenstein v Guatemala, Second Phase 1955 ICJ Reports 4 (Judgment of 6 April), 23.

[16] Rubio-Marín (2006) and Carens (2010).

[17] Bauböck's (2007).

[18] Groot (de) and Vink (2013).

[19] Joppke (2008).

[20] See Ragazzi (2014) and Collyer (2013).

official narrative of national membership. In this context, easy access to information and the variety of channels of communication and engagement made available by technological development seem to support the claim of emigrants to extraterritorial inclusion. In recent years, corporate migration has become a topic of discussion in the field of international taxation. The e-residency gives innovative possibilities also from this perspective.[21]

Estonia is the first country in the world that started to issue e-residency cards.[22] In 2014, Estonia adopted an e-residency legislation by which non-resident foreigners can obtain an Estonian digital identity card.[23] Nevertheless, it cannot be treated as e-citizenship.

It must be noted that digital signatures are already legally binding in all the EU member states. Directive 1999/93/EC searched to establish mutual recognition of digital signatures, but not all states were ready to follow it. The directive did not provide a comprehensive cross-border and cross-sector framework for secure, trustworthy and easy-to-use electronic transactions. A new regulation, No 910/2014, that is mandatory to follow will be applicable from the 1st of July 2016 and seeks to change this.[24] Outside the EU, the recognition of digital signature is recognised, if mutual agreements are in place.

## 4 E-Citizenship, Electronic Voting and Developments in ICT Field

ID cards issued to the e-citizens or e-residents are also used for electronic voting and are/form a part of the e-citizenship concept in Estonia. However, this raises issues related to the European digital divide between citizens. Some worry that, if e-voting were to be implemented, this would skew political participation towards the more affluent socio-economic groups. In the EU, for example, there are persistent differences with regard to Internet dissemination, as comparisons between Finland in the north and Portugal in the south or between Ireland in the west to Slovakia in the east part show. Council of Europe has issued a recommendation on standards for e-voting.[25]

---

[21] Kelder (2015).

[22] See more about e-residency in the chapter written by Särav and Kerikmäe.

[23] Identity Documents and State Fees Amendment Act, RT I, 29.10.2014, 1.

[24] REGULATION (EU) No 910/2014 OF THE EUROPEAN PARLIAMENT AND OF THE COUNCIL, of 23 July 2014, on electronic identification and trust services for electronic transactions in the internal market and repealing Directive 1999/93/EC.

[25] Council of Europe's Recommendation on legal, operational and technical standards for e-voting, Rec (2004) 11, September 2004. http://www.coe.int/T/e/integrated_projects/democracy/02_Activities/02_e-voting/.

Voting in elections is one of the principal mechanisms through which citizens exercise their right to participate in the political process. This is, however, not the only channel available for citizens to express their political preferences. The debate on whether direct democracy should be promoted is not a new one. Political philosophers and theorists have long debated about the virtues of direct participation. Sceptics, such as Bobbio, argue that "there is simply not enough time in the day for voters to consider all the elements involved in each and every issue put to the vote".[26] The act of voting should not be seen as an end in itself but, rather, as a mechanism through which preferences that crystallise from the process of deliberation are transmitted.

European Union citizenship can be connected to the e-citizenship powered by the chip card that gives a possibility to also vote at the EU Parliament elections. It can increase the participation in the European Parliament voting as it will be made so easy. A good example of developed e-voting system can be found in Estonia.

Unlike other e-democratic initiatives, such as e-forums, which have a bottom-up element and can develop in the absence of public authorities, the implementation of e-voting requires a top-down element—financial, logistic capacity of the state and changes in electoral law. Moreover, there are also fundamental questions regarding the role of public authorities. By introducing an ICT element into the electoral process, there is a danger that the state may become uncomfortably dependent on the skills and resources of private organisations. It would be difficult to envisage the implementation of e-voting systems without some degree of involvement from the private sector. This solicits the question of whether the organisation of democratic elections has to be the exclusive obligation of the state and whether underlying parts of the electoral process can be outsourced also to private organisations. For some states, the involvement of private intermediaries in the electoral process could be problematic, for others it may be less so. Opponents of e-voting have pointed out that the state should keep its monopoly position with regard to the organisation of elections and any type of public–private partnership should be avoided.

## 5 EU Citizenship and Its Development

The Treaty of Amsterdam of 2 October 1997 added a sentence to the Treaty that the "*Citizenship of the Union shall complement and not replace national citizenship.*"[27] European citizenship disconnects citizenship from belonging to a particular territory as the EU and a country that is part of the EU. This type of belonging gives some particular value. There are some positive and negative aspects of EU

---

[26] Quoted in Trechsel and Mendez (2005), p. 4.

[27] Previous Treaty Article 8(1) was repealed with "1. Citizenship of the Union is hereby established. Every person holding the nationality of a Member State shall be a citizen of the Union. Citizenship of the Union shall complement and not replace national citizenship."

citizenship. From the negative side, it should be mentioned that the European Union citizenship practice can be limited by lack of resources, which is not the case with the state-based citizenship. From the positive side, it should be mentioned that it gives practical direct value (free movement rights) or additional representative rights (voting for EU Parliament members) and it can be practised individually or in a community of belonging without respect of nationality status, ethnicity, religious creed. It does not challenge or replace national identity or national citizenship; it gives voluntary identity and capacity to act and enlarges the possibilities and rights. Moreover, the ECJ has proactively sought to expand and defend the rights of EU citizens with respect to non-discrimination and the freedom of movement and residence within the territory of the member state.[28]

Articles 20–27 of the Treaty on the Functioning of the European Union (hereinafter TFEU) of 2009 created new political and electoral rights. While the Lisbon Treaty did not make major changes to the provisions on EU citizenship, it linked these rights more closely to the prohibition on discrimination on the grounds of nationality. The Lisbon Treaty in the context of new emphasis on representative and participatory democracy has introduced a new agenda setting citizen's initiative. The EU citizens have a right to start an initiative for creating legislation at the EU level. There should be at least 1 million EU citizens from 7 different EU states supporting the action. Still the democratic deficit is haunting the European Union. In this context, the question that arises is whether a future European ID card could boost EU citizens' participation in the EU and thus narrow the EU's widely commented democratic deficit related to the representation of citizens.

Furthermore, EU e-citizenship can lead to the more contributory participation also in other fields to facilitate free movement of capital of foreign investors. The idea of contributory citizenship is not as abstract as it seems. There are many countries that grant citizenship to people who, among others, contribute to the country by bringing in investment or other financial assets.[29] Although these practices are normatively controversial, claims based on (economic) contribution play an important role in a number of citizenship debates, such as on citizenship entitlements of emigrants.[30] In the context of the European Union, the association between citizenship and investment has recently led to a heated debate when Malta proposed to grant citizenship to people who invest a certain sum in the country without having to take up residence in the country.[31] As EU citizenship gives the right to move to another EU country, live and work there, the right to use the social benefits, create businesses and use other benefits that emerge from the rights derived from the EU.

[28] C 430/10 Hristo Gaydarov, 17 November 2011; C 48/75 Rojer [1967] ECR 497, paras 31–33, C-184/99 Grzelczyk [2001] ECR I-6193.

[29] Dzankic (2012).

[30] Barry (2006).

[31] Ayelet and Bauböck (2014).

In 2014, Malta created Individual Investor Programme, which generated new debates at the EU level of the value of the EU citizenship. Maltese individual investor programme tries to attract any person who is at least 18 years old and proposes to make a contribution and who meets the application requirements. The European Commission deemed that the initiative contravened Malta's obligations to the EU because it circumvented the common EU migration policies. No such concerns can be raised in the case of Estonian e-residency scheme because the benefits provided by it rely exactly on non-immigration to the EU. So it is in fact opposite action to Maltese policy of granting investors a citizenship.

E-citizenship for the EU member state citizens can give further possibilities to feel themselves as part of the European Union and not only as citizens of a member state, which EU citizenship has contributed to. It increases the membership possibilities. It enables to develop more cross-border services, including e-commerce, e-governance and other electronic services that can move cross borders without physical change of the place.

Besides, as the e-citizenship or e-residency concept differs from the classical citizen or residency concept, it is also politically not as sensitive as granting national citizenship to foreigners. It contributes also to the development of and access to Internet banking systems of the other member states as a secure online identification is primary part of the e-citizenship card.

Furthermore, it is beneficial for the cooperation between states, cross-border companies, agencies as it makes easier and faster the practical activities such as signing agreements and developing, initiating and opening companies. Sharing of cross-border services without a need to move physically to the state of the service provider appears as a clever way to make use of technological development for tapping (economic) resources without having to compromise on important political aspects such as immigration and citizenship as it is an electronic residence without physical residency. However, the association between e-residency and citizenship raises normative issues in the context in which physical residence becomes less important as a normative basis for membership and when contribution-based arguments for membership are brought back to the fore. As other digital initiatives, the scheme also raises issues about equal access, privacy and state surveillance. As long as the scheme is designed and presented as a mere bundle of services and transactions empowered by technological innovation, there are no important concerns with regard to its implications for citizenship.

## 6 Conclusion

Technology developments are changing the current understanding of citizenship connections with residency and identity. E-residency as developed in Estonia does not bring more residents in a physical manner, but it is becoming a virtual residency with different benefits of using e-services, e-signature, e-voting and investment opportunities. As mentioned before, Estonian citizens living in another country may maintain their e-residency in the country of origin; foreigners living abroad can apply for e-residency in another country. These types of technological changes are changing our identities as nationals of one country. Also, the article has shown how technological changes trigger changes in conceptualisation and practices of citizenship. We need to establish new citizenship concepts and laws in order to catch up the possibilities that technological developments bring us. The current Estonian e-residency scheme is a special case and can be seen as a pilot project of attracting foreign investors without real need to change the physical residency, and furthermore the e-residency can be developed further to the common e-citizenship of the European Union.

E-citizenship for the EU member state citizens can give further possibilities to feel themselves as part of the European Union and not only as citizens of a member state which EU citizenship contributes to. It increases the membership possibilities. It enables to develop more cross-border services, including e-commerce, e-governance and other electronic services that can move cross borders without physical change of the place.

Moreover, as mentioned in the article, the e-citizenship or e-residency card of the European Union could be also granted to long-term residents of the European Union as by Directive 2003/109/EC, the long-term residents of the EU enjoy similar rights as EU citizens and the electronic version of the citizenship also gives them access to same services as are given to EU citizens. This idea needs further elaboration, and several opportunities and threats need to be investigated.

Besides, as the e-citizenship or e-residency concept differs from the classical citizen or residency concept, it is also politically not as sensitive as granting national citizenship to foreigners.

Definitely, this type of card connected to the EU citizenship rights is more useful to those EU citizens who use their EU citizen's rights to move within the EU. But even for those who do not move the electronic voting or electronic services, it can be something that they might also benefit from. It also contributes to the development and access to Internet banking systems of the other member states as a secure online identification is a primary part of the e-citizenship card.

Besides that, the e-citizenship helps to engage in public and economical life by giving opportunities of signing documents digitally. It increases the speed and inclusiveness in not only the political but also business life.

Furthermore, it is beneficial for the cooperation between states, cross-border companies and agencies as it makes the practical activities such as signing agreements and developing, initiating and opening companies easier and faster by sharing of cross-border services without a need to move physically to the state of the service provider.

## References


Ayelet S, Bauböck R (2014) Should citizenship be for sale? European University Institute, EUDO Observatory on Citizenship, San Domenico di Fiesole

Barry K (2006) Home and away: the construction of citizenship in an emigration context. N Y Univ Law Rev 81(11): New York, New York University

Bauböck R (1994) Transnational citizenship. Membership and rights in international migration. Edward Elgar, Aldershot

Bauböck R (2007) Stakeholder citizenship and transnational political participation: a normative evaluation of external voting. Fordham Law Rev 75:2393–2447. New York: Fordham University School of Law

Bentivegna S (2006) Rethinking politics in the world of ICTs. Eur J Commun 21(3):331–343: Sage Publications

Bosniak L (2006) Citizen and the alien: dilemmas of contemporary membership. Princeton University Press, Princeton

Carens JH (2010) Immigrants and the right to stay. MIT Press, Cambridge

Chadwick A (2006) Internet politics: states, citizens, and new communication technologies. Oxford University Press, New York

Coleman S, Gotze J (2001) Bowling together: online public engagement in policy deliberation. Hansard Society, London

Collyer M (2013) Emigration nations: policies and ideologies of emigrant engagement. Palgrave Macmillan, Basingstoke

Dumbrava C (2014) Nationality, citizenship and ethno-cultural belonging: preferential membership policies in Europe. Palgrave Macmillan, Houndmills, Hampshire

Dzankic J (2012) The pros and cons of ius pecuniae: investor citizenship in comparative perspective. EUI Working Paper RSCAS 2012/14 (Available online at: http://cadmus.eui.eu/handle/1814/21476)

Groot (de) G-R, Vink MP (2013) The relationship between citizenship and residence in the citizenship laws of the Member States of the European Union. In CARIM-India Research Report 2013/25. European University Institute, Robert Schuman Centre for Advanced Studies, San Domenici di Fiesole

Joppke C (2008) Comparative citizenship: a restrictive turn in Europe? Law Ethics Hum Rights 2(1)

Joppke C (2011) Immigration, citizenship, and the need for integration. In: Smith RM (ed) Citizenship, borders, and human needs. University of Pennsylvania Press, Philadelphia, pp 157–192

Karakaya Polat R, Pratchett L (2013) Citizenship in the age of the Internet: a comparative analysis of Britain and Turkey. Citizenship Stud 18(1):63–80. doi:10.1080/13621025.2013.780765

Kelder KAM (2015) E-residentsuse varjatud karid ehk mis juhtub kaugjuhitava äriühinguga? http://www.maksumaksjad.ee/modules/smartsection/item.php?itemid=1612. Accessed 30.06.2015

Kymlicka W (1995) Multicultural citizenship. Oxford University Press, Oxford

Lips AMB (2006) E-government under construction: challenging traditional conceptions of citizenship. In: Koutrakou V, Nixon P (eds) Ctrl, Alt, Delete: re-booting the state via E-government. Routledge, London

Marshall TH (1965) Class, citizenship and social development: essays. Doubleday, Garden City

Mossberger K, Tolbert CJ, McNeal RS (2008) Digital citizenship: the internet. Society and participation. MIT Press, Cambridge

Ragazzi F (2014) A comparative analysis of diaspora policies. Pol Geogr 41:74–89: Pergamon

Rubio-Marín R (2006) Transnational politics and the democratic nation-state: normative challenges of expatriate voting and nationality retention of emigrants. N Y Univ Law Rev 81:117–147

Sassen S (1996) Losing control?: Sovereignty in an age of globalization. Columbia University Press, New York
Soysal YN (1994) Limits of citizenship. Migrants and postnational membership in Europe. University of Chicago Press, Chicago
Trechsel AH, Mendez F (2005) The European Union and E-voting addressing the European Parliament's internet voting challenge. Routledge, London
Van Dijk J, Hacker K (2003) The digital divide as a complex and dynamic phenomenon. Inf Soc 19 (4):315–326
Young IM (2000) Inclusion and democracy. Oxford University Press, Oxford

# E-Residency: A Cyberdream Embodied in a Digital Identity Card?

Sandra Särav and Tanel Kerikmäe

**Abstract** Estonia—the small yet digitally advanced EU Member State—is the first country to open up its e-services to the world by issuing e-residencies, the Estonian equivalent to digital identity, to non-nationals. The Estonian digital identity or an e-residency grants its holder several rights unbeknownst to, or at least unapplied in, the majority of the EU Member States and in the world at a larger scale. Being an e-resident of Estonia, one can use the digital services of the country even if there had beforehand been no prior connection to Estonia, provided the potential e-resident shows legitimate interest. The digital services include possibility to digitally sign documents (legally enforceable in any EU Member State), do online banking, encrypt documents, as well as establish and manage a company in Estonia and declare its taxes online via the state-proven digital identity card issued and backed by the Estonian government. The given chapter scrutinises the perception of e-residency and discloses the problematical unbalanced aspects of it, pointing out that although secure from a technical point of view, e-residency lies on a defective concept and conflicting Estonian national regulatory framework that does not fully support the integration of the idea.

## 1 Introduction

In October 2014, as a response to Apple's introduction of a possibility to sign PDF documents using a trackpad, the Prime Minister of the Republic of Estonia, Taavi Rõivas, posted a bold tweet on his Twitter account, stating: "Dear Apple, If you are interested in how files are really signed digitally, contact any Estonian. Best rgds, Taavi."[1] Indeed, the people of Estonia are e-conscious—as of 3 May 2015, 1,246,723 Estonians have active ID-cards, which have been used for electronic

[1] Hereinafter weblinks available at the end of chapter in the References list.

S. Särav (✉) • T. Kerikmäe
Jean Monnet Chair of European Law, Tallinn Law School, Tallinn University of Technology, Akadeemia tee 3, 12618 Tallinn, Estonia
e-mail: sandra.sarav@ttu.ee; tanel.kerikmae@ttu.ee

 
T. Kerikmäe, A. Rull (eds.), *The Future of Law and eTechnologies*,
DOI 10.1007/978-3-319-26896-5_4

authentication as many as 344,654,526 times and for signing documents digitally 214,363,679 times.[2] As there are approximately 1,320,000 Estonians, this means that roughly 95 % of Estonians really do know how files are signed digitally. Using their ID-cards and having e-solutions available, Estonians lead a digital lifestyle—in 2015, 96 % of taxpayers declared their taxes electronically,[3] 99.6 % of the bank transactions are being done online[4] and 33 % of eligible voters e-voted during the 2015 national parliamentary elections.[5] The confidence of the citizens appears to be further supported by the fact that Estonia is among the most wired and technologically advanced countries[6] having freedom of speech and expression protected by the Constitution[7] and the Internet established as a human right.[8]

Simultaneously listed amid countries with lightest content restrictions, Estonia appears to be in a digital fairy tale—with its numerous e-government services, the country is regarded as a "model for free access as a development engine for society".[9] This is supported by facts from the European Digital Agenda country Scoreboards placing Estonia to the forefront in offering and using digital public services,[10] as well as by reputable media issues worldwide declaring Estonia to be "a leader in technology", "a place where cyberdream is already reality" and "a country famed for its digital infrastructure".[11] Other governments yearn for Estonian best practices too—towards the end of the year 2014, a novel union was formed by representatives of the Republic of Korea, the UK, Estonia, New Zealand and Israel by a mutual agreement to establish a network called D5, comprising the most digitally advanced governments in the world, with the common goal to share best practices and make the digital governments of the

---

[2] Statistics from official ID-card and Mobile-ID portal.

[3] In fact, Estonia adopted the system of electronic declarations in 2000; 3 % of the people declared their taxes online back then; within 15 years, this number has increased by 94 %. Statistics from Estonian Tax and Customs Board Yearbooks.

[4] Estonian Information System Authority.

[5] Statistics about Internet Voting in Estonia from Estonian National Electoral Committee. For more information, see, for instance, Madise and Vinkel (2014), pp. 53–72.

[6] Freedom House Freedom on the Net 2014. Estonia country report.

[7] § 45 of the Constitution of the Republic of Estonia.

[8] Pursuant to §44 of the Constitution, Estonia, everyone is entitled to free access to information disseminated for public use; it is laid down by the Public Information Act, §33, that "Every person shall be afforded the opportunity to have free access to public information through the Internet in public libraries, pursuant to the procedure provided for in the Public Libraries Act".

[9] Freedom House 2014 Freedom of the Net Estonia report.

[10] Digital Agenda for Europe. Progress by country. Estonia Scoreboard.

[11] See, for instance, the Economist explains: How did Estonia become a leader in technology? The Economist. 30 July 2013, by A.A.K, describing Estonia as having a "strong tech culture." As well as "Digital identity cards. Estonia takes the plunge." The Economist. 28 June 2014. Furthermore, Elisabeth Braw, "'E-stonia' Attempts to Become the Uber of Economies by Introducing Virtual Residency." 30 October 2014. Newsweek, etc.

participating states more efficient.[12] Estonian rapid developments with regard to e-solutions and digital infrastructure are undeniably sought after.[13]

Recently, Estonia opened up its digital borders to anyone legitimately interested in the country's e-services—this small yet tech-savvy European Union Member State has become the first country in the world to have rendered accessible some of its e-government and private sector e-services to non-Estonians in the form of something now known as e-residency—the Estonian equivalent to digital identity. Within the first month and a half, 650 applications were filed and 463 e-residencies issued. Majority of applications came from Finland (239), Russia (118), Latvia (39), the United States (36) and the United Kingdom (24), but e-residency had raised fascination across the world—numerous applications were additionally submitted from unanticipated countries, such as Venezuela, Sri Lanka as well as Mexico.[14]

The intent of this chapter is to familiarise the reader with the innovative concept of e-residency from three different angles. The first viewpoint presented in the second section of the given chapter provides an overview of the concept itself, including the technological basis, objectives for Estonia and expectations from the e-resident. The third main division scrutinises the Estonian national regulatory framework with regard to issuing the e-residencies; subdivisions present the clash between e-residency and Estonian legislation and indicate the discrepancies between e-residency and the EU principles of data protection. The fourth section seeks and provides an answer to the question whether the e-residency is the key to sought-after global digital identity management. Therewith, the purpose of the next pages is not to offer solutions to the various problematic aspects of e-residency but rather to initiate critical discussions and provide food for thought for further analysis.

## 2 The Concept of E-Residency Outstretched

As stated above, Estonian technological advancement has been noted internationally. Estonian citizens and residents are privileged in being able to manage most of their public and private affairs digitally. The plan to share that privilege with the

[12] "The D5 will provide a focused forum to share best practice, identify how to improve the Participants' digital services, collaborate on common projects and to support and champion our growing digital economies." The D5 Charter.

[13] Another Estonian success story is the Data Exchange Layer X-Road that was launched in 2001 to enable secure Internet-based data exchange between the state's information systems. President Ilves has claimed that the system was adopted merely because Estonia was too *poor* to afford a central server. In 2013, Finland and Estonia signed an MoU on cooperation in the field of ICT, one of the objectives of which was to implement the source code of the X-Road for practical use in Finland as a national data exchange layer. Another interesting fact is that the same MoU was the first international intergovernmental digitally signed agreement.

[14] The Minister of the Interior of the Republic of Estonia, Mr Hanno Pevkur at 05.02.2015 weekly press conference of the Government of the Republic of Estonia. It must be noted that up-to-date statistics on the number of applicants and e-residencies issued are not available to the public.

rest of the world was presented in the Estonian Development Fund competition and the price-winning development idea was titled "10 million e-Estonians by 2025".[15] The concept of e-residency was born, and thus it had to be introduced to the wider public: "E-resident is a foreigner, to whom Estonia has created a digital identity based on identity of the country of citizenship and issued a digital identity card—digital-ID of an e-resident."[16] To give a more tangible framework to the innovative idea, the Digital Agenda 2020 for Estonia designated the opening of Estonian "secure and convenient services" to foreign nationals as one of the priority initiatives of the named strategy.

Impetus for Estonia? Apparently, the country is aspiring to become as renowned for its e-services as Switzerland is for its banks.[17] Accordingly, the Digital Agenda 2020 for Estonia puts down the intent to retain the image of a tech-savvy country, whereas the concept of e-residency is emphasised as being one of the key factors in achieving that goal.[18] However, issuing digital identities is not only about Estonia's reputation, but it also has a multifaceted effect. In addition to marketing Estonian e-services, the legal foundation for the e-residency—the Identity Documents Act of Estonia—introduces as the objective of the issuing of e-residencies the advancement of Estonian "economy, science, education or culture by providing access to e-services with the Estonian digital document"[19]; and thirdly, as laid down by the Concept, the e-residency programme further ought to contribute to the enhancement of the policy of the Estonian compatriots programme supporting Estonians and Estonian culture abroad.[20] Here it remains inscrutable whether the incentives are indeed systematically organised layers of a deliberate compound programme or the concept of e-residency has been "squeezed in" to any more or less agreeable initiative to justify its existence.

---

[15] The idea was introduced by Taavi Kotka, Ruth Annus and Siim Sikkut. Estonian Development Fund is a public institution subject to the Parliament investing in innovative companies for the purpose of contributing to Estonian economic development.

[16] Issuing digital identities to non-residents: creating e-residency. Concept. Appendix to explanatory memorandum to draft legislation of Estonian Identity Documents Act and State Fees Act. Appendix 1." [Mitteresidentidele digitaalse isikutunnistuse väljaandmine: e-residentsuse loomine. Kontseptsioon. Isikut tõendavate dokumentide seaduse ja riigilõivuseaduse muutmise seaduse eelnõu seletuskirja juurde. Lisa 1.] 2014. Available only in Estonian. Hereinafter referred to as the Concept.

[17] Digital Agenda 2020 for Estonia.

[18] The Digital Agenda 2020 has submitted as among its objectives the maintaining of Estonian image as a technologically advanced country and well-developed information society, as well as creating awareness of e-Estonia in the world.

[19] Identity Documents Act of the Republic of Estonia. § $20^5$. E-resident's digital identity card. Hereinafter referred to as IDA.

[20] The supporting of Estonians and the Estonian culture abroad is organised through the national compatriots programme led by the Ministry of Education and Research and implemented in cooperation with the Ministry of Culture and the Ministry of Foreign Affairs.

## 2.1 Technological Basis (PKI)

Due to the fact that Estonia already had a functioning system for digital identity documents, it was not seen as a technological impediment to effectuate a system of secure digital ID-cards for e-residents.[21] The idea of prior existing ID-cards itself was first introduced in 1998, and in January 2002, the first ID-cards were issued to citizens.[22] The chip embodied in the national ID-cards and now also in the digital ID-cards of e-residents uses a 2048-bit public key encryption (the old versions of the card had a 1024-bit version), which confirms the definite proof of the identification in any electronic environment supporting the Estonian system.[23] Insofar as the e-resident's ID-card functions as an authentication tool similarly to citizens' and residents' ID- card, it is a national state-backed Public Key Infrastructure (PKI), thus ensuring that the state undertakes to assure its existence and functioning.

The Public Key Infrastructure (PKI) is the literal key for the secure authentication and digital signing. The key can be referred to as a sophisticated code kept on the electronic chip of the ID-cards (both Estonian national ID-cards and the novel e-residency digital identity cards).[24] This is subsequently comprised of two parts, i.e., two keys: a public encryption key and a private decryption key. To exemplify, the digital signature is created in combination of the two: first, by using the data necessary for giving the signature that is contained in the secure signature creation device—*the private decryption key*—and, second, by using the data that is needed for verification of that signature and uniquely corresponds to the first—*the public encryption key*.[25] There are two certificates[26] within the contact chip or microchip of the card which can be used for authentication and digital signatures respectively, whereas by using the same software that is compatible with Estonian ID-cards.[27] Therewith, the card can be used for digital signatures and authentications by installing the necessary software and using either an ID-card reader attached via USB to a computer (some have built-in hardware) or a Mobile- ID whereat the users can sign in without a card reader, by only using their phone. Simply put, the card works on two-factor authentication—in order to access a digital service or to sign digitally, secure PIN codes previously provided to the e-resident must be entered.

To elaborate on the security aspect—one part of that set of two keys is kept in the public part of the chip, which means that the ID-card readers, whether installed in the hardware or separately attachable by a USB cable, access system card readers,

---

[21] The Concept, supra note 16.

[22] Chronology of ID-Card from the Official ID-Card and Mobile-ID portal.

[23] Electronic ID-Card information from E-Estonia site.

[24] Public Key Infrastructure. PKI. Estonian Information System Authority.

[25] § 2 (2) of the Estonian Digital Signatures Act.

[26] A certificate is an electronic certification that binds the data necessary for certifying the authenticity of a person and the digital signature with the person and certifies the identity of the person. See more from the ID-card and Mobile-ID Portal "What are certificates."

[27] IDA, Supra note 19. § $9^4$. Entry of certificates in document.

web services or any other ID-card based application, can read that information. The certificate that has been placed in this part of the key, including the personal data, is the electronic proof accessible via the PKI.[28] The secret key of the set is saved in the protected part of the chip and can only be accessed by the PIN codes which were given to the owner. To illustrate: the public and private keys are in mathematical connection, but it is not, however, possible to derive the private key on the basis of the public key. The information encrypted by the public key can only be unencrypted with the personal secret key, which means that the confidential message is only readable by its addressee. Therefore, by authenticating oneself with the ID-card, the web server sends the owner a session key that is being encrypted with that person's public key and can only be encrypted with that specific authentication key (inserting the PIN).[29]

The further, perhaps more easily conceivable, security aspect lies in the fact that merely knowing other persons' PIN codes will not suffice to abuse the ID-card—the physical possession of the ID-card is required to authenticate oneself for the purposes of using the e-services. This works vice versa as well—if the physical card gets into wrong hands, the e-services are still not available if the public key infrastructure cannot confirm the validity of the certificates. Moreover, the chip on the card has a counter of wrong entries, which means that the PIN will be blocked after three erroneous attempts to identify oneself (and it can be unblocked by a PUK code).[30] The possible attacks on the system can include, for instance, a specifically designed malware which could imitate the utility or plug-ins in the browser attempting to redirect the user who has authenticated oneself or tries to change the details of a bank transfer. However, both of these presume that it is the computer that is compromised, not the e-ID system.

With a view to future developments and taking into account what Estonia has already achieved at national level, the near future will enable the use of Mobile-IDs[31] outside of Estonia. Once the e-resident exchanges the existing SIM card with the PKI-capable one (meaning that enabling the use of Mobile-IDs requires a contract with an Estonian mobile network operator), the authentication and verification of digital identities via a mobile phone offers the same potentiality and quality as it is through a computer—only more convenient; the authentication and giving of digital signatures will no longer be dependent on having access to a computer; along with an ID-card reader and the software, it will suffice to have access to a mobile phone (does not necessarily have to be a smartphone) or a tablet. Mobile-IDs provide the same access to the services by remembering PIN codes

[28] §5 (1) of the Digital Signatures Act: "... a certificate is a document which is issued in order to enable a digital signature or digital seal to be given and verified and in which a public key is uniquely linked to the certificate holder".

[29] ID-Card. Computer protection. Information security signpost. [ID-kaart. Arvutikaitse. Infoturvalisuse teeviit.]

[30] *Ibid.*

[31] About Mobile ID from the official ID-card and Mobile-ID portal.

1 and 2, and the data exchange takes place over an encrypted connection, which thus ensures the same level of security.[32]

## 2.2 Political Aim

An e-resident will receive an identification card which, though, does not have a photo on it and thus cannot be used as a travel document, for instance. Accordingly, an e-resident's identity card is first and foremost a digital document[33] embodying a variety of e-services which are opened to the new e-resident in the form of an ID-card bearing a microchip with security certificates similar to national ID-cards.[34] The focus point is that irrespective of nationality and whatever the digital service is, an e-Estonian can authenticate oneself with just a few clicks. Until the first e-residency was issued towards the end of 2014,[35] only citizens of some other EU Member States who operated a digital identification system similar to Estonians were able to authenticate themselves in the same way (access was granted for specific services exclusively, e.g., the e-Business Register) as those owning an Estonian ID-card. However, due to the minimal number of such ID-cards and their users in the rest of the EU[36] (Estonia has been accepting the certificates of Belgium, Finnish, Portuguese and Lithuanian ID-cards since 2008), as well as considering that there was no effective solution for involving third country nationals, it was perceived that the Estonian economy, culture, education and science could not be advanced sufficiently without foreigners taking up the use of Estonian digital services, and hence the e-residence was created as a solution addressing the issue.[37]

This is explicated in the concept of e-residency, which marks attracting and involving foreign expertise and investment as the only possibility (if not a prerequisite) for Estonia to establish itself in today's globalised world where economic, political and cultural development is mostly based on international communication and cooperation.[38] The drafters[39] of the Concept stipulated that the contribution of such experts ought not to be dependent on their physical location, and therefore the

---

[32] Martens (2010), p. 217.

[33] IDA, supra note 19, § $20^5$. The Identity Documents Act differentiates between a digital identity card §2 ($1^1$) and a digital document prescribed for digital identification of a person §3 (3).

[34] *Ibid*, § $20^2$. Digital data to be entered on digital identity card.

[35] The first e-resident was the British journalist, Senior Editor to the Economist Magazine, Edward Lucas. See, for instance, his foreword to the e-Estonia newsletter.

[36] Estonian ID-card and e-ID are actually quite similar to Belgium card. See Martens (2010), p. 216.

[37] The Concept, supra note 16, p. 4.

[38] *Ibid*, p. 3.

[39] The proposals in the Concept were developed in joint effort of representatives from Estonian Ministry of the Interior, Republic of Estonia Government Office, Ministry of Economic Affairs and Communications, Information System Authority, Police and Border Guard Board, Estonian

e-residency would be a perfect solution for giving interested foreigners the premises to participate in everyday affairs with digital solutions equal to those available to Estonian citizens and residents, without actually having to be physically present.[40]

What concerns the compatriot policy is that the instigators of e-residency see it as an appropriate medium for keeping emigrant Estonians in connection with their roots by offering the possibilities to get access to digital services regardless of their citizenship or state of residence. It is laid down: "insofar as the Estonian identity is first and foremost based on language and culture deriving from it, the Estonian language based communication with emigrant communities in other states becomes important [. . .]. Thus the probability that current emigrants as well as second and third generations will maintain their connection to Estonia, some of them returning to Estonia or keeping cross-border connections, will increase."[41]

By receiving a verifiable digital identity and a digital ID-card, the e-resident becomes identifiable with an ID-card and can authenticate oneself, as well as provide digital signatures in an electronic environment instead of physical signatures or facial recognition, which in turn means access to digital services offered by Estonia, as well as, in the near future, use of electronic identification and trust services in cross-border electronic transactions within the EU Digital Single Market.[42] Even though some services of the private sector, such as Internet banking, telecommunication operators self-service, etc., along with, e.g., Eesti.ee (Estonian Point of Single Contact[43]), Estonian Tax and Customs Board, are accessible online without the ID-card via a bank link, this is not as secure or as convenient as is access with the digital ID-card authentication.

## 2.3 *Ambiguities of the Concept*

At the moment, the list of possible (non-exhaustive) users for utilisation of the "regular" ID-card include private and public services, e.g., access to governmental institutions, e-voting, e-school and e-kindergarten, banks, university study information systems, telecommunication and Internet service providers, insurance, e-health system, etc., yet not all of them are accessible with the e-resident's

Internal Security Service, Estonian Tax and Customs Board, Certification Centre, with consultations from other interested parties.

[40] The Concept, supra note 16.

[41] *Ibid*, p. 6. This argument is based on an analysis on multiple citizenship, conducted by the Ministry of the Interior in 2013 [Mitmikkodakondsus. Analüüs. Siseministeerium 2013].

[42] The Regulation (EU) No. 910/2014 on electronic identification and trust services for electronic transactions in the internal market (eIDAS Regulation).

[43] The Points of Single Contact (PSCs) are e-government portals for entrepreneurs active in the service sector. It is a legal requirement to have a PSC in each EU country since December 2009 as set out in the EU Services Directive.

ID-card.[44] The e-residency card of digital Estonia nonetheless opens the virtual doors to registering a company online (via the Business Portal), signing documents digitally, exchanging encrypted documents, doing online reporting to business register, conducting secure online bank transfers,[45] declaring taxes online, submitting annual reports online, as well as accessing digital prescriptions in Estonian pharmacies.[46] The potential users of such services have been set forth in the Concept:

- foreign investors and the employees of companies founded by such investors;
- foreigners who are taking part in the management of such companies (in the managing board or council) or participate in the venture;
- foreign experts and employees in Estonian companies;
- foreign clients and partners of Estonian undertakings;
- foreign researchers, scholars, students;
- representatives of other states and international organisations in the Republic of Estonia (e.g., NATO Cyber Defence Centre of Excellence, EU IT Agency);
- family members of the aforementioned persons.[47]

Assessing the target group and the threefold objective for issuing e-residencies, i.e., (1) attracting people to use the country's e-services; (2) boosting Estonian economy and educational, scientific and cultural development by taking the services to an international arena; and (3) pursuing the compatriot policy, the concept comes across a bit diffusive. It is apparent that the focus is almost entirely on people with a financial interest in Estonia. As there is no mention of former Estonian citizens who have emigrated, the aim of contributing to the compatriot policy becomes obsolete.[48] Retaining that by using Estonian e-services via the digital identity card an e-Estonian is imposed with the responsibility to contribute to the development of Estonian economy, culture, education or science, it seems that this specific objective is not too forethoughtful. Apart from foreign researchers, scholars and students, it is difficult to find a target group who would promote Estonian culture, science or education. Simultaneously, the evaluation criteria indicating the assessment of increase of respective aspects are undefined or merely not made public—it is not explained how the e-Estonian should prove that due to the activism of him or her using Estonian e-services, the level of science would be raised by a certain percentage, and considering that the e-residency is not an infinite benefit, it

---

[44] These are listed as possible uses of ID-card. For more, see the ID-card and Mobile-ID official portal.

[45] An e-resident *may* be eligible to open a bank account in Estonia; however, it still requires a physical visit to Estonia, to the bank, and does not guarantee the opening of a bank account as it is up the bank to make the decision.

[46] Services for the so-called hassle-free transaction of affairs; see more at the e-Estonia website.

[47] The Concept, supra note 16, p. 6.

[48] To overly criticise, it seemed obsolete from the beginning. If the aim of the compatriot policy is to increase *communication* in Estonian language between migrant (ex)citizens, e-residency is surely not the tool bearing in mind the penetration of social media sites.

is not clear how the e-resident should indicate the contribution to increase in Estonian development, in order to avoid being subjected to revocation of the e-identity.[49] It is quite apparent that the most desirable e-resident is a business-oriented person, boosting primarily economic development.[50] This is, of course, very remunerative for local businesses—engaging in business relationships with foreign colleagues and investors via digital and legally effective communication—and, of course, a thrust for the Estonian economy. Yet the added value of using e-services to scientists, artists or academic persons remains, at least at this point, ambiguous.

## 3 The Conflicting Regulatory Framework

Estonia is undeniably leading a digital way of life and disclosing this lifestyle to foreign nationals. Although the same safe software is used for Estonian citizens' ID-cards, residents' ID-cards and e-residents' ID-cards, the digital identity of an e-resident is distinguishable from the digital identities of the former two by the certificates, hence ensuring that by having the digital identity the legal status of the person using the e-services remains legible.[51] Consequently, the service providers can separately monitor the use of e-residents' digital identifications or restrict access to them whenever necessary. Even though e-services that are meant for citizens only—for instance, e-voting—are not accessible to e-residents, which is made clear at authentication, providing a digital identity still requires scrutinising the applications and e-activity of the e-resident to see whether or not a person is a suitable candidate for becoming an e-Estonian and whether the person who has already received the e-residency is using it judiciously.[52]

As is oft emphasised in the introductory concept of e-residency, it must be born in mind that the digital identity of an e-resident is a benefit, not a right,[53] implying that the Estonian officials deciding over its issuing can require something from the person seeking to have a digital liaison with Estonia and can take the privilege away if the e-resident's activities do not comply with Estonian regulations or codes of conduct. The Estonian Identity Documents Act formulates the prerequisites for obtaining e-residency—the person applying for an Estonian digital identity must

[49] Pursuant to IDA, supra note 19, § $20^6$ (4), the card may be revoked if the basis specified in subsection (1), i.e., having a relationship with the Estonian state or legitimate interest in the use of e-services of the Estonian state, of this section ceases to exist.

[50] The Ministry of Economic Affairs and Communications introductory page to e-residency, under the title "Why are we doing it?" declares—"Registration of businesses will bring investments to Estonia and create jobs and will thus accelerate the economic growth." Nothing about culture, education or science.

[51] The Concept, supra note 16, p. 4.

[52] *Ibid*, p. 12.

[53] *Ibid*, Section 2.1. Underlying Principles [Aluspõhimõtted].

have either "a relationship with the Estonian state" *or* "legitimate interest in the use of e-services of the Estonian state".[54] Even though the Act sets forth the criteria of legitimate interest or previous relationship, it does not elaborate on the principles and leaves both open to interpretation. Previous relationship [in Estonian: "eelnev seos"] has an implausibly wide scope and could mean anything from a visit to Estonia to formerly renounced Estonian citizenship. By the same token, it is rather challenging to identify a legitimate interest to use the e-services if there is no formal way of formulating it.

## 3.1 *Issuing, Suspending, Revoking the E-Residency Applications*

The procedure of dispensing digital identity cards foresees that the potential e-resident has to substantiate legitimate interest in the form of a written statement or other proof laying down the intent and circumstances of use[55] (the assessment of which is, in fact, not defined anywhere) or a prior connection with Estonia (not defined either), as well as provide the Estonian Police and Border Guard Board with personal data (including sensitive data, i.e., biometrical data).[56] Subsequently, the application undergoes a review and processing of the information handed to Estonian officials from the Police and Border Guard Board in order to establish whether the applicant would be a proper Estonian e-citizen. Thus, it is the Police and Border Guard Board who has the right to decide over the application,[57] identify and verify the person,[58] as well as exercise state supervision over issued e-residencies, together with the Estonian Internal Security Service and the Estonian Tax and Customs Board.[59] Even though at the launch of the e-residency programme the applicant was obliged to travel to Estonia twice (once to submit the application and identify oneself and for the second time in order to obtain the document—identity documents cannot be posted), from April 1, 2015, it has been made possible to apply in Estonian embassies and consular offices in 38 foreign representations, or

---

[54] IDA, supra note 19, § $20^6$ (1). Conditions for issue, suspension of validity and revocation of e-resident's digital identity card.

[55] §$10^2$ (1) of Regulation of the Government of the Republic laying down the list of certificates and information to be submitted upon application and terms for the issue of an identity card, a residence permit card, a digital identity card, an Estonian citizen's passport, a seafarer's discharge book, a temporary travel document, a travel document for a refugee or a certificate of record of service on ships.

[56] IDA, supra note 19, § 9. Standard format of documents and data entered in documents.

[57] IDA, supra note 19, §$11^1$. Identification of person and verification of identity upon issue of document; § $12^1$. Issue of document; §15 Organisation of issue and revocation of document, (4). See also Estonian Ministry of the Interior website.

[58] *Ibid.* §$20^9$. Identification of person and verification of identity of e-resident.

[59] *Ibid.* §$20^8$. Exercise of state supervision. See further Chapter 6 of the Estonian Aliens Act.

online,[60] whereas applications are still sent to Estonia for review.[61] After submitting the application, the Police and Border Guard Board is granted the discretion to decide upon the issuing of e-residency to the applicant.[62] During the evaluation of the eligibility of the candidate and even after the issuing, for the purpose of follow-up monitoring, the Board officials can exercise the authority to check the reliability of an e-resident from all accessible sources, whereas they can involve relevant institutions and make inquiries into necessary data collections for verification of identity and process data without prior notification or consent.[63]

At the stage of application, whereas the Police and Border Guard Board is responsible for receiving the information from the application on the reason for applying, it is an intricate task assigned for the Board to determine whether that specific applicant, by using Estonian e-services (e-prescription or banking system, for instance) will be able to contribute to Estonian culture, education, science or economy. Starting from the latter, it is perhaps the easiest to decide upon the economic aspect—if the applicant proclaims that the legitimate interest is establishing a business in Estonia—this most likely enhances the business environment and possibly even economy. However, it must be awfully difficult, if not impossible, for the Board to determine whether the fact that a person who has twice visited Estonia (and thus has a previous relationship with Estonia?) will be able to promote the country's culture, education or science. Accordingly, it appears that the tasks concerning the evaluation of the effect of the e-resident's use of e-services are in general uncharacteristic to the work of the Estonian Police and Border Guard Board.

Moreover, in view of the aforementioned, if the Police and Border Guard Board accepts, handles the inquiries, decides upon issuing and exercises control over the applications,[64] the institutional capacity of the Board must be increased to face the amplified working load.[65] With that regard, it must be emphasised that there is a very obvious discrepancy between what the Digital Agenda 2020 for Estonia has laid down and what the developers of the idea had in mind in terms of number of e-residents. The former set a goal of 5000 e-ID cards issued to non-residents,[66] by

[60] Since May 13, 2015, an online application site has been accessible at https://apply.e-estonia.com/, rendering obligatory merely one visit to the consular office, embassy or Estonian Police and Border Guard Representation necessary for obtaining the document.

[61] IDA, supra note 19, §$20^7$ ($1^1$).

[62] *Ibid*, §§ $20^6$ and $20^7$.

[63] The Concept, supra note 16, p. 9.

[64] Even if initially submitted to foreign missions, the applications are referred for examination to the Board officials in Estonia.

[65] After opening the online application site, the workload for the Police and Border Guard Board has further increased; at the moment of writing this article, it seems that the amplified load is a problem insofar as according to the official application website, the review process has slowed down: "Due to high volume of applications, the application review process will currently take longer than expected. Thank you for your patience."

[66] Digital Agenda 2020 for Estonia, p. 30.

2020, which would roughly mean a thousand new e-residents per year. The latter goal, namely 10 million e-Estonians by 2025, would either indicate that within the remaining 5 years there would be an additional 9,995,000 e-residencies issued or a "less intense" division over 10 years, i.e., a million new e-residents per year. A simple calculation shows that between the period of 1 December 2014 until 31 December 2024, this would entail issuing e-residencies for roughly 2715 people per day, i.e., in case of a 24-h working system, including full time on weekends and public holidays, 113 people per hour. With the above-mentioned pace at 463 - e-residents per month and a half, not only the goal will not be achieved unless the institutional capacity is enormously increased, but the concept itself must be made more attractive to receive more than 600 applications within 36 days.

## 3.2 *Legal Certainty for E-Residents*

The fact that a relationship with Estonia or a legitimate interest is a prerequisite for becoming an e-resident, whereas it is not clearly indicated what those are, indicates that the Estonian system can be considered to lack complete articulation and contain regulatory ambivalences. The Estonian Identity Documents Act has left much discretion for interpretation in terms of to whom the e-residencies and under which circumstances are issued which may create obscurity in terms of legal certainty of the e-residency candidates and e-residents. Even though marketed as the key for using Estonian e-services, the Concept provides that there is no ubiquitous access to what Estonia offers its residents and/or citizens. The e-residents can be bound by limits that private sector service providers choose to impose on accessing their services.[67] Therefore, on the premise that a service provider deems it more appropriate to offer its facilities only to residents and/or citizens, there is discretion to leave the e-residents out of the scope of their services. In addition, the official explanatory concept lays down that it is plausible, in duly justified cases [põhjendatud juhtudel], to limit the access of e-residents to public digital services or to set forth additional preconditions, which help to reduce the risks accompanying e-residency.[68] The aforementioned combined means that the e-resident cannot and perhaps should not expect unlimited access to the realm of e-Estonia.

In accordance with the Identity Documents Act and pursuant to the Concept,[69] the legal status of an e-resident is similar to the status of an alien and is analogous to the situation of issuing a visa—there exists no subjective right to stay in Estonia or a right to obtain an identity document from Estonia. Furthermore, the issuing, refusal to issue or exercising supervision does not require further reasoning on behalf of the

[67] The Concept, supra note 16, p. 8.

[68] *Ibid*, p. 8.

[69] The Concept, supra note 16, p. 10.

state.[70] Thus, it is emphasised that neither the latter mentioned actions nor suspension of validity or exercising state supervision can violate *a non-existing fundamental right or freedom* insofar as the situation of an e-resident is analogous to that of a person on temporary stay.[71] This leaves the legal status of the e-resident abstruse—that he or she is not a resident or a citizen of Estonia is clear; however, having received a digital identity and an identity number based on which that person can be identified through the use of national public key infrastructure should give that person a fiduciary relation with Estonia beyond that of an alien on temporary stay. On top of it all, the authors of the Concept must have failed to understand the meaning of fundamental rights and freedoms.

## *3.3 More Security: Less Privacy?*

As outstretched in the preceding section, the Police and Border Guard Board, to whom the e-residency candidates submit (via embassies or online) the personal data, decides over the granting of the e-ID by identifying and verifying the applicants and assessing their justification of interest. The potential digital resident submits to the Estonian authorities the standard format of documents and data (including biometric data[72]) that is also required for issuing national identity documents, i.e., passports and Estonian identity cards that can be used for physical identification, e.g., for travelling purposes. In accordance with Estonian law, the identity documents, together with the data submitted, are stored in a specific government-established database, the purpose of which is to "ensure the interior security of the state by keeping record of the identification of persons and the issue and revocation of identity documents".[73] Services accessed with digital authentication via the X-Road system are stored in state information system databases which are interfaced with the data exchange layer of the state information system.[74]

The data processed in IT systems are secured by a three-level IT baseline security system (ISKE) which was specifically adapted for Estonian public sector based on a German information security standard—IT Baseline Protection Manual (IT-Grundschutz in German)—and is mandatory to be followed by state and local government institutions handling databases/registers.[75] Pursuant to ISKE, there are three levels of security, low (L), medium (M) and high (H). The information stored

[70] *Ibid*, pp. 10–11 and the IDA, supra note 19, § $20^7$ (3).

[71] The Concept, supra note 16, pp. 11–12.

[72] IDA, supra note 19, §9.

[73] *Ibid*, §$15^2$.

[74] Public Information Act, § $43^2$. State information system.

[75] Government Regulation No. 252 of 20.12.2007, Information systems security measures sytem [Infosüsteemide turvameetmete süsteem]. Only available in Estonian. For an overview in English, please see the Information Systems Authority website.

in the identity document database has the highest security level (H). As explained in Sect. 2.1 regarding the technological basis for the e-IDs, there is one single authentication system that has proven to be secure and reliable for both national identity cards as well as e-resident cards. Nevertheless, on top of this, in order to support the system of digital identities and ensure its integrity at the core, biometric data of all individuals who have applied for or own Estonian identity cards, irrespective of whether they are national identity documents or digital identity documents meant exclusively for e-identification, are stored in digital database cards, archived and retained for 50 years[76] (in case of e-residency, this is done to avoid conferring duplicate identities to one person[77]).

The integration of biometric features in passports and travel documents is being done in accordance with EC Regulation 2252/2004,[78] whereas the pressure for the EU to introduce the biometric passport in the first place came from the US government in their context of "war on terror",[79] *inter alia*, for aligning the Member States' legislation with the US relevant legislation for the purpose of being eligible to participate in the United States Visa Waiver Program in order to allow the EU nationals to enter the US territory without a visa.[80] From the perspective of e-residents, this is immaterial—the digital identity documents issued do not serve as travel documents, as has been established above. Nevertheless, due to the fact that under the Estonian Identity Documents Act the term "digital identity card" denotes both the e-IDs of nationals as well as e-residents' e-ID cards, the requirement of biometric identifiers also applies to both.

Drawing on the aforementioned, the authors of the given chapter claim that the failure to differentiate between the two types of documents leads to unnecessary collection of biometric data that is in contradiction with the Data Protection Directive Article 6 principles of purpose and proportionality[81] (Article 5 in the draft Data Protection Regulation[82]). Article 29 Data Protection Working Party has acknowledged that the increased use of biometrics presents specific data protection risks which are further increased if biometric identifiers are kept in external databases, whereas if there are alternative less intrusive means available, biometric

[76] Government Regulation No. 109 of 03.07.2008, Statutes on maintaining the database on identity documents. [Isikut tõendavate dokumentide andmekogu pidamise põhimäärus] §§4 and 18. Only available in Estonian.

[77] The Concept, supra note 16, p. 9.

[78] Council Regulation (EC) No 2252/2004 of 13 December 2004 on standards for security features and biometrics in passports and travel documents issued by Member States.

[79] Goncalves and Gameiro (2012), p. 324.

[80] Background to Regulation 2252/2005, available at EUR-Lex.

[81] Directive 95/46/EC.

[82] Proposal for a Regulation on the protection of individuals with regard to the processing of personal data and on the free movement of such data (General Data Protection Regulation). COM (2012) 11 final.

data should not be used.[83] They have accentuated that there should at the outset be clear determination for which such data will be used, and subsequently the taking of personal data should not be excessive in relation to the purposes for which they are collected; "[i]n other words, authentication/verification applications which can be carried out without a central storage of biometric data should not implement excessive identification techniques."[84]

Bearing in mind that the e-residents' identity card is only valid for digital identification and not for physical identification, the requirement for biometric data seems to be straightforwardly unreasonable and disproportionate and Estonian legislation on e-residency contradicting the aforementioned assertions from every angle. The necessity of the use of biometrics for physical identifications as prescribed by the EU regulatory framework should not extend to digital identification; various authors have avouched that even for use in travel documents and passports, the advantages of biometrics are often overshadowed by subsequent storing of the data that results in non-repudiation use of biometrics, such as increased levels of control and surveillance, leading to a "so-called big brother scenario"[85] or to a "global police state".[86] In case of e-residency, the justification for using biometrics is to avoid granting duplicate identities, as stated above. At present, it can only be speculated whether or not this is proportional and purposeful.

The authors contributing to the previous volume of this book have analysed the various challenges and novel problems with respect to privacy and protection of personal data for national and supranational legal systems in terms of intensified digitalisation and technological innovations adapted for e-governance systems.[87] Dutt and Kerikmäe, who provided introspect to the concepts and problems associated with e-democracy, saw "a secure, private and safe online identity for citizens" to be one of the key aspects for e-democracy to succeed "as a more pivotal feature of democracy".[88] However, juxtaposing the secure multi-layered technological infrastructure encircling the e-IDs with yet another security technology—the biometrics—there is a possible reverse effect to (e-)democracy. It has been ratiocinated that giving too much leeway to new technological developments without proper analysis of the fundamental rights perspective, the (often) subtle multiplication of security measures may pose an ultimate risk to democracy instead.[89] Biometrics as security technology cannot be "thrown in" for good measure, as

[83] Article 29 Data Protection Working Party. Working Party on Police and Justice. The Future of Privacy. Joint contribution to the Consultation of the European Commission on the legal framework for the fundamental right to protection of personal data, pp. 14, 26 and 27.

[84] Article 29 Data Protection Working Party. Working document on biometrics, p. 6.

[85] Schouten and Jacobs (2009), p. 311.

[86] Ashbourn (2005), p. 20.

[87] See the contributions of, for instance, Katrin Nyman-Metcalf, Ülle Madise, Priit Vinkel, Pawan Dutt, Agnes Kasper, Addi Rull, Ermo Täks and Alexander Norta in Kerikmäe (2014).

[88] Dutt and Kerikmäe (2014), p. 294.

[89] Goncalves and Gameiro (2012), pp. 322–323.

Estonia seems to have done, without proper analysis of risks for the protection of fundamental rights and freedoms, not considering whether the purpose to be achieved could not be achieved by less intrusive means.

Ten years ago, Ashbourn condemned biometrics-favouring governments, referring to them as having "rushed headlong into what can only be described as a frenzy of biometric related initiatives accompanied by clouds of emotionally misleading and technically incorrect rhetoric".[90] Even though innovative identity verifications pose interesting technological challenges—he wrote—we should not act as children playing with technological toys.[91] Prior to introduction of e-residency, Nyman-Metcalf, a notable e-governance expert, professed, when considering legal framework of e-governance, including the future of digital identities, that fields such as e-signatures or e-identification demand special or specifically customised existing legislation for their proper regulation.[92] She emphasised that law is the background against which to assess the applicability of new technological developments.[93] Estonian way for "making room" for e-residency within the Identity Documents Act is not precisely in harmony with the range of prospective challenges to violation of use of biometrics but rather resembles attempts to play with that technological toy. Thus, from legal point of view, it looks like the introduction of the concept was pushed through too abruptly, not fully considering the multitude of facets surrounding e-residency.

## 4 Can E-Residency Create a Global Digital Citizen?

Despite the contradictions presented in the preceding sections, the e-residency concept in itself is innovative and unforeseen, corresponding to the need for a cross-border recognition of digital identities—it has been noted that due to ongoing technological developments and enormous increase in information flow, secure and reliable dissemination of information, especially what concerns digital verification of the individual, is certainly challenging. Scholars, such as Al-Khouri, argue that the lack of secure and dependable tool connecting physical and digital identities impedes development and precludes the use of full potential of cross-globe digital economy.[94] His argumentation relies on the OECD 2011 report, which accentuated the need for global digital identity management offering means for "trusted remote interactions" and further cultivating the Internet economy.[95] The report encouraged

[90] Ashbourn (2005), p. 21.

[91] *Ibid.*

[92] Nyman-Metcalf (2014), p. 41.

[93] *Ibid*, p. 34.

[94] Al-Khouri (2014). See also Graux (2013), De Andrade (2012) and De Andrade (2013).

[95] OECD (2011). Digital Identity Management. Enabling Innovation and Trust in the Internet Economy.

governments to adopt national identity management strategies, align their e-government services with the strategy and subsequently cooperate at international level for mutual recognition of enabling cross-border digital management.[96]

At the EU level, cross-border use of online services by secure electronic identification and authentication is seen as an integral part of the Europe 2020 strategy for smart, sustainable and inclusive growth.[97] In the process of effectuating the strategy, a regulation was proposed and adopted for the EU-wide mutual recognition of e-identification and digital signatures[98] in order to provide a framework for secure and trustworthy cross-border digital communication and an interoperable system of e-government services between citizens, businesses and public authorities across the EU.[99] The Regulation foresees, among other things, the need for creation of a public key infrastructure at pan-European level for increasing the security of digital transactions and is not intended to interfere with existing national infrastructure on electronic identity managements systems (such as Estonian national e-ID system) but enforced to make them interoperable.

An effective solution seems to subsist at the small corner of Europe, in the form of a programme providing e-trust services to foreign nationals based on the previously existing national identity documents, state-backed by the PKI, enabling access to private and public services by secure means of authentication and verification, and it is called e-residency, except that it is only there to make contributions to Estonian economy, science, education or culture and to increase the visibility of Estonia as a technologically advanced state (who perhaps had what it takes to effectuate a global—at least EU-wide—digital identity management even before the world realised they needed one) and except that it exists as a closed system not designed to serve as *modus operandi* for global effectuation of mutual digital identification management. Then again, Estonian ID-card is one of numerous national e-identity systems, although indeed one of the most successful schemes in terms of integration and use at national level. Estonian solutions stand out in the era of proliferation of identity management systems and techniques in the marketplace[100] (like the Apple's trackpad signature) as a result of the all-encompassing use of digital identification for both private and public digital services. Thus, although it can at first be perceived as the key for cross-border digital authentication, the e-residency programme has since the beginning advertised itself as being a closed, Estonia-patronising system and never shown any

---

[96] *Ibid.*

[97] Communication from the Commission Europe 2020. A strategy for smart, sustainable and inclusive growth. COM(2010) 2020 final.

[98] Regulation (EU) No. 910/2014.

[99] Even though there was a legal framework for digital signatures at the EU level even prior to the Digital Agenda 2020, it existed solely only e-signatures (Directive 1999/93/EC) and did not encompass e-identification or other trust services, e.g., time stamping.

[100] See Hoikkanen et al. (2010), p. 6.

philanthropic purpose at the global scale.[101] Therewith, e-residency should not be seen as the sought-for panacea for a global digital citizen, but considering the attention it has brought to Estonia, it seems to be an exuberant national start-up splendidly serving its purpose of retaining the image of a tech-savvy country.

## 5 Concluding Remarks

This chapter has indicated that the idea of making a foreign national, for example a Sri Lankan, an e-Estonian is a very ambitions one, and despite certain deficiencies in Estonian legal framework, as well as the dubious capacity of the responsible institutions enforcing the e-residency programme, the concept has been pushed through and has received great attention worldwide. E-residency has enticed people from across the world to become Estonian digital citizens, including, for instance, the well-known British Journalist Edward Lucas (also the first e-resident) and high-ranked officials, such as the Prime Minister of Japan, Shinzō Abe. Therefore, by virtue of the fact that e-residency was launched to operate within a closed national system providing to foreign nationals Estonian e-services and gathering them under the umbrella of Estonian e-ID system with contributions to Estonian development in mind, the programme can be regarded a successful ICT tool. What has not been successful, though, is the implementation of the e-residency concept in coordination of it with national and supranational regulatory framework.

Even though it has been made clear that the e-residency programme does not seek to serve as a model for global or EU-wide effectuation of digital identity management, certain reconsiderations should be made with regard to data protection aspects of the concept in order to make it resemble the cyberdream it has been referred to. Currently, the Estonian government plays a twofold role for e-residents—being simultaneously a friend and a foe. On the one hand, Estonia offers the proven system of secure government-provided and state-backed identity that supports the safe access via e-identification and authentication to Estonian e-services; on the other hand, there is a challenge to the data privacy in the form of long-term storage of the e-residents' personal information in Estonian databases.[102] The uptake of ICTs for e-governance solutions demands methodological approach and careful analysis for a consistent regulatory system that could coexist with innovation and technological advancements,[103] but e-residency was unsystematically merged with existing regulation.

[101] Curiously enough, Graux, when analysing the problematics of the EU eSignatures Directive, noted that the comprehensive electronic authentication framework common to the EU could be regarded as a business opportunity since the EU has failed to act upon this at supranational level. See Graux (2011).

[102] Hoikkanen et al. (2010), p. 4.

[103] Innovative technologies need e-regulation that is consistent and interoperable with "traditional" regulation. With developing implementable e-regulation, a need arises for progressive methodological basis. An example of 10 policy principles for such methodological approach are provided, for instance, by Kerikmäe and Dutt; see Kerikmäe and Dutt (2014), pp. 28–29.

The bottom line is that in terms of a general framework surrounding the concept of e-residency, the layers of protection of digital identities are sound from technical security perspective but are not completely in coherence with the EU legal principles on data protection. These indications are not meant to accuse Estonia of potential violations of data confidentiality, integrity and security or question its cybersecurity strategy but rather are intended to come across as a *caveat* for a country that will possibly be digitally storing the data of thousands of foreign nationals in the era where cyberattacks are not uncommon. Likewise, if Estonia sees the idea of 10,000 or 10 million e-residents as a tangible prospect, the authors see the re-evaluation of the current legislation supporting the e-residency—i.e., the Estonian Identity Documents Act, which was merely amended to "accommodate" the provisions related to e-residency—as indispensable.

# References

## *Books and Articles*

Al-Khouri AM (2014) Digital identity: transforming GCC economies. Innov: Manage Policy Pract 16(2):184–194

Ashbourn J (2005) The social implications of the wide scale implementation of biometric and related technologies. Background paper for the Institute of Prospective Technological Studies, DG Joint Research Centre, European Commission

De Andrade NNG (2012) Regulating electronic identity in the European Union: an analysis of the Lisbon Treaty's competences and legal basis for eID. Comput Law Secur Rev 28:153–162

De Andrade NNG (2013) "Electronic Identity for Europe": moving from problems to solutions. J Int Commer Law Technol 8(2):104–109

Dutt P, Kerikmäe T (2014) Concepts and problems associated with eDemocracy. In: Kerikmäe T (ed) Regulating eTechnologies in the European Union: normative realities and trends. Springer Verlag, pp 285–323

Goncalves ME, Gameiro MI (2012) Security, privacy and freedom and the EU legal and policy framework for biometrics. Comput Law Secur Rev 28:320–327

Graux H (2011) Rethinking the e-signatures directive: on laws, trust services, and the digital single market. Digit Evid Electron Signature Law Rev 8:9–24

Graux H (2013) Moving towards a comprehensive legal framework for electronic identification as a trust service in the European Union. J Int Commer Law Technol 8(2):110–117

Hoikkanen A, Bacigalupo M, Compano R, Lusoli W, Maghiros I (2010) New challenges and possible policy options for the regulation of electronic identity. J Int Commer Law Technol 5 (1):1–10

Kerikmäe T (ed) (2014) Regulating eTechnologies in the European Union. Normative realities and trends. Springer International Publishing

Kerikmäe T, Dutt P (2014) Conceptualization of emerging legal framework of E-regulation in the European Union. In: Kerikmäe T (ed) Regulating eTechnologies in the European Union: normative realities and trends. Springer Verlag, pp 7–32

Madise Ü, Vinkel P (2014) Internet voting in Estonia: from constitutional debate to evaluation of experience over six elections. In: Kerikmäe T (ed) Regulating eTechnologies in the European Union: normative realities and trends. Springer Verlag, pp 53–72

Martens T (2010) Electronic identity management in Estonia between market and state governance. Identity Inf Soc 3(1):213–233

Nyman-Metcalf K (2014) e-Governance in law and by law. The legal framework of e-governance. In: Kerikmäe T (ed) Regulating eTechnologies in the European Union: normative realities and trends. Springer Verlag, pp 33–52

Schouten B, Jacobs B (2009) Biometrics and their use in e-passports. Image Vis Comput 27:305–312

## *Others:*

"Digital identity cards. Estonia takes the plunge." The Economist. 28 June 2014. Available at: http://www.economist.com/news/international/21605923-national-identity-scheme-goes-global-estonia-takes-plunge.

Application for e-Residency. Available at: https://apply.e-estonia.com/

Article 29 Data Protection Working Party. Working document on biometrics. Adopted on 1 August 2003. Available at: http://ec.europa.eu/justice/policies/privacy/docs/wpdocs/2003/wp80_en.pdf

Article 29 Data Protection Working Party. Working Party on Police and Justice. The Future of Privacy. Joint contribution to the Consultation of the European Commission on the legal framework for the fundamental right to protection of personal data. Adopted on 01 December 2009. Available at: http://ec.europa.eu/justice/policies/privacy/docs/wpdocs/2009/wp168_en.pdf

Background to Regulation 2252/2005. Available at EUR-Lex: http://eur-lex.europa.eu/legal-content/EN/LSU/?uri=CELEX:32004R2252.

Communication from the Commission Europe 2020. A strategy for smart, sustainable and inclusive growth. COM(2010) 2020 final.

Constitution of the Republic of Estonia. Available in English at: https://www.riigiteataja.ee/en/eli/530102013003/consolide

Council Regulation (EC) No 2252/2004 of 13 December 2004 on standards for security features and biometrics in passports and travel documents issued by Member States.

Digital Agenda 2020 for Estonia. Ministry of Economic Affairs and Communications. Available at: https://e-estonia.com/wp-content/uploads/2014/04/Digital-Agenda-2020_Estonia_ENG.pdf

Digital Agenda for Europe (Communication from the Commission of 19 May 2010 to the European Parliament, the Council, the European Economic and Social Committee and the Committee of the Regions – A Digital Agenda for Europe [COM(2010) 245 final – Not published in the Official Journal].).

Digital Agenda for Europe. Progress by country. Available at: https://ec.europa.eu/digital-agenda/en/scoreboard/estonia

Directive 1999/93/EC of the European Parliament and of the Council of 13 December 1999 on a Community framework for electronic signatures

Directive 95/46/EC of the European Parliament and of the Council of 24 October 1995 on the protection of individuals with regard to the processing of personal data and on the free movement of such data.

e-Estonia. The Digital Society. Available in English at: https://e-estonia.com/

Electronic ID-Card. E-Estonia.com Available in English at: https://e-estonia.com/component/electronic-id-card/

Elisabeth Braw, "'E-stonia' Attempts to Become the Uber of Economies by Introducing Virtual Residency." 30 October 2014. Newsweek. Available in English at: http://www.newsweek.com/2014/11/07/estonia-attempts-boost-economy-introducing-virtual-residency-280571.html

Estonian Development Fund. Available in English at: http://www.arengufond.ee/en/.
Estonian Information System Authority. Facts about e-Estonia. Available in English at: https://www.ria.ee/facts-about-e-estonia/
Estonian Information Systems Authority website. Available in English at: https://www.ria.ee/iske-en/
Estonian Ministry of the Interior. E-residency. Available in English at: https://www.siseministeerium.ee/e-residency/
Estonian National Electoral Committee. Statistics on Internet voting. Available in English at: http://vvv.vvk.ee/voting-methods-in-estonia/engindex/statistics/.
Estonian Tax and Customs Board Yearbooks. Available in English and Estonian at: http://www.emta.ee/index.php?id=34149&tpl=1026 and http://www.emta.ee/index.php?id=14595
Foreword of Edward Lucas' foreword to the e-Estonia newsletter at: https://e-estonia.com/foreword-to-the-e-estonia-newsletter-by-edward-lucas/
Freedom House Freedom on the Net 2014. Estonia country report: https://freedomhouse.org/report/freedom-net/2014/estonia
ID-Card. Computer protection. Information security signpost. ID-kaart. Arvutikaitse. Infoturvalisuse teeviit. Only available in Estonian at: http://www.arvutikaitse.ee/arvutikaitse-algtoed/id-kaart/
Issuing digital identities to non-residents: creating e-residency. Concept. Appendix to explanatory memorandum to draft legislation of Estonian Identity Documents Act and State Fees Act. Appendix 1." [Mitteresidentidele digitaalse isikutunnistuse väljaandmine: e-residentsuse loomine. Kontseptsioon. Isikut tõendavate dokumentide seaduse ja riigilõivuseaduse muutmise seaduse eelnõu seletuskirja juurde. Lisa 1.] 2014.
Memorandum of Understanding between Finland and Estonia on cooperation in the field of ICT. Available in English at: https://valitsus.ee/sites/default/files/news-related-files/ict_mou_fi-ee_10dec2013.pdf.
OECD (2011). Digital Identity Management. Enabling Innovation and Trust in the Internet Economy. Available at: http://www.oecd.org/sti/ieconomy/49338380.pdf
Official ID-card and Mobile-ID portal. Available in English at: http://www.id.ee/?lang=en&id
Proposal for a Regulation on the protection of individuals with regard to the processing of personal data and on the free movement of such data (General Data Protection Regulation). COM(2012) 11 final.
Regulation (EU) No 910/2014 of the European Parliament and of the Council of 23 July 2014 on electronic identification and trust services for electronic transactions in the internal market and repealing Directive 1999/93/EC
Regulation (EU) No. 910/2014 on electronic identification and trust services for electronic transactions in the internal market
Regulation of the Government of the Republic laying down the list of certificates and information to be submitted upon application and terms for the issue of an identity card, a residence permit card, a digital identity card, an Estonian citizen's passport, a seafarer's discharge book, a temporary travel document, a travel document for a refugee or a certificate of record of service on ships. Only available in Estonian.
Republic of Estonia Aliens Act. Available in English at: https://www.riigiteataja.ee/en/eli/513042015008/consolide
Republic of Estonia Digital Signatures Act. Available in English at: https://www.riigiteataja.ee/en/eli/ee/530102013080/consolide/current
Republic of Estonia Government Regulation No. 109 of 03.07.2008, Statutes on maintaining the database on identity documents. [Isikut tõendavate dokumentide andmekogu pidamise põhimäärus]. Only available in Estonian.
Republic of Estonia Government Regulation No. 252 of 20.12.2007, Information systems security measures sytem [Infosüsteemide turvameetmete süsteem]. Only available in Estonian.
Republic of Estonia Identity Documents Act. § $20^5$. E-resident's digital identity card. Available in English at: https://www.riigiteataja.ee/en/eli/512112014001/consolide

Republic of Estonia Public Information Act. Available in English at: https://www.riigiteataja.ee/en/eli/522122014002/consolide

The D5 Charter: https://www.gov.uk/government/uploads/system/uploads/attachment_data/file/386290/D5Charter_signed.pdf

The Economist explains: How did Estonia become a leader in technology? The Economist. 30 July 2013, by A.A.K, describing Estonia as having a "strong tech culture." Available at: http://www.economist.com/blogs/economist-explains/2013/07/economist-explains-21.

The Minister of the Interior of the Republic of Estonia, Mr Hanno Pevkur at 05.02.2015 weekly press conference of the Government of the Republic of Estonia. Available in Estonian at: http://meediaveeb.valitsus.ee/show.php?path=/2015/pressikonverents-2015-02-05-rnd32757.f4v

The Twitter Post of the Prime Minister of Estonia: https://twitter.com/TaaviRoivas/status/523530893613617152?utm_source=fb&utm_medium=fb&utm_campaign=TaaviRoivas&utm_content=523530893613617152

# Intellectual Property Protection of 3D Printing Using Secured Streaming

**Paula-Mai Sepp, Anton Vedeshin, and Pawan Dutt**

**Abstract** 3D printing technology is a new and emerging technology which is capable of changing the world. However, an easy access to 3D printing technology makes a convenient way to illegally reproduce physical objects regardless of copyrights, license, and royalty payments. As 3D printing of physical things at home might become the "new normal," it will pose threats to traditional intellectual property laws, which were created in an era when copyright infringement of physical objects, or also defined as "physibles," was yet to come. The authors have brought forward the legal issues and have attempted to describe a unique technical solution—secured streaming which solves or at least partially solves the problem of copyrights in 3D printing. The proposed solution provides a possibility for a copyright owner to limit the number of 3D prints. He can specify the number of copies that are allowed for the manufacturer or an end user to produce. Moreover, secured streaming has detective and protective controls to detect information system compromises and to stop streaming of 3D designs to 3D printers.

## 1 Introduction

Three-dimensional (3D) space printing technology is often referred to as the new hot and emerging technology, capable of changing the world. In fact, the roots of the technology reach back to the late 1970s, when the seed for additive manufacturing

P.-M. Sepp (✉)
Ministry of Justice of Republic of Estonia, Tõnismägi 5a, 15191 Tallinn, Estonia
e-mail: paula.sepp@outlook.com

A. Vedeshin
3DPrinter OS, Mektory Innovation Center Building, Raja 15, 12618 Tallinn, Estonia
e-mail: anton.vedeshin@gmail.com; http://www.3dprinteros.com

P. Dutt
Tallinn Law School, Tallinn University of Technology, Akadeemia tee 3, 12618 Tallinn, Estonia
e-mail: pawan.dutt@ttu.ee



T. Kerikmäe, A. Rull (eds.), *The Future of Law and eTechnologies*,
DOI 10.1007/978-3-319-26896-5_5

idea was first put down as a joke, in a newspaper article by David Jones.[1] An independently filed patent application by Wyn Kelly Swainson for the same technology was granted in 1977.[2] 3D printing can be described as a method of joining materials, layer by layer, on the basis of a computer automated design (CAD) model or 3D-scanned file.[3] If inkjet printers print pixels from the screen onto a piece of paper using ink on an XY-axis, then 3D printers print using plastic string on an XYZ-axis, making the object three dimensional.[4] 3D printing technology is on the verge of a breakthrough into home use and is revolutionary in the sense that it enables everyone to become creator of things.[5] Additive manufacturing enables designers to create products with complex shape and very small detailing, which have previously been hard to execute with other methods of manufacturing.

3D printing is thus one of the automated manufacturing methods to produce physical objects by adding material layer by layer. There are many good examples of using 3D printing technology in industries and small and medium enterprises. New Balance is printing shoes by the size and exact shape of a sportsman's feet.[6] Francis Bitonti, a famous New York designer, is printing exceptional dresses and home accessories.[7] At remote locations, like aircraft carriers, oil derricks in sea, and space stations, it is important to get printable parts at the point of need and time of need without extra costs for logistics and shortest lead time. Boeing and Airbus are printing turbine parts to increase efficiency and reliability of aircraft engines. However, 3D printing is not anymore a method for prototyping at big factories and corporations. 3D printers are not yet at everyone's home, but even today they are at least accessible within walking distance in any major city. An easy access to 3D printing technology makes a convenient way to illegally reproduce physical objects regardless of copyrights, license, and royalty payments. After obtaining a printable 3D design, it can be reproduced many times without the possibility for a copyright owner to trace.

New digital technologies have made copying a lot easier than it has been before, and we have already witnessed the collateral damage in relation to copying of music and movies. As 3D printing of physical things at home might become the "new normal," it will pose threats to traditional intellectual property laws, which were created in an era when copyright infringement of physical objects, or also defined as

[1] Bradshaw et al. (2010), pp. 7–8.

[2] Ibid.

[3] Stahl (2013), pp. 3–4.

[4] Howells (2014), p. 13.

[5] Weinberg (2013), p. 1.

[6] New Balance (2013). Press release: New Balance Pushes the Limits of Innovation with 3D Printing. Available at: http://www.newbalance.com/press-releases/id/press_2013_New_Balance_Pushes_Limits_of_Innovation_with_3D_Printing.html (accessed 20.08.2015).

[7] See examples of high-end 3D designs from Francis Bitonti Studio web page. Available at: http://www.francisbitonti.com/ (accessed 20.08.2015).

"physibles,"[8] was yet to come. What also makes 3D printing stand out is the speed to market—it enables people to scan and create a physical product in a matter of hours. In particular, the intellectual property issues are paramount in relation to copyrights because they are free and exist automatically for a work that has been fixed in a tangible form. Other forms of intellectual property are not left untouched, as problems will also arise in the field of patents, trademarks, and industrial design protection. Another reason why copyrights have the biggest likelihood of becoming the object of infringement is that most items available for home 3D printing include designs of decorative nature or fan fiction art, which does not entail a useful feature.[9] The leading approach to 3D printing originates from the U.S., because the legal side of 3D printing has been dealt with more extensively there. The main elements of 3D printing technology are the physical 3D object and digital CAD files, which can be obtained through designing process in a CAD software or by 3D scanning. The digital CAD file and the physical 3D printed object easily meet the fixation requirement of copyright protection.[10] It is fundamental to recognize that CAD files differ from MP3 files used as music carriers and MP4 files used for audiovisual content, for which the suitability for intellectual property protection is not under doubt.[11] Because 3D printing contains both digital and physical characteristics, it is hard to determine whether the main characteristics and related intellectual property issues should be evaluated separately or as a whole. Scholarly opinions are roughly divided into two in deciding whether the CAD file or the 3D printed object poses a more pivotal question for the suitability for intellectual property protection.[12]

Gartner estimates that by 2018, 3D printing will result in the loss of at least $100 billion per year in intellectual property globally.[13] This creates a completely new problem of copyright protection, as it is relatively easy to copy and reproduce objects, and in some cases 3D printing even creates a threat on the society if parts are produced from not original or compromised designs.

[8] The online peer-to-peer sharing site, The Pirate Bay, launched a category for 3D designs called "physibles." See, for example: Walters (2012).

[9] Doherty (2012), p. 358.

[10] Dasari (2013), p. 279.

[11] Twomey (2014), p. 33.

[12] See: Dolinsky (2014), pp. 629–631. According to Dolinsky, there is no question in the copyrights of 3D printed objects, which are protected as "pictorial, graphical and sculptural works," and the main question will be the copyrightability of CAD files. See also: Rideout (2011), pp. 167–168. Rideout on the contrary states in his work that the copyrightability question of a CAD file is conditional to the eligibility of copyright protection of the 3D printed object. According to Rideout, it is the CAD files that would likely fall under "pictorial, graphic and sculptural works" and more specifically under "technical drawings, diagrams and models."

[13] Gartner (2013). Press release: Gartner Reveals Top Predictions for IT Organizations and Users for 2014 and Beyond. Available at: http://www.gartner.com/newsroom/id/2603215 (accessed 20.08.2015).

In this chapter, the authors will look into the legal issues and will attempt to describe a technical solution—secured streaming which solves or at least partially solves the problem of copyrights in 3D printing. The solution provides a possibility for a copyright owner (CO) to limit the number of 3D prints. CO can specify the number of copies that is allowed for the manufacturer or an end user to produce. Moreover, secured streaming has detective and protective controls to detect information system compromises and stop streaming of 3D designs to 3D printers.

## 2 Why Protecting Printable 3D Designs Has Become So Important

One would ask why copyright protection in automated manufacturing and 3D printing particularly is so important. Society has lived a long time without a special solution or just using Digital Rights Management (DRM) to secure CAD designs.

About 60–70 years ago we were at "paper age"; most of the products' technical drawings were done on paper. Imagine an individual who wants to copy the product; he makes pictures of the sketches. Now he needs to find a production technology, train engineers, set up a factory and production lines to produce prototypes and then a real product. Let's assume this would take around 2 years.

Then about 15–20 years ago we entered the digital age, which offered us the use of CAD tools. However, these tools were used mostly to create a virtualization of a product to make right measurements, different types of simulations, quicker changes to the structure after prototype testing cycles. If somebody would get such CAD design, he would still need to find a production technology, train engineers and set up a production facility; compared to the paper age example, this would take half a year to produce a real product.

Nowadays, at 3D printing age, CAD intended for 3D printing already has all important information inside to produce the real object. If one would compromise such a design, he can get to the market with the product in just a few days. As usually, the 3D design intended for 3D printing has all the needed information to manufacture a product according to all specifications, tolerances, durability and taking into account force distribution and dispensation.

## 3 What Are Current Technical Solutions Stating?

With the development of technology, the security requirements evolve too. Most of 3D printers connected to networks do not have enough protection against today's threat of digital theft. See Fig. 1 for a detailed 7 action (A1 . . . A7) and 6 transition (T1 . . . T6) steps of a CAD design life cycle from a product idea to a physical object

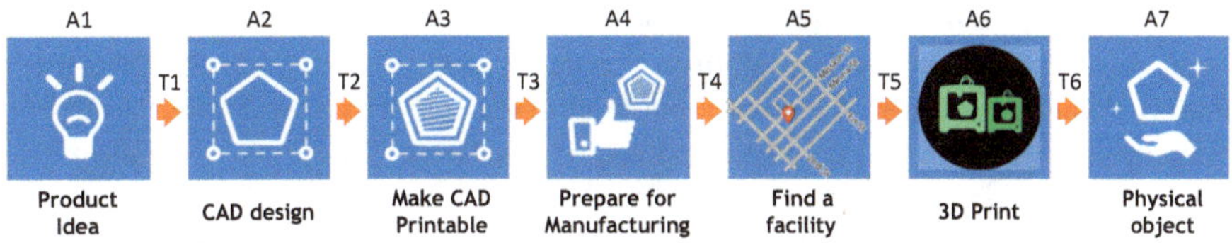


**Fig. 1** 7 action and 6 transition steps of a CAD design lifecycle: from a product idea to a physical object

manufacturing process. This is an illustrative model to represent the life cycle of a CAD design and in practice could contain more or less steps from product idea to a physical object. At every action or transition step, there is a special CAD or other software involved, and at transition steps in-between action steps there are different types of storage or information transfer technology used.

Action steps A1, A2, A3, A7 are possible to secure using different types of cloud CAD solutions from numerous companies[14]; however, none of these software packages offer end-to-end functionality or integrated security for the whole life cycle of a printable 3D design, which makes them vulnerable at least at steps A4, A5, A6, A7 and T3, T4, T5. Users use email, USB sticks, SD cards, network drives to share CAD designs with their colleagues or partners at steps T3, T4, T5 and frequently at steps T1, T2.

Transition steps T1, T2, T3, T4, T5 are possible to secure by existing technologies; however, most of the solutions are based on DRM model, which is vulnerable by its nature, or even if it is secured during the transition, it is still vulnerable at the end of transition step' for example, in sending files using SSL—when the file is received—it could be copied, or for example if file is downloaded from cloud storage, such as Google Drive, Box.com, or Dropbox, in the end of transition—saving to the hard drive of the personal computer—it becomes vulnerable. Some companies implement nondisclosure agreements (NDA) with employees and partners, which will not help either to protect digital content in a long-term perspective.

T5 is usually a USB or local network connection, which in case of modern 3D printers in not ultimately secured.

Some steps still are not possible to ultimately secure or alternatively could be solved at other than software level. T6 is delivery and a handover of a 3D printed physical object to the user. A7 is usage of the printed object by an end user. At T6 and A7 steps, object could be disassembled and scanned or reverse engineered in a different way for further reproducing.

In the following sections of this chapter, we will introduce an innovative method of securely streaming CAD designs seamlessly through A1–A6 and T1–T5 steps of CAD design lifestyle without exposing it to all involved parties.

NDA, DRM, and existing digital media streaming will not help.

[14] For example: Solid Edge from Siemens, Inventor from 3D Systems, Autodesk, Solid Works, etc.

Signing an NDA with employees or collaboration partners is a usual practice used within big, small, and medium-size organizations. Once the digital content is exposed due to intentional or nonintentional disclosure of information, there is no way to stop copying it or getting it back. Thus NDA is not anyhow helping to protect 3D designs long term.

Another method which is frequently used to secure digital content is DRM. Classical DRM works in a way that digital content is encrypted (usually the whole file) and then using email, web browser, CD/DVD disk, USB flash drive, or SD card is sent/given to an end user, who using a key decrypts the digital content and consumes it (please see figure below). If the content is stolen and the key is compromised or calculated (which is just a matter of time and computing power) then the content secured with DRM technology could be copied and used as many times as individuals want, there is no way to stop reproduction of such content. Good examples are numerous software packages, operating systems like Windows, DVD movies, games, MP3 media, etc. This is exactly the content Torrent networks and Pirate Bay like sites are full of. Not only DRM technology is an easy target of intellectual property copyright violation; moreover, malicious software and viruses are distributed together or inside packages with cracked DRM software, movies, and music.

Up to now many companies in digital media sector, such as Netflix, YouTube, Spotify, TuneIn, have used media and secured media streaming. From the first sight it seems that this would probably work for 3D designs too, as 3D designs are media to some extent. Media streaming also protects the content, even better than DRM. At a closer look, in order to stream media, it should be in streamable format, and information should not be anyhow available to download or obtain in a different way prior to digital media consuming session. Copyright protection is achieved by the complication of getting the stream, converting it to a different file format, and then distributing it. Sometimes the quality of media is not there, so it does not make any sense to grab, for example, a video from YouTube, or it is too complicated for the end user to go through all procedures to store one song or a movie to the hard drive of his computer; in 95 % of the cases it is easier to pay, as in case of streaming media businesses' business models, the subscription price is comparably low, compared to the cost of ownership of a song album or a DVD with movie. Many businesses use nowadays media streaming (not necessarily secured) as a sort of protection; most of the people pay for the service, and of course there is a minority who still can compromise the stream and copy the content. Another problem is that the content should be possible to find. Assume there is an individual who decoded and copied the song or a movie from stream of YouTube, where should he put it so other people can easily find it? Potential consumers of this media probably already have subscriptions to the services if they consume a lot; if not, then even 5–10 % of the cases will not affect the revenue and loss of royalty payments much. Many software companies went similar way; for example, Microsoft Office 365 allows you to use this product on a monthly basis, without need to own a license and with the possibility to opt out any time.

Why could the same or similar media streaming technologies not be applied to 3D printing? There is a huge difference in the requirements for streaming between printable 3D files and media like movies or songs. In case of streaming video or music, if the stream got recorded this is not a big problem; as we described above, such copy will have quite a short life in torrent networks, and the same user will watch or listen to it for hundreds/thousands of times; in case of 3D printable object, this could be massively reproduced by a first-hand consumer. Another important difference is connected to the quality of stream; for example, if during the movie-watching process few frames would drop or music will skip half a second few times, this is not a big deal. However, in case of the stream going to 3D printers, every byte and every bit should be delivered and in the right sequence. In the best case, user will get bad quality product and probably reprint it or use a competitive product. The worst case, as 3D printers are very precise and expensive machines, wrong sequence of codes or some bytes missing can break the 3D printer. In comparison with video and music—it is not possible to break a TV or a monitor with the wrong video/music stream. Finally even the worst case, 3D design could be compromised on the storage server or on the way to 3D printer; if it is a mission critical part, for example airplane turbine part, then the authors believe the reader of this book by all means would not like to be a passenger of that airplane. In comparison with video and music—the end user will soon understand that actors in the movie are different or that the song is performed by, for example, Jennifer Lopez. These points have the biggest impact on the fact that video or music streaming is not a suitable solution, and there is a space for next generation streaming solution, which delivers right data, at the right place, in the right time without compromising security or, even better, with ultimate security.

## 4 Understanding the Legal Aspects of 3D Printing

As 3D printing is a completely unregulated field, regulating it will pose different challenges to legislators because the implementation of any regulative measure can have unforeseeable effects to further developments of 3D printing technology. The possible options of regulation may entail in the enforcement of hard regulation by the state, community self-regulation, or leaving the industry unregulated for as long as possible and pose regulations only after the industry has had time to mature. The existing legislation for copyrights usually involves an unlimited list of protected works, which allows for the interpretation of new technologies and mediums under copyright protection, meaning that drafting a specific regulation for 3D printing is not essential in such an early phase of technological developments. Nevertheless, scholars have proposed different existing categories of work, which could be treated as analogs to 3D printing, for the reason that it has not been explicitly regulated. Examples on how to deal with the rapid technological developments of 3D printing from the legal perspective can be found in case law dealing with disruptive technologies that have changed the world.

Experience in the United States and the United Kingdom (where many of these issues have been dealt with first) has shown that attempts to ban hardware or to outlaw devices are especially problematic. This is certainly true for those devices which have legitimate as well as illegitimate applications. This is very often the case where the hardware is distributed through distributors who are not in a position and have no effective means of monitoring usage by an end user of the devices.[15] Often, copyright exceptions are carved out for private users as a way of conciliation of interests of copyright owners, the equipment industry, and ultimately the consumers. This is to ensure that creators are rewarded but not at the cost of disadvantaging consumers in an unreasonable manner.[16]

Historically speaking, it could be said with some conviction that the law of copyright owes its development to significant advances in technology, starting from the invention of the printing press itself. However, it should also be noted that the judiciary has preferred to defer to the wishes of the legislature in this regard and has been consequently hesitant to expand protections under the copyright regime without explicit guidance from Parliament. This view has gained traction all the more for reasons that the legislature alone has constitutional authority and institutional ability to take into account the various competing interests in society which tend to surface every time a new path-breaking invention is brought into commercial existence.[17] It is important for the law to encourage innovation and to invigorate commercial activities, rather than sacrificing the above ideals on the ground of mere possibility of misuse of new technology to the detriment of some copyright owners.[18] After all, it must also be understood that the Charter of Fundamental Rights recognizes the freedom to conduct business.[19]

Fair dealing provisions are useful in this regard as they generally provide important limitations to owner's rights (for the purposes of noncommercial research or private study, critical reviews, and news reporting).[20] However, in most jurisdictions these provisions are fairly restrictive, unlike under the United States law.[21] It is important to note that in the United States, only guidelines regarding fair use are provided, and these apply to all types of work, although this can be controversial.[22] The role of transformative use (i.e., making a new work by adding newness,

---

[15] Copinger and Skone James (2005), p. 1452.

[16] Xiaoxiang Shi (2012), p. 533.

[17] Sony Corporation of America v Universal City Studios, Inc., 464 U.S. 417 (1984), p. 431.

[18] Merges et al. (2012), p. 720.

[19] Nyman-Metcalf et al. (2014), p. 37.

[20] Copinger and Skone James (2005), p. 481.

[21] Copyright Act 1976, 17 U.S.C., Section 107.

[22] Copinger and Skone James (2005), p. 481, and also see fn. 14 on that page where criticisms regarding the US approach and their contrast with the principle of statutory construction noscitur a sociis (i.e., that the meaning of a doubtful word may be ascertained by referring to the meaning of words associated with it) is discussed.

either in purpose or character) is also important for furthering the cause of copyright law through the implementation of the fair use doctrine.[23]

It should always be borne in mind that the concept of vicarious liability has given rise to complications under copyright laws since this branch of law rarely renders anyone expressly liable for infringement activities committed by another. The doctrine of "contributory infringement" is after all "….merely a species of the broader problem of identifying the circumstances in which it is just to hold one individual accountable for the actions of another."[24] Sale of articles which can be used for infringing as well as other and lawful uses is not sufficient to render the seller as a contributory infringer since such an absurdity would "block the wheels of commerce."[25]

Also of interest is the "Staple Article of Commerce" doctrine, which emphasizes upon the rights of others to engage in commerce which is of such a nature as being substantially unrelated with infringement of an owner's copyright. Thus, a product which can be used widely for legitimate and unobjectionable purposes and which is capable of substantial noninfringing use would not come under the purview of the doctrine of contributory infringement.[26] Time and again various authors have reasoned that copyright should not be stated as violated if new technologies are developed which possess both types of applications—namely, infringing and noninfringing.[27] This is especially the case when the courts must assess the public interest in accessing that article of commerce while deciding on the merits of the matter.[28] This should, however, not be confused with the inducement rule, whereby one who distributes a device with the sole objective of promoting infringement of copyright becomes in turn liable for the infringing acts of third parties.[29] Although the "Staple Article of Commerce" has its roots in patent law (whereby distribution of a component of a patented device will not lead to infringement of the patent, provided that it is suitable for other uses), it is noteworthy that the aforementioned defense (used successfully in the Sony case outlined below) is not absolute, and indeed the courts now also consider whether the infringing activity outweighs the noninfringing activity.[30]

---

[23] Khaosaeng (2014), p. 241.

[24] Sony Corporation of America v Universal City Studios, Inc., 464 U.S. 417 (1984), p. 435.

[25] Ibid, p. 441.

[26] Ibid, p. 442.

[27] For example, see Raval (2012), p. 98, where controversies regarding gaming consoles and rights of gamers to make modifications in the software are explored in the prism of dichotomies under US and Australian copyright laws.

[28] Merges et al. (2012), p. 363.

[29] As held in Metro-Golwyn-Mayer Studios Inc. v. Grokster, Ltd. Supreme Court of the United States 545 U.S. 913 (2005).

[30] Haque (2008), p. 377. where the author discusses the case Metro-Goldwyn-Mayer v Grokster (9th Cir) 380 F.3d 1154 (2004).

## 4.1 *Case Laws Dealing with Disruptive Technologies*

It would be of interest to see how the courts have dealt with issues regarding technological progress in the face of copyright law concerns in the 1980s and 1990s, in order to seek to foretell where the issue of 3D printers is headed. Attempts to outlaw video recorders, tape-to-tape recorders, and MP3 players will be studied, since each represents an advancement of technologies lying at the intersection of computer technology and the Internet frontier. Efforts to restrict the above devices (and their leapfrogging technology enablements) have consistently failed to fructify, and it should be of no surprise that 3D printing devices too will face similar birth pangs (in issues concerning legality thereof).

### 4.1.1 The Sony Case: Time Shifting[31]

This United State's Supreme Court case from the early 1980s dealt with home video tape recorders. The legal issue which was raised here was regarding the sale of copying equipment (namely, Betamax video tape recorders) by the petitioners to the general public and the perceived sense of consequent violation of copyright vested in the respondents. The respondents commenced the proceeding in the District Court by contending that some individuals had infringed the respondent's copyrights by using the Betamax tape recorders to record copyrighted works which had been exhibited on commercially sponsored television. Interestingly, the respondents sought no relief against the Betamax consumers per se. Rather, in an unprecedented move, they sought to impose liability upon the distributors of copying equipment by making the petitioners liable for the copyright infringement by their customers on the ground that the marketing style and process of the Betamax machines by the petitioners was at fault. The respondents thereby sought monetary damages and an equitable accounting of profits, coupled with injunctions against the manufacture and marketing of the Betamax machines.

Underlying the tensions in this particular case was the novel concept of "time shifting" which had been propagated by the petitioners. Time shifting was designed to help average members of the public to use Betamax tape recorders as a means for recording a televised program which he is unable to view at the time of telecast, with the intention to watch the recorded program at a later time. Further, tapes could be reused, recorded programs could be erased, a "timer" function enabled recording of programs from TV when the owner was not at home, and the machines were equipped with a pause button and fast-forward control mechanisms. All in all, this provided a significant leap in the arena of home entertainment systems.

Since the nature of the copying through tape recorders was uniquely private, enforcement of copyright was seen as overreaching and excessive as it would require the monitoring of private behavior and acting against end users who

[31] Sony Corporation of America v Universal City Studios, Inc., 464 U.S. 417 (1984).

committed the above acts in the privacy of their homes. This was also seen as giving rise to a conflict between fundamental human rights and copyright enforcement.[32]

It must be noted that in the 1980s, domestic videocassette recorders were used widely for the purpose of recording broadcasts, despite the fact that it was unlawful to do so. In fact, the laws were amended (no doubt encouraged by the above judgment) to facilitate such recording for purposes of time shifting![33]

What is interesting to consider in this case was the assertion of the United State's Supreme Court that:

There should be a balance between the interests of authors and inventors on one hand and the interest of society in the free flow of ideas, knowledge and commerce. Also of note is the fact that copyright protection never gives the owner complete control over all the possible ways and means in which his work can be used.

The respondents were neither able to prove that the practice of time shifting had caused any impairment to the commercial value of their copyrights, nor could they elucidate (through a preponderance of evidence) upon the potential for harmful effects of this practice in the future.

Nothing should be done to enlarge the scope of the respondents' statutory monopolies under the Copyright Act by means of enjoining the distribution of Betamax tape recorders, collecting sales royalties on above-listed equipment, or other such coercive reliefs. This was especially important since the Betamax tape recorders were held by the court to be "articles of commerce" and consequently were not seen as being subject to copyright law and such attempts by the respondents were seen as an expansion of copyright privileges beyond the limits of the grants authorized by the Legislature.

The noncommercial nature of the use, coupled with the private nature of the recording and playing activity committed entirely within the environs of one's house, readily applied itself to the doctrine of "fair use" of copyrighted works. This sort of activity was seen to be in tune with the legislative goal of serving public interest through open access to information via public airwaves.

The petitioners were merely in the business of supplying a piece of equipment that was generally capable of being used for making authorized or unauthorized copies of copyrighted works and are thus absolved of vicarious liability. What is lacking in this instance is that the petitioner ever had constructive knowledge of the fact that its customers may make use of the tape recording machines for producing unauthorized copies of copyrighted materials. This distinction between copyright and patent laws needs to be stressed upon.

Assuming without accepting that home-use recording of copyrighted material was a form of infringement of copyright therein, an injunction against the Betamax tape recorder would appear to be harsh and inordinate and would result in depriving the public of access to and ability to legally use the machine for the purposes of

[32] Karapapa (2011), p. 257.

[33] Copinger and Skone James (2005), p. 568.

recording noncopyrighted material or material which is capable of being legally copied due to express permission of the copyright owners.

The respondents do not represent all copyright holders, and the petitioners have shown that televised sports events, religious broadcasts, and educational programs comprise a substantial category of copyrighted works—works whose owners welcome the use of Betamax tape recorders for the purposes of legitimate copying of their freely accessible works.

As is the norm, the court took note of surveys, opinion evidence, etc. tendered by the parties to the dispute. These supported the petitioners' claims that substantial numbers of copyright owners did not find the practice of "time shifting" to be objectionable and that harm from "time shifting" is not only highly speculative but also minimal in nature.

Thus, it was held by the Court that sale by the petitioners of such equipment to the public did not constitute contributory infringement of the copyright vested in the respondents.

In hindsight, it can be seen that Hollywood was incorrect when it predicted disaster due to Sony's video tape recorders. Instead, what was noticed is that the movie industry discovered new business opportunities in video rentals and sales. This shows that content industries predict doomsday scenarios on a regular basis when they are confronted with new technologies that threaten existing business models, but subsequently the more resilient businesses find new ways and means to profit from the advancement in technology.[34]

This case (among other notable ones) is the reason why the United States' leadership in the development of new technologies related with time shifting has been globally recognized, and the legal approach adopted by the United States with regard to IP development and consumer rights is often seen to inspire intellectual property (IP) laws enacted in foreign countries (and subsequently eyebrows are raised when the United States' approach is ignored).[35]

However, it must be noted that even in the United States it is now widely acknowledged that the above Sony case did not address the new protections afforded by the Digital Millennium Copyright Act, 1988, and thus equipment manufacturers need to ensure avoidance of a circumvention claim rather than to negate a claim of copyright.[36] Further, the approaches towards this issue have been diluted post 2005, since the Grokster decision. However, a review of the post-2005 period analysis in different countries has proven to be uneven, perhaps being a sign of the far-reaching impact of the Sony decision and the inability of subsequent judgments to completely erase Sony's lucent primacy with respect to developing technologies.[37] Another good indicator is also the Napster case, where the court

[34] Merges et al. (2012), p. 608.

[35] Giblin (2012), p. 639, where the author analyzes the situation in Australia.

[36] Merges et al. (2012), p. 692.

[37] Daly (2007), pp. 319–324, where the author has conducted a review of post-2005 peer-to-peer file sharing issues.

held that the "shifting" analyses of the Sony and Diamond (discussed below) cases were not applicable since in these two cases the methods of shifting resulted in exposure of the material only to the original user and not to the general public.[38]

### 4.1.2 The Amstrad Case[39]

In the mid 1980s in the United Kingdom, another interesting development in home entertainment music systems took place, pushing the boundaries of "home taping" a step further. Amstrad commenced the manufacture, marketing, and sale of double cassette deck audio systems. The speciality of these systems was that they facilitated the recording from one tape deck to the other at twice the speed of a normal playback, thereby enabling the owner of the machine to copy favorite cassettes at twice the normal playing time. This raised the ire of the majority of record and cassette manufacturing companies, which contended that Amstrad was encouraging home taping of prerecorded cassettes, something which was obviously hurtful to their interests. The owners of the relevant copyrights also sued Amstrad for infringement of copyright in this regard.

Since copyright can be infringed either directly by the infringer or by someone who authorises the infringement, it necessarily thereby follows that a person liable for authorizing infringement will be liable as a joint tortfeasor and also vicariously liable for the acts of his subordinates or agents.[40] Although proof of an act of direct infringement would be required, judicial decisions in this regard are unclear.[41] It was alleged that Amstrad and others were supplying the above equipment in breach of a common law duty of care owed to copyright owners. Further, it was alleged that there was also a breach of an equitable duty of care not to allow goods likely to be used for the purposes of infringement to pass out of Amstrad's hands, without first taking certain necessary and reasonable precautions to ensure that copyrights were not infringed by the usage of such equipment.

However, it should be noted that merely putting into another person's hands the means to do something (which could be infringing or legitimate) is not enough. It should be shown that the supplier has some control over how the means will be used.[42] This is essentially what a grant entails—that the grantor can somehow exercise control over the acts of the grantee.[43] Thus, mere facilitation or giving the users technical means to infringe would not suffice, since users are responsible

---

[38] Akester (2005), p. 106.

[39] CBS Songs Ltd v Amstrad Consumer Electronics Plc [1988] A.C. 1013.

[40] Copinger and Skone James (2005), p. 449.

[41] Monotti (2013), pp. 325–326.

[42] Yan (2012), p. 123.

[43] Copinger and Skone James (2005), pp. 450–451.

for their own acts (albeit with a few caveats—as such an approach would not work today in a Pirate Bay website type of situation).[44]

One of the interesting causes of action raised in this matter was the offense of incitement to commit offenses under the relevant copyright act, propped up in part on the grounds that the advertising by Amstrad was particularly effective in this aspect and was viewed as encouraging/inciting the general public to buy these machines with the view to copy the contents of their favorite cassettes, thereby breaking the copyright law. The court, however, held that Amstrad could persuade a purchaser to buy a machine through its advertisements but could not possibly influence his decision to infringe copyright.[45]

This case could be seen as a continuation of the rather long and convoluted history wherein the recording industry has tried, without much success, to stop the so-called illicit copying of recordings (as manifested in the present case by tape-to-tape copies). It is interesting to note that the recording industry has targeted not only pirates but also domestic copyists who copy for themselves or people they know.

Interestingly, the House of Lords noted that home copying was widespread, was unpreventable, and brought the law into disrepute, and thus the law should be amended or repealed.[46]

Some of the interesting points noted by the House of Lords in this case were as follows:

The issue of Civil Liability in the form of tort—Even if Amstrad marketed and advertised these equipments in a way which encouraged purchasers to copy their favourite cassettes, thereby giving rise to the accusation of incitement to breach other people's copyrights, none of the parties to the suit were able to prove that Amstrad had been sufficiently party to any actual infringement which could render it to be an infringer and thus a joint tortfeasor. For such a tort to take hold, the incitement would have to be shown to have been directed to particular persons who could be identified or deemed identifiable at the date of the incitement. Consequently, no civil liability could arise if the incitement was merely directed towards the public at large.

The issue of criminal liability could not be conclusively established, and the court contented itself by conceding that it was the duty of Parliament, and not the Judges, "to provide new remedies for new wrongs."

In order to enable a plaintiff to sue for an injunction to restrain a criminal act, it is not deemed sufficient for him to merely show that the criminal act interferes with some property interest of which he is the owner.

In view of the fact that the copyright law provides for both civil and criminal liabilities, it could be inferred that since the act in question creates an obligation and enforces the performance in a specified manner, that performance cannot then be enforced in any other manner.

---

[44] Savola (2014), pp. 285–286.

[45] Ibid, p. 287.

[46] Key-Matuszak (2013), p. 440.

Where it so occurs that the copyright owners have no recourse to practical remedies as such against the actual infringers, then the courts are powerless to stop such activities and the Parliament alone is adapted best to deal with such situations (through the use of levies on the sale price of recording equipment, etc.).

### 4.1.3 The Diamond Rio MP3 Case: Space Shifting[47]

The third and final case which will be examined herein pertains to the digital revolution which, coupled with the Internet, led to the creation of a revolutionary novel method for distribution of music, thereby dealing more deadly blows to the music industry. In the late 1990s, an attempt was made once again by copyright owners in the United States to enjoin the manufacture, sale, marketing, and distribution of a portable entertainment system, namely the Rio MP3 player. The Rio was a small pocket-sized device with headphones. Its main feature was the ability to allow a user to download MP3 audio files from a computer and to listen to them at any place at his convenience.

The convenience of such a device cannot be understated. One just has to see it in the historical context to realize that the jump in recording technology from analog to digital had far-reaching benefits for the music listener. While earlier, if a person wanted to make a copy from a record or a compact disc, he could only use a cassette tape recorder. This was an analog-style recording, and it had its negative aspects/shortcomings. Consequently, every analog recording led to the intolerable situation that each successive generation of copies suffered progressively from high levels of degradation in the quality of the sound. On the other hand, digital copying does not show any degradation in the sound quality. This makes digital copying very attractive to music pirates who can make perfect copies of commercially prepared recordings, thereby infringing the copyrights subsisting therein.

This switch from analog to digital recording technology itself was of little consequence towards mass copying and distribution. This was because of the inherent limitations in the nature of the Internet itself in the early 1990s. Since the digital information contained within the average-sized music computer file tended to be excessively large, storing the same took an inordinate amount of space (requiring vast amounts of computer floppy discs) and downloading it from the Internet could take hours. This situation changed dramatically with the introduction of compression algorithm technology (including standard, nonproprietary, and freely available MPEG-1 Audio Layer 3, also known as MP3), which allowed an audio file to be easily made smaller by limiting its bandwidth.

Although this made downloading of music files from the Internet easy, it still meant that users could only listen to these songs by using speakers or headphones, while seated next to their computers. This was changed by the introduction of the

[47] Recording Industry Association of America v Diamond Multimedia Systems Inc 180 F. 3d 1072 (1999).

Rio device, whose main selling point was that it allowed for portability. Namely, the audio file could be downloaded from the Internet (or a compact disc player) onto the computer hard drive and then onto the Rio itself by plugging the Rio into the computer and with the aid of some special software known as the Rio Manager. It should be noted that the Rio device itself could not affect such a transfer and needed to be connected to a personal computer which had the Rio Manager software. The Rio could store vast amounts of sound files (up to 1 h of music and 16 h of spoken material such as eBooks, etc.), and with the addition of flash memory cards it was possible to store much more data content. The Rio could only be used for listening to the stored audio data via headphones but could not be used to make duplicates of any stored digital audio files. It could also not be used to transfer or upload such a file to any computer/device/Internet. However, by using a flash memory card, audio files could be removed from one Rio and played back in another.

The court examined the following pertinent points and drew far-reaching conclusions:

Although the predominant use of MP3 was stated to be trafficking of illegally downloaded audio recordings, especially by various pirate websites, leading to discouragement of legitimate purchases of audio recordings (losses alleged by the plaintiff were to the tune of over 300 million US Dollars), the court concluded that the legitimate business of sale and provision of free samples of audio files (including pre-recorded music) online by independent and wholly internet based record labels was growing rapidly and was according to some estimates worth more than a Billion US Dollars and therefore could not be ignored.

The Rio device was not required to meet the stringent requirements of the Audio Home Recording Act of 1992 with regard to the provisions for employment of Serial Copyright Management Systems that are designed to send, receive, and act upon information about the generation and copyright status of the files that it plays. This was because the Rio was held not to be a digital audio recording device (as defined by the Act) since it could only make copies from a computer hard drive and could not reproduce a digital music recording, either directly or from a transmission.

Even though there exist judicial precedents to the effect that straightforwardness of statutory command would bar any resort to legislative history, the court looked at both the plain language of the definitions of the Act and the legislative historical context (for interpretational purposes) and concluded that nothing could be seen as defining a digital musical recording as one which included songs fixed on computer hard drives. Notwithstanding the primary purposes of the recording function, it should be noted that a machine or a device is not to be considered a digital audio recording device even though it may have the technical capability to do so.

Limiting of the legislative exemption to computer programs meant that "any recording device could legally evade regulation by passing the music through the computer and ensuring that the MP3 file resided momentarily on the hard drive," and this was held to be indicative of legislative intent to create a specific loophole (perhaps in deference to the wishes of the powerful computer industry).[48]

The Rio facilitated personal, portable use for private, noncommercial purposes. This gave rise to the term "space-shifting" (of those files which already resided on a user's hard drive) and could be considered as "fair use."

Thus, it can be seen that the court followed the precedent laid down by the United States Supreme Court in the Sony case (regarding time shifting being fair use) by holding that space shifting was "paradigmatic noncommercial personal use."[49]

## *4.2 Possible Legal Solutions for Lawful 3D Printing*

Looking forward, it could be said that the most promising analogies (among others) include architectural plans and blueprints, other technical drawings, computer programs, computer-generated works, and sculptures.[50] Different aspects of the existing categories ruin their suitability for 3D printing. For example, architectural plans may be similar to 3D printing in the sense that they exist first in the form of a CAD drawing and are later executed into physical objects.[51] Same goes for technical drawings, which usually consist of technical plans that normally would not be copyrightable but have been granted an exception under U.S. copyright law. Analogy to architectural plans or technical drawings would lead to a dual protection desired by the designer, meaning that both the CAD file and the 3D printed end result would be protected.[52] The main difference comes from the fact that the CAD file for an architectural building or a technical drawing includes guidelines for humans to interpret, while CAD files of a 3D printable object include information for a 3D printer to execute, and this underlying difference makes the analogy unsuitable.[53] 3D printed objects could easily fall under the copyrightable category of sculptures, but as some of them are not merely decorative and incorporate a utilitarian purpose, the objects sometimes fall out of the scope of copyright.

The analogy of 3D printing to computer programs can give different outputs to legal research. Firstly, the definition of computer programs could be used as analogous to 3D printing, and secondly, the anomaly of encompassing computer programs under copyright protection, as such, could give guidelines on how it would be possible to regulate and also encompass 3D printing technology under copyright protection. Computer programs under U.S. Copyright Act are defined as

[48] Ibid, p. 1079.

[49] Merges et al. (2012), p. 712.

[50] Dolinsky (2014), pp. 627–629.

[51] Osborn (2014), p. 829.

[52] Dolinsky (2014), pp. 629–631.

[53] Ibid.

"a set of statements or instructions to be used directly or indirectly in a computer program in order to bring about a certain result."[54] Some scholars have found the definition of computer programs perfectly compatible with CAD files because CAD files also "contain all the information to be used by a printer to print a three-dimensional model."[55] Why application of this analogy is not suitable is that a designer normally never writes the code of the CAD program but only uses the software to create a CAD design, which is not the equivalent of a software code written by a programmer.[56] Some CAD programs are even simplified to the extent that the designer only picks predesigned objects and aligns them according to his needs.[57] Thus, the copyrightability of computer programs extends to the software itself rather than to the work produced via the software.[58] Computer programs were protected as literary works, but the definition of a computer program in the EU computer programs directive was not very specific, in order to avoid the term becoming outdated and to allow for legal rules to follow the rapid development in technologies.[59] The regulation of computer programs was already established prior to them becoming more widespread for home use, and possibly the legal regulation played a part in the success and innovation that followed computer programs. Though many categories could suffice to act as an equivalent to either CAD files or 3D printed objects, none is capable of simultaneously encompassing both the digital and physical features accompanying the technology. Due to the complex nature of the whole 3D printing technology and the different steps from CAD file to the actual 3D printing process, it could be reasonable to try and regulate it more specifically, by setting up a legal framework to improve legal clarity.

CAD files and 3D printed objects are a unique form of expression to copyright law and do not completely comply or fall under any of the existing categories of copyrightable subject matter and due to their complexity pose new issues and questions about the suitability under copyright protection regarding the functionalities of CAD file and the 3D printed end result. For these reasons, it has been proposed by scholars that it would be reasonable to establish a sui generis copyright-like protection for 3D objects. Whenever a novel technology accompanied with economic benefits emerges, policy makers need to make considerations in order to provide suitable legal framework for the new technologies to operate,

[54] 17 U.S.C. section 101.

[55] Osborn (2014), p. 824.

[56] Ibid, p. 829.

[57] Ibid.

[58] Dolinsky (2014), pp. 637–639.

[59] Directive 2009/24/EC of the European Parliament and of the Council of 23 April 2009 on the legal protection of computer programs. OJ L 111/16, 5.5.2009, recital (7). The term "computer program" has been somewhat defined for the purpose of the directive under the preamble, and it "/../shall include programs in any form, including those which are incorporated into hardware. This term also includes preparatory design work leading to the development of a computer program provided that the nature of the preparatory work is such that a computer program can result from it at a later stage."

because the protection of such works will have impact on the technological development.[60] In the EU, sui generis protection has been granted for databases with the database directive.[61] Though the originality and suitability of many databases under copyrightable subject matter is doubtful, the objectives of granting databases a sui generis protection under copyrights include the substantial investments required from the maker of the database in order to create the database and the fact that copyrights remain the most appropriate form of IP protection for authors of databases.[62] So far, databases, which do not qualify for traditional copyright protection, are the only exception of works to be granted sui generis protection under EU copyright law, but it has been previously suggested by scholars that computer programs should have also been protected with a sui generis right. Computer software falls somewhere in between copyright and patent rights, and it has been declared that copyrights provide insufficient protection, while patent law is too restrictive for innovation and development of the technology.[63] In practice, protecting computer programs as literary works within the meaning of the Berne Convention can already be seen as implementing a sui generis right because the traditional copyright rules have been widened and altered to comply with the distinctive technological characteristics of computer programs.[64] Taking into account the fact that no such subject matter has previously existed in the realm of copyright protection and that it incorporates digital and physical aspects both seeking copyright protection, the sui generis proposals by scholars for 3D printed objects is not an entirely unexpected line of thought. The sui generis right that Rideout proposes for 3D printing technology is to establish a copyright-like protection for even those 3D printed objects that incorporate a useful article and, as previously determined, would thus fall out of the scope of copyright. Rideout generates the idea on the basis of sui generis right granted for vessel hulls under U.S. copyright law, which resembles industrial design protection and applies to the appearance and utilitarian function of the vessel hull.[65] Thus, he proposes that the necessary practice of protecting works with a sui generis right under the scope of copyright exists and it could be easily broadened to encompass 3D printed objects as well.[66] Creating a sui generis protection for 3D printing technology would merely constitute a method of encompassing all 3D printed objects, as such, under copyright protection. It would make it very convenient for designers, as there will be no reason for obtaining industrial design protection or trademark protection to pursue their intellectual property protection, because copyrights for

---

[60] Mylly (2009), p. 880.

[61] Directive 96/9/EC of the European Parliament and of the Council of 11 March 1996 on the legal protection of databases OJ L 077, 27.03.1996.

[62] Ibid, recital (5), (7).

[63] Toeniskoetter (2005), p. 76.

[64] Mylly (2009), p. 880.

[65] Rideout (2011), p. 175.

[66] Ibid.

3D printed objects would exist automatically. This solution could possibly decrease destructive effects of regulation to 3D printing industry, as the protection of works can create a higher incentive for designers to create and share their designs. On the other hand, it could also have a negative effect on the traditional intellectual property regulations in place because it is capable of creating multiple layers of protection by different forms of IP; for example, the end result can be simultaneously protected by copyright and design right, which can end in overprotecting of works, which is also unreasonable and not the purpose of setting the sui generis protection.

Michael Weinberg and other scholars have expressed concerns that such sui generis copyright-like protection for functional objects will create a patent-like protection, without the novelty requirement and strict period of protection, which is usually granted for 20 years.[67] Patents are meant to protect useful creations and are rewarded to inventions, which are novel and have inventive step. The application process is complicated and costly, which is why they are hard to ascertain. 3D printing can bring forth problems for 3D enthusiasts, even when they independently create the design for an infringing object, which is not the case with copyrights.[68] On the other hand, taking into account the desktop 3D printer quality and materials currently available, there might not be many patented objects that could be executed through 3D printing.[69]

Copyrights and design rights are very similar to one another, as the object of protection for both is the visual appearance of a work. In the EU, a great emphasis is put on highlighting the importance of design and to support that, a harmonized Community Design system is established with Council Regulation 6/2002. The harmonization is carried from the idea of creating a designer-friendly environment, in which innovation of, development of, and investments into new products are encouraged.[70] In case of copyrights and design rights, one does not exclude the other, and they can exist cumulatively for a work. Design is a key element for being successful in business and competition—it helps for the product to stand out in the variety of others. 3D printing is especially beneficial for designing new test products, as it helps to make the design from digital to physical in a matter of hours, simplifying the creation of test products and making the production process and entering to market much faster than it has been before.[71] At the same time, the digital era is a stepping stone for designers, who now have to think about protecting their works more than ever prior to publishing any of their designs and making them vulnerable for intellectual property infringements, which can be utilized into a product in a very small time frame. Design law and copyright law are closely related when it comes to 3D printing, mainly for the reason that if and when the

[67] Ibid.

[68] Doherty (2012), p. 359.

[69] Bradshaw et al. (2010), pp. 26–27.

[70] Council Regulation (EC) No 6/2002 of 12 December 2001 on Community designs, recital (7).

[71] Lewis (2014), pp. 315–316.

range of materials for 3D printing escalates, it will enable printing of many different utilitarian works, such as leather shoes, clothing, and so on, which are generally excluded from the protection of copyrights, due to their utilitarian nature, and are the reason why design law was generated. In general, it is possible that the CAD files could acquire copyright protection, while 3D printed objects which are on the borderline of copyrights, but suitable for design protection, will fall under the scope of design protection. In the case of adequate design regulation, it would be a clear and good solution, which would eliminate the need to expand copyright law to functional objects and would help to avoid duplicate layers of IP protection for 3D printed objects.

## 5 A Possible Technical Solution for Effective and Lawful 3D Printing Using Secured Streaming of 3D Designs

The whole value chain from idea to a physical object should be secured, as the design could be potentially compromised at any step. It is not just a new type of streaming; it is a comprehensive set of tools combined on an ultimate cloud security platform, which includes 3D printing copyright protection available to use at every step through the whole value chain, secured streaming to 3D printers and between secured cloud servers, detective and protective controls allowing to detect intruder even before he can compromise secured stream to 3D printers. Secured streaming of 3D designs is built on the philosophy cloud versus hacker—a human being with a cloud for hacking. In the age of cloud computing, intrusion to almost any system is a matter of time and computing power. One important integral part of the solution for 3D design cloud storage and streaming is the ability of the system to set time-based limitations. Simplified IP-secured delivery process is shown in Fig. 2.

Majority of 3D printers that are available on the market are not network enabled; most of 3D printers utilize USB. Industrial and professional printers do have network connectivity but in most of the cases for file transfer only; the printing process and settings of the machine happen inside the machine through the touch screen interface or special software. In Fig. 3 there are three different approaches how secured stream can reach the 3D printer. The preferable approach is embedded cloud client, which is also a decrypting module for the secured streaming; this

**Fig. 2** Simplified IP secured delivery process

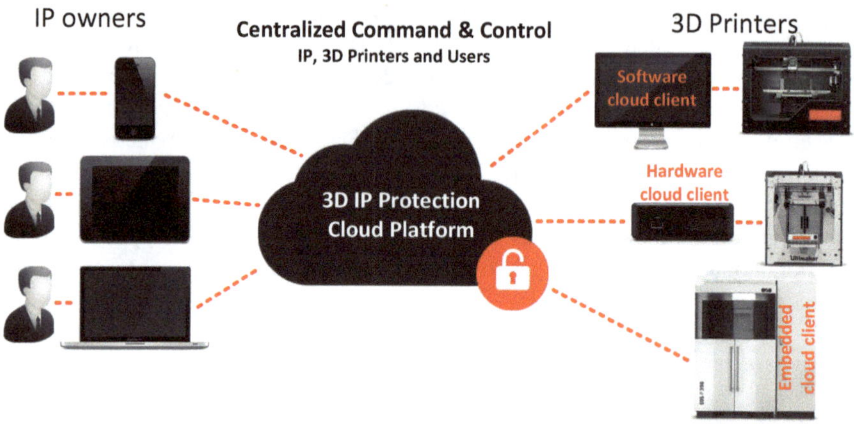


**Fig. 3** Secured streaming cloud client types and methods of connection

approach is the most secure, and cloud client is implemented on a hardware chip, which is installed as a part of 3D printer main board. This approach is valid for newly produced printers or disassembly, and change to hardware is needed. Hardware cloud client is the second preferable solution from a security point of view, easy to implement too; the requirement is to keep a decryption box as close as possible to the printer, as USB connection still could be vulnerable. Hybrid solution is also possible; when decryption box decrypts the stream and encrypts it for USB-secured transfer, this type of encryption needs less code on the printer side and could be just included into 3D printer firmware. For example, 3D printer open source firmware Marlin could be changed in a way that it decrypts secured USB connection.

In Fig. 4, you can see the conceptual diagram of high-level cloud architecture which gives a general idea on how secured storage and streaming is built. It consists of four main components: Web, File Segments, Key and Streaming Cloud Module, and one optional (smart card). To mitigate intrusion, the information is segmented within the cloud platform.

It is important to understand that File Segments machines on the left and Key machines on the right are autonomous and proactive, which means there is no way to query or send a command to them; they behave according to their internal rules, monitor Web machines on the top and Streaming machines on the bottom of the figure above, make decisions whether it is secure and as regards the right moment to transfer any information. So basically the intruder has to analyze for a long time the behavior of File Segments and Key machines to get any idea how exactly they are operating and what the possible vulnerabilities are; by that time, the intruder will be detected and measures will be taken.

The whole process starts from the Web cloud module. Web server receives a file. File Segments machine is monitoring the web server for new files. As soon as there is a new file, it is taken by the File Segments machine. Key machine also monitors

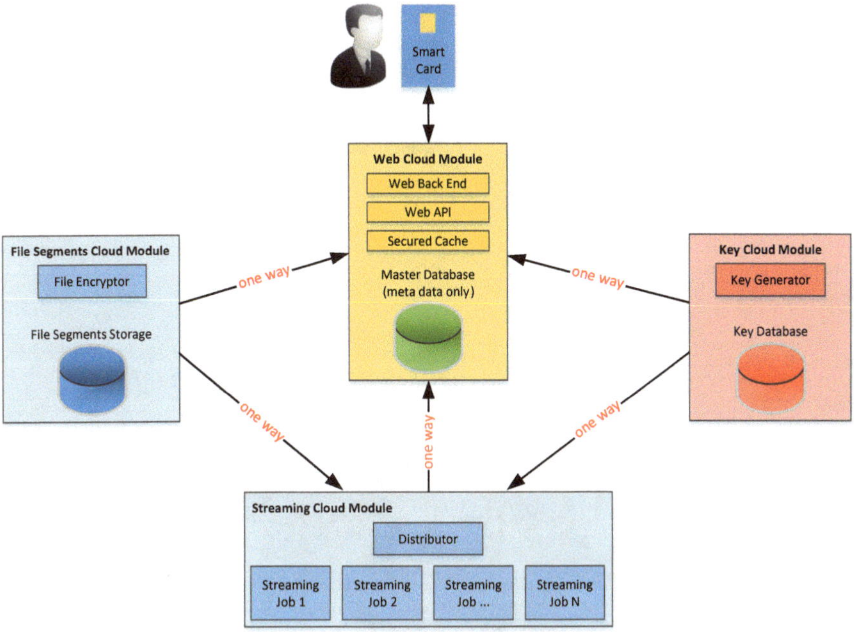


**Fig. 4** Secured storage and streaming high level cloud architecture conceptual diagram

the Web machine and is ready to generate a set of asymmetric key pairs. Usually there are thousands of keys generated. Private keys are kept on the Key machines and never exposed until streaming process. A File Segments machine collects the keys, splits the file into thousands of pieces, and encrypts each segment with its own key. File Segments are kept on File Segments machine until streaming process starts. There is no way to get all segments at the same time slot. File Segments module has a special type of storage which will physically allow to get more segments than a 3D printer is physically able to print. The next step is secured streaming process. User sends a command to print a design. Web module stores a request in the queue. All three servers (File Segments, Key, Streaming) analyze the metadata on the web machine and make a decision to start the streaming process. Streaming machines create a temporary virtual machine or a container for the moment of streaming, which will be deleted right after the streaming process. Streamer communicates and gets ready the 3D printer to receive the stream. File Segments issue a first segment of a file and sends it to the streamer virtual machine created for that exact job. Key module waits till all the servers are ready and sends over a private key for that exact segment. Streamer receives a key, decrypts a segment, and encrypts it for streaming. Streaming encryption works as all-the-time-changing hash table.

Thus, there is no single point of failure in case of intrusion, and until more than 1 server type is compromised the system is not vulnerable. In production system, each type of servers is actually a cloud by itself, so imagine 10–100 virtual

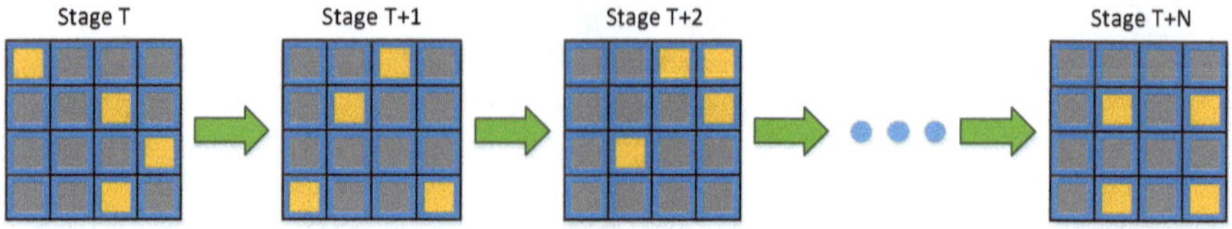


**Fig. 5** Live matrix concept, changing state millions of times per short time frame

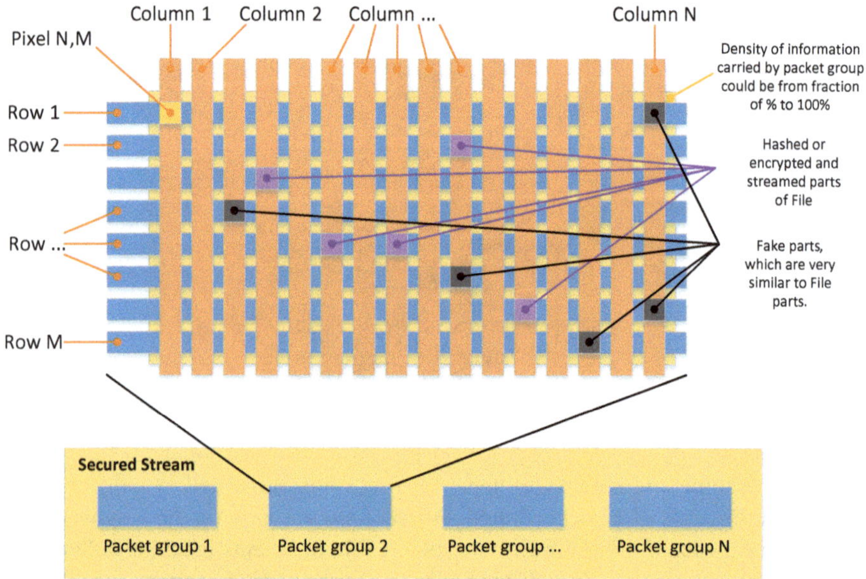


**Fig. 6** Simplified principle of a live matrix concept

machines in the place of each block on the figure below. And the data is segmented within this sub-cloud, which makes it even harder to compromise.

The data is kept in so-called live matrixes, a hash-table-like structure, which change their state millions of times per short time slot. A live matrix is calculated on a server and in decryption module. There is no physical possibility to keep more than 2–3 versions of these structures in decryption module; basically, it makes impossible to decrypt parts of the stream half a minute later. If hacker will record the whole stream going to 3D printer, half a minute later even decryption module could not decrypt it, so it is not possible to "replay" the stream, as it is sometimes possible in case of media streams. In Fig. 5 is a conceptual diagram showing so-called live matrix life cycle.

In Fig. 6, you can see a detailed view on the live matrix structure and how it works. The file is split into thousands of splits, each split is split into many parts, every part is hashed and is located at its own place in the matrix, and the matrix is changing its state all the time by rehashing the values. The same function runs in a decryption box of a 3D printer, and when a new hash is coming, it is being looked up in the live matrix. Fake parts could be added to make cracking more complicated.

## 6 Applications of Secured Streaming in Real Businesses

3D design marketplaces use secured streaming technology to protect IP of designers. Now it is possible not only to protect 3D designs on the way to 3D printer but also to provide a possibility to sell one-time-print licenses, which allow end users to print the desired object only once. In case of a technical problem, user is allowed to print one more time, but in order to do that, he needs to make a picture of a failed object and send it to a support desk, then another one time license is granted. This market is just evolving, but already today there are good examples like Pinshape, which serves as a marketplace for downloading or streaming of 3D printable models.[72] A typical secured streaming and 3D-copyright-protection-enabled 3D marketplace business process is shown in Fig. 7.

Many companies will change their business models because of advancing 3D printing technology. For example, LEGO—"Will 3D printing turn Lego into an intellectual property publisher?"[73] There is a true story—a child once a week was sending to LEGO HQ a 3D printed part; initially it was rough and not fitting well,

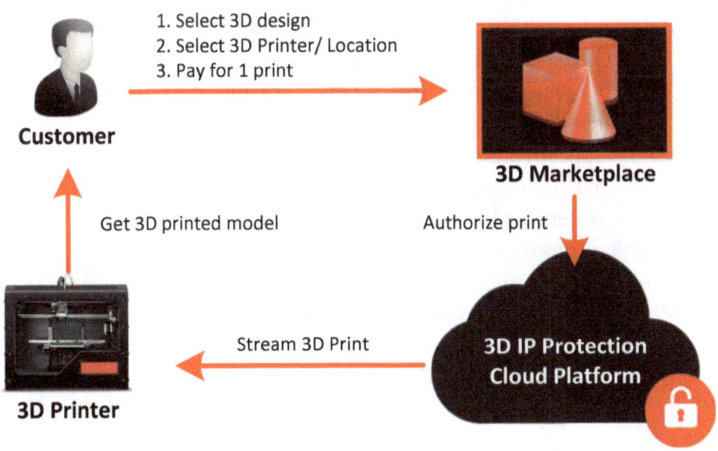


**Fig. 7** Typical secured streaming and 3D copyright protection enabled 3D marketplace business process

[72] See more from: www.pinshape.com.

[73] Levine (2014). Will 3D Printing Turn Lego Into an Intellectual Property Publisher? Available at: http://venturebeat.com/2014/03/03/will-3d-printing-turn-lego-into-an-intellectual-property-publisher/ (accessed 20.08.2015).

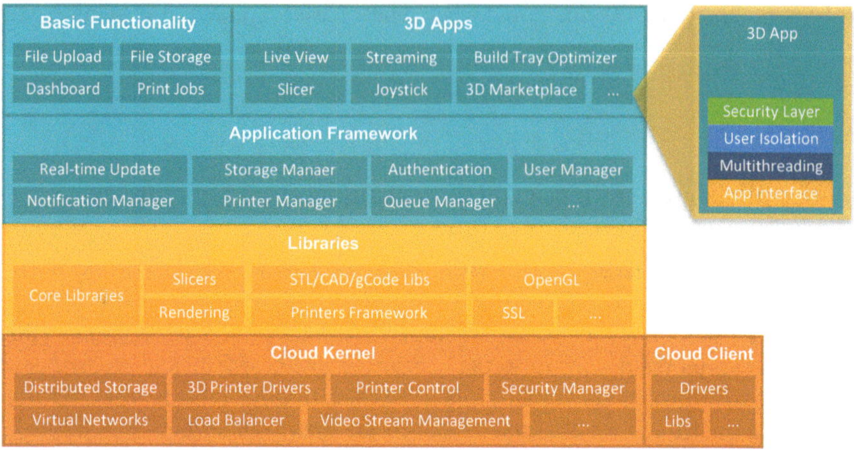


**Fig. 8** 3DprinterOS—general architecture of open operating system for 3D printers

and Lego executives did not take it seriously; however, half a year later, a teenager could so well fine-tune printing settings of his 3D printer that the plastic part fitted perfectly. The same way when 15 years ago many industries switched to media streaming through the Internet instead of CD/DVDs, now we are at the edge of next revolution when 3D printing will change the way companies operate. So maybe in 3–5 years people would buy a license to print a Lego set, instead of buying one.

Due to the need for end-to-end 3D printing, copyright solutions to secure the whole value chain cloud software platforms evolve. An interesting example is 3DprinterOS represented in Fig. 8—a cloud-based open operating system for 3D printers.[74] It is like an Android for 3D printers but runs its apps in the cloud. Compared to usual AppStore or Google Play applications, one of the essential things for every app developer is to implement the security layer, which is compatible with secured streaming of 3D designs. This has the potential to secure the IP of the whole ecosystem and 3D printing value chain.

There are many more examples of famous designers, design bureaus, 3D print hubs, 3D printer manufacturers, 3D marketplaces, schools and universities, 3D print shops, production and prototyping companies that every day in their business process already use secured streaming of 3D designs to protect their copyrights and prevent the stealing of their IP.

[74] See more from: www.3dprinteros.com.

## 7 Conclusion

Thus, we have seen that the existing measures for enforcing copyright protection need to be reviewed in order to comply with the complex nature of 3D printing technology. Based on an analysis of existing copyright regulation in relation to 3D printing, a conclusion can be made that the existing copyright regulations are not capable of encompassing the entire process of 3D printing. Some analogies are compatible at parts, but none is fully suitable, and it could even be possible that CAD files can be protected under copyrights and the physical 3D printed objects under design rights. In terms of existing regulation, it definitely needs to be reviewed before introducing the subject matter of 3D printing under copyright regulation. Because no such subject matter has been regulated before, the different alternatives also need to be carefully considered and reviewed; the possible outcomes of implementing regulative measures should be evaluated, to achieve an efficient regulative solution for 3D printing. Perhaps to refrain from interfering with the innovation and technological development, the industry should rather be left unregulated for as long as possible, to allow for it to mature and develop. Applying strict DRM and copyright protection cumulatively can lead to overregulating the industry and might end in decreasing innovation, which is why a DRM-like solution should consider the industry-specific characteristics to provide a suitable solution. The world of 3D printing is exciting and is capable of offering endless opportunities to different fields of use, if we only allow. The authors have brought forward the legal issues and have attempted to describe a unique technical solution—secured streaming which solves or at least partially solves the problem of copyrights in 3D printing. The proposed solution provides a possibility for a copyright owner to limit the number of 3D prints. He can specify the number of copies that are allowed for the manufacturer or an end user to produce. Moreover secured streaming has detective and protective controls to detect information system compromises and to stop streaming of 3D designs to 3D printers.

## References

Akester P (2005) Copyright and the P2P challenge. Eur Intellect Prop Rev 27(3):106–112

Bradshaw S, Bowyer A, Haufe P (2010) The intellectual property implications of low-cost 3D printing. ScriptEd 7(1):7–8

Daly M (2007) Life after Grokster: analysis of US and European approaches to file-sharing. Eur Intellect Prop Rev 29(8):319–324

Dasari H (2013) Assessing copyright protection and infringement issues involved with 3D printing and scanning. Am Intellect Prop Law Assoc Q J 41:279

Doherty D (2012) Downloading infringement: patent law as a roadblock to the 3D printing revolution. Harv J Law Technol 26:358

Dolinsky K (2014) CAD's cradle: untangling copyrightability, derivative works, and fair use in 3D printing. Washington Lee Law Rev 71:629–631

Garnett KM, Davies G, Harbottle G (2005) Copinger and Skone James on Copyright. Sweet & Maxwell, London
Giblin R (2012) Stranded in the technological dark ages: implications of the Full Federal Court's decision in NRL v Optus. Eur Intellect Prop Rev 34(9):632–641
Haque H (2008) Is the time ripe for another exclusive right? Eur Intellect Prop Rev 30(9):371–378
Howells JAJ (2014) The intellectual property right implications of consumer 3D printing. Available at: http://pure.au.dk/portal-asb-student/files/71036699/The_Intellectual_Property_Right_Implications_of_Consumer_3D_Printing_Final.pdf (accessed: 06.08.2015), p 13
Karapapa S (2011) Padawan v SGAE: a right to private copy? Eur Intellect Prop Rev 33 (4):252–259
Key-Matuszak P (2013) Time-shifting after NRL v Optus: a need for amendments. Eur Intellect Prop Rev 35(8):439–444
Khaosaeng K (2014) Wands, sandals and the wind: creativity as a copyright exception. Eur Intellect Prop Rev 36(4):238–249
Lewis A (2014) The legality of 3D printing: how technology is moving faster than the law. Tulane J Technol Intellect Prop 17:315–316
Merges RP, Menell PS, Lemley MA (2012) Intellectual property in the new technological age. Wolters Kluwer Law and Business, Aspen Casebook Series, New York
Monotti AL (2013) Liability for joint infringement of a method patent under Australian law. Eur Intellect Prop Rev 35(6):318–326
Mylly UM (2009) Harmonizing copyright rules for computer program interface protection. Univ Louisville Law Rev 48
Nyman-Metcalf N, Dutt PK, Chochia A (2014) The freedom to conduct business and the right to property: the EU technology transfer block exemption regulation and the relationship between intellectual property and competition law. In: Kerikmae T (ed) Protecting human rights in the EU. Springer, Berlin, pp 37–70
Osborn LS (2014) Of PhDs, pirates and the public: three-dimensional printing technology and the arts. Texas A&M Law Rev 1
Raval MI (2012) Game over for mod chips? The aftermath of Sony v Stevens and the Australian-US Free Trade Agreement. Eur Intellect Prop Rev 34(2):95–107
Rideout B (2011) Printing the impossible triangle: the copyright implications of three-dimensional printing. J Bus Entrep Law 5:167–168
Savola P (2014) Blocking injunctions and website operators' liability for copyright infringement for user-generated links. Eur Intellect Prop Rev 36(5):279–288
Stahl H (2013) 3D printing–risks and opportunities. Öko-Institut e.V. Institute for Applied Ecology, pp 3–4
Toeniskoetter SB (2005) Protection of software intellectual property in Europe: an alternative sui generis approach. Intellect Prop Law Bull 10
Twomey P (2014) A new dimension to intellectual property infringement: an evaluation of the intellectual property issues associated with 3D printing. Trinity Coll Law Rev 17:33
Weinberg M (2013) What's the deal with copyright and 3D printing?. White paper from Public Knowledge's Institute for Emerging Innovation, p 1
Xiaoxiang Shi S (2012) Time shifting in a networked digital world: Optus TV Now and copyright in the cloud. Eur Intellect Prop Rev 34(8):519–533
Yan M (2012) The law surrounding the facilitation of online copyright infringement. Eur Intellect Prop Rev 34(2):122–126

## *Others*

Sony Corporation of America v Universal City Studios, Inc., 464 U.S. 417 (1984).

CBS Songs Ltd v Amstrad Consumer Electronics Plc [1988] A.C. 1013
Recording Industry Association of America v Diamond Multimedia Systems Inc 180 F. 3d 1072 (1999)
Metro-Golwyn-Mayer Studios Inc. v. Grokster, Ltd. Supreme Court of the United States 545 U.S. 913 (2005).
Copyright Act 1956 (UK)
Copyright act 1976, 17 U.S.C.
Digital Millennium Copyright Act, 1988
Directive 96/9/EC of the European Parliament and of the Council of 11 March 1996 on the legal protection of databases OJ L 077, 27.03.1996.
Charter of Fundamental Rights of the European Union (2000/C 364/01)
Council Regulation (EC) No 6/2002 of 12 December 2001 on Community designs
Directive 2009/24/EC of the European Parliament and of the Council of 23 April 2009 on the legal protection of computer programs. OJ L 111/16, 5.5.2009.
Levine, B. (2014). Will 3D Printing Turn Lego Into an Intellectual Property Publisher? Available at: http://venturebeat.com/2014/03/03/will-3d-printing-turn-lego-into-an-intellectual-property-publisher/ (accessed 20.08.2015)
Gartner, (2013). Press release: Gartner Reveals Top Predictions for IT Organizations and Users for 2014 and Beyond. Available at: http://www.gartner.com/newsroom/id/2603215 (accessed 20.08.2015)
New Balance (2013). Press release: New Balance Pushes the Limits of Innovation with 3D Printing. Available at: http://www.newbalance.com/press-releases/id/press_2013_New_Balance_Pushes_Limits_of_Innovation_with_3D_Printing.html (accessed 20.08.2015)
Walters, R. (2012). The Pirate Bay Declares 3D Printed "Physibles" as the Next Frontier of Piracy. Available at: http://www.extremetech.com/electronics/115185-the-pirate-bay-declares-3d-printed-physibles-as-the-next-frontier-of-piracy (accessed 06.08.2015).

# From Bitcoin to Smart Contracts: Legal Revolution or Evolution from the Perspective of *de lege ferenda*?

**Kaido Künnapas**

**Abstract** Bitcoin has raised many debates dealing with fundamental issues of decentralised law and virtual currencies. Is it money? Is it payment system? Is it bilateral agreement or just a computer game? Regulatory bodies have decided not to act and see what risks emerge. In areas important to governments—i.e. taxation and anti-money laundering—initial regulatory approaches already emerge. Contract law and P2P relations are, however, not addressed. As so-called Bitcoin 2.0. or "smart contracts" are dealing much with P2P relations and rock the fundamentals of contract law, the law seems to be not able to address these new appearances. This article discusses nature of Bitcoin, *de lege lata* and *de lege ferenda* regulatory developments in this area and some fundamental regulatory problems emerging with smart contracts as Bitcoin 2.0.

## 1 Introduction

### *1.1 The Problem*

Overwhelmed by the prosperity of Bitcoin, global community is experiencing the same daze Marco Polo had seven centuries ago, when he saw "crazy Chinese" using stamped strips of paper as means for payment instead of metal coins kept in

K. Künnapas (✉)
Advokaadibüroo LMP, Tallinn, Estonia

Faculty of Social Sciences, Institute of Law, Tallinn University of Technology, Tallinn, Estonia

Faculty of Law, University of Tartu, Tartu, Estonia
e-mail: kaidokynnapas@gmail.com



T. Kerikmäe, A. Rull (eds.), *The Future of Law and eTechnologies*,
DOI 10.1007/978-3-319-26896-5_6

emperor's chambers.[1] Bitcoin has raised many intriguing legal issues and debates about crypto-anarchism[2] and extinction of centralised law.[3] The idea of privatisation of money is, though, not so new. In 1991, it was discussed by scholars that full privatisation of currency requires that government currency be fully replaced by privately issued bank notes and token coins.[4]

Further developments in the field of blockchain technology and smart contracts have addressed these topics even more vigorously. Several groups have proposed successor Bitcoin 2.0 designs that incorporate more sophisticated forms of smart contracts, which have blockchain similar to Bitcoin, but allow complex contracts to be created and automatically enforced.[5] Such math-based law aims to be revolutionary development not only for virtual currencies but also to have much wider application in contractual relations, in which regulatory contracts are replaced by self-enforcing contracts and court bailiffs and judges are set aside. Or this is the idea at least.

Bitcoin and smart contracts have raised one fundamental question—whether and how should law regulate such phenomenon? Author takes over a thorough discussion presented by Sergii Shcherbak in "*How Should be Bitcoin Regulated*?"[6] and critically discusses and develops some aspects highlighted there. The purpose of this paper is to (1) outline the main characters of Bitcoin and smart contracts and (2) generate some ideas on regulatory developments for Bitcoin and smart contracts. Author argues that Bitcoin and smart contracts are not so revolutionary measures from a legal point of view and it is possible to place them into existing legal framework without a need to create wholly new type of decentralised law. Author uses mostly traditional dogmatic method.

---

[1] Wolman (2014), p. 13. This monetary system collapsed after the rulers of Yuan dynasty gave way to most known temptation among money issuers and printed paper money way more they had assets (coins) covering it. It became trust-based fiat money without a trust, which obviously was not viable.

[2] Suede (2012).

[3] On the other hand, it is found that Bitcoin system is not as decentralised at is looks at first glance. A large number of centralised services currently hosting Bitcoin, as well as privileged rights retained by Bitcoin developers, may undermine the democracy among Bitcoin users. Gercais et al. (2014), p. 10.

[4] Woolsey (1991), pp. 86–87.

[5] Omohundro et al. (2015). The idea of smart contracts is actually much older, developed by Nick Szabo in 1993 in one of his works. According to Szabo, smart contracts combine protocols, users' interfaces and promises expressed via interfaces over public networks. This gives us new ways to formalise the digital relationships which are far more functional than their inanimate paper-based ancestors. Smart contracts reduce mental and computational transaction costs, imposed by either principals, third parties or their tools. The law of the Internet, and the devices attached to it, will be provided by a grand merger of law and computer security. Szabo (1997).

[6] Shcherbak (2014), pp. 45–91. S. Shcherback has LLM in Law and IT from Stockholm University. Author finds that this is one of the most thorough analysis on the Bitcoin's regulatory needs. As per taxation issues, doctoral thesis of Aleksandra definitely stands out (available online: https://openaccess.leidenuniv.nl/handle/1887/29963).

## 1.2 Technical Assumptions: Mechanics of Bitcoin

By technical nature, Bitcoin is a computer program/network/file having two major dimensions: P2P user network (operating network) and units of Bitcoins (encrypted files, BTC). To interact on the Bitcoin network, users first need to download the free and open-source software.[7] Each Bitcoin and each user is encrypted with a unique identity, and each transaction is recorded on a decentralised public ledger (also called a blockchain) that is visible to all computers on the network but does not reveal any personal information about the involved parties. The public ledger verifies that the buyer has the amount of Bitcoin being spent and has transferred that amount to the account of the seller. Bitcoin is sometimes referred to as a cryptocurrency because it relies on the principles of cryptography (communication that is secure from view of third parties) to validate transactions and govern the production of the currency itself.[8]

Bitcoin aims to be better due to its trust-free nature. Money-alike instruments with digital signatures provide part of the solution, but the main benefits are lost if a trusted third party is still required to prevent double spending.[9] It is similar to the event where a constitutive certificate of debt is signed digitally by the issuer and it is sent to two or more parties. If it covers all the assets of the issuer, it has spent three times more than it has assets to spend. This can seem as a simple example of triple spending. Satoshi Nakamoto proposed a solution to the double-spending problem using a peer-to-peer network. The network timestamps transactions by hashing them into an ongoing chain of hash-based proof-of-work, forming a record that cannot be changed without redoing the proof-of-work. The longest chain serves as not only proof of the sequence of events witnessed but also proof that it came from the largest pool of CPU power.[10] To take the debt certificate example above and improve it as proposed by Nakamoto, the time stamp should be added to the digital signature and an entry to the public register should be made which would prevent spending one asset twice or more times. Figure 1 shows the basic structure of Bitcoin network and transactions.

---

[7] Elwell et al. (2014), p. 2.

[8] Elwell et al. (2014), pp. 1–2.

[9] Clearing and double-payments are indeed a problem for current banking systems regardless of international card organisations' efforts to provide flawless payment structures. It is not rare when payment terminals verify that there is certain small amount of money on the bank account and, after doing so, enable transactions with much higher value (such as automated gas stations having special place in MasterCard rules). This may result in committing a computer related fraud in the meaning of article 8 of Convention on Cybercrime. Please see: *Convention of Cybercrime* (2015).

[10] Nakamoto (2009).

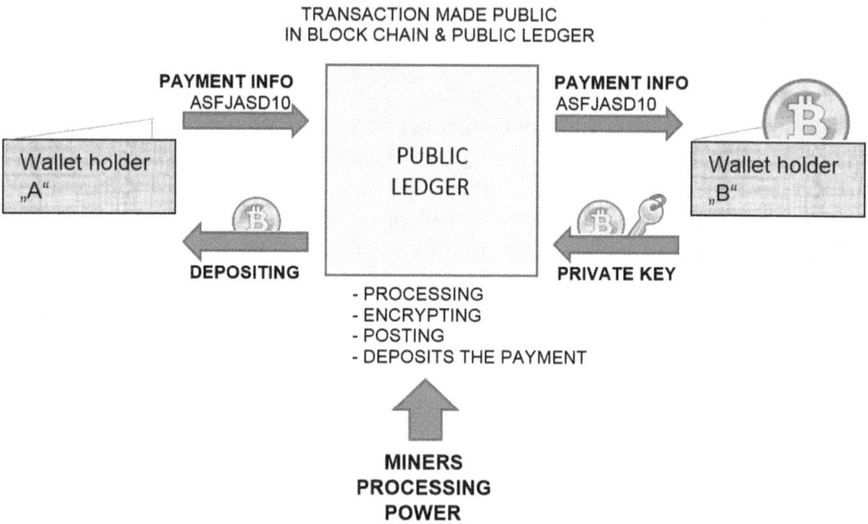


**Fig. 1** Simplified BTC P2P transaction structure

# 2 Bitcoin Under *de lege lata* in the EU

## *2.1 Emerging Tendencies*

In legal world, categorisation works mostly through defining legal phenomenon. European Central Bank (ECB) has defined Bitcoin as high-risk, decentralised, peer-to-peer network-based, unregulated digital money scheme which has certain innovations that make its use more similar to conventional money.[11] Two main arguments can be drawn from the ECB's definition: first, it is a money scheme having characteristics of both digital money and conventional money, and, secondly, there are no existing regulations which are clearly applicable to Bitcoin.

This unregulated nature is true in the sense of EU law. Many states and central authorities have stated that their position is to watch and see what will happen to Bitcoin and, based on that, decide whether and how to regulate it, if at all. Legislators desire to first experience to which interests and problems they must address the regulation.

Emerging national laws tend to distance themselves from defining Bitcoin and regulating P2P and contractual relation. As per P2P relations, it is possible that if no significant problems emerge, it may remain unregulated and follow the principle of freedom of contract and the legal status of the Internet. Most of the recommendations and consultations tend to support non-regulation as the best and only effective solution.

[11] European Central Bank (2012), p. 27.

**Table 1** Bitcoin regulations in selected jurisdictions

| Jurisdiction | Legal tender | What it is? |
|---|---|---|
| Australia | No | Commodity |
| China | No | Commodity; banned for payment institutions |
| Denmark | No | Electronic service |
| Estonia | No | Decentralised virtual currency |
| Finland | No | Commodity (trade). Exchange is financial service under EU VAT directive and therefore exempt from VAT |
| France | No | Object of payment services under supervision, taxed as property |
| Germany | No | Alternative private means of payment, contractual mechanism |
| The Netherlands | No | Alternative virtual currency |
| Portugal | No | Bidirectional virtual currency payment model |
| Spain | No | Digital goods |
| UK | | Single purpose vouchers (from tax point of view) |

When it comes to legal areas important for governments—i.e. taxation and anti-money laundering (AML)—the situation differs a lot. The fundamental question "What is Bitcoin?" gets attention where necessary to governments, and the answer to this question is often diverging and goal-oriented, aiming for reducing money laundering and not capping potential tax evasion schemes involving Bitcoin. An FBI intelligence assessment specifically pinpointed Bitcoin as "likely [to] continue to attract cybercriminals who view it as a means to transfer, launder, or steal funds as well as a means of making donations to groups participating in illegal activities".[12] As P2P transactions are fundamentally discrete and often require disproportionate amount of resources from public authorities to address their attention to these transactions and start any tax procedures or money laundering investigations, the first regulatory mechanisms are most likely to emerge in the form of national supervision over certain services provided by operators, such as Bitcoin exchange and merchants. This has been the main method for anti-money laundery so far.[13]

From the overview of "Regulation of Bitcoin in Selected Jurisdictions", the following legal attitude can be seen towards Bitcoin.[14]

As it can be seen from Table 1, none of the states recognise Bitcoin as legal tender equal to money. It is in most cases treated as commodity, and transactions with it are treated as exchange of assets as any other. Income from such transactions is usually subject to income tax. As Bitcoin transactions are falling outside the scope of payment services and intermediary and exchange services, such

[12] Kleiman (2013), p. 74.

[13] Main function of the Estonian Money Laundering and Terrorist Financing Prevention Act and EU's III anti-money-laundering directive is to regulated registration, supervision and some aspects of transaction compliance.

[14] The Law Library of Congress, Global Legal Research Center, Global Legal Research Directorate Staff (2014).

transactions are subject to VAT/GST (the latter one is, however, to be analysed by the Court of Justice of the European Union in case C-264/14 concerning VAT treatment of Bitcoins' exchange to fiat currencies). Finland and the UK are interpreting Bitcoin exchange as payment service which is not subject to VAT under section 135 of VAT Directive (see Sect. 2.3).

## 2.2 *E-Money and Payment System Laws*

Bitcoin does not fall under the definition of e-money provided in E-Money Directive 2009/110/EC[15] (EMD). Article 2 clause 2 defines e-money as electronically stored monetary value as represented by a claim on the issuer which is issued on receipt of funds for the purpose of making payment transactions and which is accepted by a natural or legal person other than the money issuer. Bitcoin falls clearly outside of the scope of EMD as it does not generate a claim against the issuer of Bitcoin.[16] There actually is no central issuer of money. Regardless of this, Bitcoin can actually meet all other criteria of e-money and therefore is a close institute to e-money.

Bitcoin does not fall under the Payment Services Directive 2007/64/EC[17] as well. It may seem surprising as Bitcoin was originally designed to be an electronic payment system independent from trust.[18] Its architecture involves the payment system providing public ledger for transactions. Bitcoin is used by an ever-increasing number of Bitcoin stakeholders (users) who can be conditionally divided into four main categories: users, miners, exchanges and merchants. They use the system for transferring value in the form of Bitcoin and, eventually, using it for buying commonly used products and services. But as the Payment Service Directive is applicable only to certain type of payment service providers which are legal entities, Bitcoin cannot be classified as payment service provider—it is not a legal entity.[19]

## 2.3 *VAT and Income Tax Laws*

### 2.3.1 Taxation of Bitcoin Transactions: Digital "Cayman Islands"

When it comes to legal areas which have significant importance for the governments and states want to have their own "share", i.e. taxation, classification of

---

[15] Directive 2009/110/EC.

[16] Shcherbak (2014), p. 61.

[17] Directive 2007/64/EC.

[18] Nakamoto (2009).

[19] Shcherbak (2014), p. 60.

Bitcoin as electronic commodity or good has met more confident approach by legislators or revenue authorities. In March 2014, the Estonian Tax and Customs Board stated that providing alternative payment service does not fall under the VAT exemption provided for ordinary financial services.[20] Turnover from transactions with Bitcoins is subject to VAT. This means that Bitcoin transactions are treated as service under section 2 sub-section 3 clause 3 of Estonian Value-Added Tax Act, which are carried out by electronic means.[21]

HM Revenue and Customs (HMRC), UK tax authority, has issued Brief 09/14 on VAT and virtual currencies. According to this, the following turnover/income will be outside of the scope of VAT or exempt under article 135 (1) (d) of VAT Directive: (1) income received from Bitcoin mining activities is exempt; (2) income received by miners for other activities, such as for the provision of services in connection with the verification of specific transactions for which specific charges are made, is exempt; (3) when Bitcoin is exchanged for sterling, euros or foreign currencies, no VAT will be due on the value of the Bitcoins themselves; (4) charges (in whatever form) made over and above the value of the Bitcoin for arranging or carrying out any transactions in Bitcoin will be exempt from VAT under Article 135 (1) (d)[22] of VAT Directive.[23] However, in all instances, VAT will be due in the normal way from suppliers of any goods or services sold in exchange for Bitcoin or other similar cryptocurrency. The value of the supply of goods or services on which VAT is due will be the sterling value of the cryptocurrency at the point the transaction takes place.[24] Finland has adopted a similar approach.[25]

The UK's approach differs from the Estonian one. The reason for this is the different understanding on the nature of Bitcoin and, consequently, the services related to it. The UK has taken direction towards recognising it as means of payment which deserves to enjoy some benefits similar to money. HMRC stated in the Brief that there are already a number of outlets, including pubs, restaurants and Internet retailers, that accept payment by Bitcoin in the UK. The reason for such is regulatory approach may be emerging public acceptance of Bitcoin.

Bitcoin's VAT treatment may be the first significant step towards identifying Bitcoin's legal status. On June 2, 2014, the Supreme Administrative Court of

[20] Council directive no 2006/112/EC of 28.11.2006.

[21] Under this, "services" means the provision, in the course of business activities, of benefits or the transfer of rights, including securities, which are not goods, and obligations to refrain from economic activity, to waive the exercise of a right or to tolerate a situation for a charge. Software and information transmitted by electronic means, and data media carrying software or information that are especially compiled or adjusted according to the purchaser's specifications are also services.

[22] Article 135 (1) (d) states: Member States shall exempt the following transactions: transactions, including negotiation, concerning deposit and current accounts, payments, transfers, debts, cheques and other negotiable instruments, but excluding debt collection.

[23] HM Revenue & Customs (2014).

[24] Ibid.

[25] Stanley-Smith (2014).

Sweden[26] lodged a request for a preliminary ruling with the European Court of Justice (Case C-264/14), asking whether the exchanging of Bitcoin for fiat currencies, and vice versa, is a transaction liable to VAT.[27] Exact questions posed by Sweden were the following: (1) Is Article 2(1) of the VAT Directive to be interpreted as meaning that transactions in the form of what has been designated as the *exchange of virtual currency for traditional currency* and vice versa, which is effected for consideration added by the supplier when the exchange rates are determined, constitute the supply of a service effected for consideration? (2) If the answer to the first question is in the affirmative, is Article 135(1) to be interpreted as meaning that the abovementioned exchange transactions are tax exempt?[28] The ruling of the court does not, however, provide a definition of and an overall legal treatment of Bitcoin but only indicates whether the exchange transactions made with virtual currencies are subject to VAT or not.

When it comes to income tax, Bitcoin is classified as monetarily appraisable property, and income from transactions (either sale or exchange) with Bitcoin is subject to income tax under section 15 of Estonian Income Tax Act.[29] This approach is indeed interesting as when it comes to analysing Bitcoin as money, the major counterargument has been that Bitcoin does not store value (see Sect. 3.1.2). The treatment of income in the UK is similar to Estonian. The profits and losses of a non-incorporated business on Bitcoin transactions must be reflected in their accounts and will be taxable on normal income tax rules.[30]

### 2.3.2 Procedural Issues with Respect to Prevention of Tax Frauds

As Bitcoins are assets regardless of their legal positioning, there may be several reasons for seizing Bitcoins. For instance, when facing tax assessment procedure, possible tax liability may drive taxpayers to hide their assets or, at least, to become apathetic towards the well-being of their businesses. It can be a consequence of a *mala fide* or *bona fide* acts, as well as wilful or negligent acts. Regardless of their intentions, compulsory execution of tax liability may thereof become considerably more difficult or impossible. In order to prevent such situations with negative value output, the right to secure or enforce payment of potential tax liability before it may be possible under customary procedure may be granted to revenue authority.[31] In

[26] *Högsta förvaltningsdomstolen.*

[27] Lomas (2014).

[28] OJ 2006 L 347, p. 1.

[29] Estonian Tax and Customs Board (2014). As 'monetarily appraisable property' is defined in section 15 sub-section 1 of Estonian Income Tax Act by open definition, Tax and Customs Board statement does not provide much information for defining Bitcoin more thoroughly.

[30] HM Revenue & Customs (2014).

[31] Please see U.S. Internal Revenue Code sections 6851 and 6861, section $136^1$ of the Estonian Taxation Act.

such situation, a question arises: how is it possible to seize Bitcoins, being basically files kept in digital wallet?

There have been numerous arrests and asset seizures related to Bitcoin use. Two of the more notable incidents occurring in 2013 include the crackdown on the Silk Road website. By October 2013, government authorities seized more than 33.6 million USD worth of Bitcoins belonging to the owner or website.[32]

In principle, it is possible to seize Bitcoins by gaining access to private key protecting the Bitcoin as password. It is possible to make a transaction and change the owner of the Bitcoin. Authorities could get that either with his cooperation or if he had stored it somewhere now accessible to the authorities. This raises significant legal issues. In the US, lawyers have argued that forcing someone to hand over their encryption keys violates the Fifth Amendment right to protection from self-incrimination.[33] The same issue emerges in the EU under article 6 clauses 1 and 2 of the European Convention on Human Rights,[34] which protects individuals against self-incrimination.[35] Request to hand over the private key may be unlawful with regard to the aforementioned reasons.

It is evident that prosperity of Bitcoin-alike virtual currencies having no central structure place enormous pressure to authorities to find ways to seize property for whatever legal purposes, considering the effects of non-self-incrimination right. As this relates to supranational interests, such as prevention of terrorism financing and money laundering, a need to seize Bitcoins and gain access to these may affect the legal approach to this field of financial law in general, providing relieving detour.

## *2.4 AML Laws*

Bitcoin's anti-money laundering treatment has been the centre of interest for governments and agencies. In Estonia, Tallinn Administrative court made the first

[32] Kien-Meng Ly (2014), p. 603. Following this raid, the market value per Bitcoin fell from $141 to a low of $109.70. Furthermore, this seizure resulted in the U.S. government holding 22 % of the Bitcoin market. Mirjanich (2014), p. 221.

[33] Silk Road shutdown: how can the FBI seize Bitcoins? (2013).

[34] The European Convention on Human Rights – Rome, 4.11.1950.

[35] See for instance: ECHR judgment *Engel and Others v The Netherlands*. In addition to this, the right to peaceful enjoyment of possession, as well as right to ownership regulated in article 1 of the First Protocol (the Protocol) to the Convention, has relevance as well in seizing property. One type of interference to the substance of property regulated under article 1 of the Protocol is interference justified by the need to secure payment of taxes (Sermet 1998, p. 8). Such right is not absolute (ECHR judgment *Sporrong and Lönnroth v Sweden*) and must meet a certain test of rule of law, proportionality and legality. In addition to procedural limits, such as non-self-incrimination right, there are many other regulations which must be taken into account when designing measures for seizing property with the purpose of securing payment of taxes as well for other similar purposes.

and only decision[36] so far concerning Bitcoins and AML regulations on 18.11.2014. The main issue of this case is more of an administrative procedure issue, discussing whether Financial Intelligence Unit (FIU) was allowed to collect information on the services (if any) provided by Mr Voogd in order to decide whether the service fell under AML laws or not. However, the FIU argued that dealing with Bitcoins fall under this regulation as being alternative means of payment. Namely, under section 6 sub-section 4 of Estonian Money Laundering and Terrorist Financing Prevention Act, service of alternative means of payment means buying, selling or mediating funds of monetary value—through a communications, transfer or clearing system—by which financial obligations can be performed or which can be exchanged for an official currency. It follows that FIU sees Bitcoin as a fund with monetary value which is possible to use for performing financial obligations, i.e. it functions as certain type of money.

The regulators need to decide on which way to fight emerging money laundering activities involving Bitcoin and other cryptocurrencies as well. Author supports the approach that regulation of such currencies should occur at the point where law enforcement can most effectively punish civil and criminal violations with the least overhead. Because Bitcoin is a decentralised, peer-to-peer virtual currency, it makes little sense to regulate entities other than Bitcoin currency exchanges. Increased pressure on users will only serve to increase the cost of enforcement in the long run.[37] As Bitcoin is used outside of the financial world more and more, with possibility to change it for commodities and services in shops and markets, it is definitely appropriate to subject it to AML laws. The public acceptance of Bitcoin has provided justification to such approach.

# 3 Possible Scenario of *de lege ferenda* of Bitcoin in the EU

## *3.1 Idea Behind Bitcoin: Virtual Fiat E-Money*

### 3.1.1 Philosophical Retrospect on the Idea of Money

In order to regulate something, it must be first identified what it is and where it can be placed in existing legal system. There is no uniform legal definition for money, which makes it difficult to position it, at least for lawyers. For economists, money has been understood as a special good or verifiable record which can be exchanged for another good or service in a particular country of socio-economic context, made

[36] Tallinn Administrative Court ruling of 18.11.2014 no 3-14-50581 *Otto Albert de Voogd v Financial Intelligence Unit*. – Not available publicly. There have been also two criminal cases in Estonian court in which illegal use of Bitcoins for purchase of drugs were discussed.

[37] Bryans (2014), p. 472.

so desirable due to its extremely liquid form.[38] Evolution of money has always been directed towards liquidity.[39] Historically, there have been three forms of money, reflecting the level of liquidity and substantiation of value in the money.

First, *commodity money* is the money whose intrinsic value is determined by the commodity the money is made of. Silver or ancient gold coins are examples of commodity money, so were bird feathers and certain type of shells.

Uncomfortable form of commodity money led to *representative money*, providing more portable and divisible means for exchange. Its intrinsic value is backed by a certain commodity this money is redeemed for. Mere paper sheet can reflect—or represent as reflected by its name—the value of certain good. Fine examples are tokens and gold certificates.[40] Value and stability of representative money is backed with the value of the good it is representing. The most commonly used asset behind representative money has been gold. Unfortunately, it represents the idea of representative money the least. The gold itself, on the other hand, is not an asset with intrinsic value. By nature, it is a shiny mineral which can be used for a few practical purposes. The value of it is again emotional and conventional and is based on natural desire for shiny assets. As it is the common feature of all nations, it is accepted as asset which can be represented by certificate. The idea of gold-based money is shortly but sharply described by David Wolman, stating that promise behind fiat money can be described as "We promise that these papers will have a value in some day. It is, however, important that nobody asks whether this day is today".[41] It is significant that back in 1869 in the U.S. Supreme Court case *Hepburn v. Griswold*, justice Salmon P. Chase decided the legal tender issued by the U.S. government to be unconstitutional as having no legal basis there. This decision was quickly overturned by two justices appointed at the same day.[42]

Third type of money is *fiat money*,[43] which is not made of or backed by any commodity and has no intrinsic value. Fiat money is a legal tender put into circulation and backed traditionally by a government. It is a promise made by the issuer of money, and its value is based on the mere trust for the issuer and its future endeavours. Currency is the most common form of fiat money and is a fungible, transferable, divisible and recognisable legal tender. The exchange value of the

---

[38] Eamets (2005), p. 100. Mishkin (2013), p. 8.

[39] There are, however, notable exceptions as regard liquidity. In Micronesia, for instance, large rock discs named *Rai* were used for buying goods and services. It is significant that there was no need to transfer actual possession of *Rai* to its new owner—acknowledgment basis was enough. Some wealthy families had never seen their *Rai*s, but their wealth was not questioned. It is yet another example of money which value is based on acceptance by community. Please see: Friedman (1991), pp. 1–2.

[40] Shcherbak (2014), p. 57.

[41] Wolman (2014), p. 35.

[42] Wolman (2014), p. 36. About case *Hepburn v Grisworld*, please see further online: https://supreme.justia.com/cases/federal/us/75/603/case.html (25.04.2015).

[43] In Latin, '*fiat*' means 'so be it'. It refers to creating something by word or from emptiness.

**Table 2** Money matrix

| | | | |
|---|---|---|---|
| Legal status | Unregulated | Certain types of local currencies | Virtual currency |
| | Regulated | Banknotes and coins | E-money |
| | | | Commercial bank money (deposits) |
| | | Physical | Digital |
| | | Money format | |

currency directly depends on the governmental policy and the national economy.[44] Considering the prosperity of digital economy, the logical form following cash is digital money in its various forms (e-money, virtual currencies) stored in digital wallets. By its nature, e-money is still a fiat money as long as its value is based on currency.

It is argued that there is now existing a fourth type of money in the form of Bitcoin—*factum money*[45] or just a novel type of money.[46] Whereas fiat money is put into existence, and maintained, by a government (or, theoretically, some other kind of agency) producing it, factum money just is.[47] The author does not agree that it is fully correct to name such type of money "just is" money as even Bitcoins must be created by miners as a result of a cryptographic process. Difference appears in decentralisation and source of legitimacy of the money. This, however, does not reflect either the liquidity or substantiation of value but who controls issuance of money. Bitcoin aims to be a fiat money, following the natural endeavour towards liquidity and being made by word from "emptiness". The difference between traditional fiat money and Bitcoin is not so huge as often thought, and its validity is based on similar "asset"—trust and hope.

Current types of money can be placed in a money matrix presented by European Central Bank's report. Bitcoin belongs to digital unregulated money box named virtual currency.[48] In order to swap from virtual currency to e-money box, either the problem with the claim against the issuer must be solved or the definition of e-money must be changed. Simplified money matrix is presented in Table 2.

### 3.1.2 Functional Definition of Money

European Central Bank has explained the definition of money functionally. Regardless of the form of money, it is traditionally associated with three different functions. Firstly, money is used as *medium of exchange*, an intermediary in trade to

[44] Shcherbak (2014), p. 57.

[45] Buterin (2014).

[46] Shcherbak (2014), p. 58.

[47] Buterin (2014).

[48] European Central Bank (2012), p. 11.

avoid the inconveniences of a barter system, i.e. the need for a coincidence of wants between the two parties involved in the transaction. Secondly, money is a *unit of account*. Money acts as a standard numerical unit for the measurement of value and costs of goods, services, assets and liabilities. Lastly, money can be saved and retrieved in the future for *storing of value*.[49] This requires money to be reliable and safe for its users.

Bitcoin has proven to have characteristics of medium of exchange and unit of account. Its ability to store value has been, though, highly questionable. It is not backed by any good or commodity, and its trust is not generated by underlying government. Although the fiat money is not backed with certain commodity either, the whole structure of state turns into people's trust towards money. Rapid and vast changes in its exchange rates have been extreme proof on Bitcoin's volatility.[50] As said by Gavin Andresen, lead developer of the Bitcoin virtual currency project, *Bitcoin is an experiment, treat it like you would treat promising internet start-up company*.[51] Being indeed a psychosocial experiment, the value of Bitcoin is based on subjective value given to this instrument, which is based on the fact that certain groups of persons are accepting it.[52] As writer Kurt Tucholsky noted about the self-defining source of value of fiat money: *Money has value because it is accepted everywhere, and it is accepted everywhere because it has value*.[53]

The author finds that both Bitcoin and legal tender share the characteristics of fiat money, provided the Bitcoins are acknowledged by merchants regardless of governments' opinions and regulations. The intrinsic value of Bitcoin can be created by public acceptance of such means of payment regardless of its volatile and decentralised nature. Let us emphasize that the value of our currencies (such as euro) is our estimation to the soundness of our governments and reflection of our hopes for the future. The same seems to be with Bitcoin. As it is not backed by whatsoever goods or assets, it leads us to the problem of the functional definition of money and the question whether Bitcoin falls within this definition. As the current financial system operates, thanks to financial stability, growing amount of virtual currency users may start to threaten this monopoly. This may be the reason why decentralised virtual currencies tend to face not-so-positive reaction by legislators, and it has not been treated as money by global trendsetters.

---

[49] European Central Bank (2012), p. 10.

[50] In February 2014, Bitcoin prices fell on the news from a high of $831 to a low of $658 before rebounding to $719 in a few days.

[51] European Central Bank (2012), p. 27.

[52] Bitcoin has been compared to socio-economic psychology-based irrationalities that have emerged throughout history, such as gold rush in the nineteenth century and "tulip bubble" in sixteenth and seventeenth centuries in the Netherlands. Please see: Desjardins (2014). Such bubbles are founded on people's faith, desires and expectations towards certain values and beliefs. Case of South Sea Company in the 1720s reminded the role of management and trust related to it in creating economic bubbles. History has proven that bubbles based on faith, desires and expectations do not tend to survive.

[53] Wolman (2014), p. 17.

### 3.1.3 Possible Scenarios for Bitcoin Regulation

Sergii Shcherbak argued that the balanced regulation of Bitcoin aiming to ensure the balance between the interests of Bitcoin stakeholders and the interests of regulatory bodies is achievable in the form of the partial regulation of the Bitcoin usage by Bitcoin stakeholders; the interests of regulatory bodies is achievable in the form of the partial regulation of the Bitcoin usage by Bitcoin stakeholders through the implementation of the proposed strategy comprising of four interconnected aspects.[54]

These four aspects cover different levels of Bitcoin's functionality:

(1) conceptual level—Bitcoin should be recognised officially as unregulated technology; it is similar to the Internet and e-mail and should be treated the same;
(2) the level of user interaction—Bitcoin users who transact directly between each other should be officially excluded from the scope of regulatory scrutiny;
(3) the level of interaction between users and merchants—this level should be regulated; Bitcoin merchants and their consumers should be subject to requirements in the relevant law;
(4) the level of interaction between users and exchanges—this should be the most regulated area, falling under anti-money laundering rules and Payment Services Directive and also investments regulations.[55]

The regulative area within Bitcoin system with users, miners, exchanges and merchants can be schematised as showed in Fig. 1. Regulatory area presented in Fig. 2, however, proves to be vague. Regulations cover professional participants such as MERCHANTS and EXCHANGERS. Transactions between USERS and MINERS remain unregulated. Anti-money laundering rules and other rules applicable to consumer protection naturally apply. Exchangers should be treated as payment service providers and treated accordingly.

The statement on unregulated nature on user level is actually not fully true. The usual contract law principles apply as two entities agree on something, such as transfer of Bitcoins. While the definition of agreement varies a lot among jurisdictions, the idea is the same—when one party bindingly undertakes to perform an act or omission, the legal regulation provided by law for certain transactions apply. Bitcoin as P2P instrument is used for transferring a value under an agreement of two participants. A transaction is a transfer of value between Bitcoin wallets that gets included in the blockchain.[56] So by nature it functions as a performance of agreement or agreement and performance of agreement in one.

Let us take one Estonian example. If one party A provides a loan[57] to the other party B in BTC, the regulation to loan agreements apply. If the loan in BTCs is

[54] Shcherbak (2014), p. 91.

[55] Ibid, pp. 89–91.

[56] How does Bitcoin work? (2015).

[57] Under Estonian law, the loan can be provided in the form of money or substitutable asset.

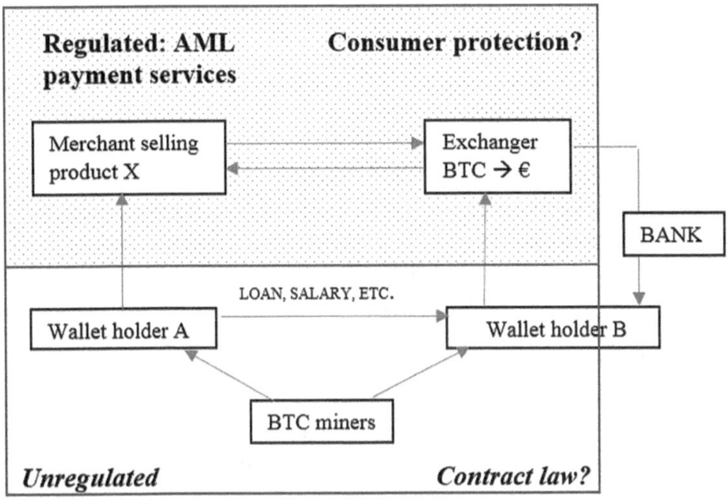


**Fig. 2** Regulatory area of Bitcoin

provided in economic or professional activities (can be a natural person), there is an obligation to pay interests even if there is no agreement on that. Section 397 (1) of Estonian Law of Obligations Act states that the interest shall be paid on loans granted in economic or professional activities; in the case of other loan agreements, interest shall be paid only if so agreed. Should the interest be paid in BTCs or in euros as legal tender if not agreed specifically? As interests are considered to be in monetary form, the current law refers to euros and the lender does not have a right to claim BTCs. But is this consequence the one what average parties acting in similar conditions would expect, lending "virtual" money?

Another example: contract price is paid in BTCs. The performance is with deficiencies, and there is a need to reduce price. Under section 112 (1) of Estonian Law of Obligations Act, if a party accepts defective performance, the party may reduce the price payable by the party by the proportion of the ratio of the value of defective performance to the value of conforming performance. Is it reduced in BTCs, or is the value of BTCs converted to euros and reduced then? Again, this one occasion which may cause disputes between contracting parties requires developing a new case law.

These examples do not provide answer to the question how Bitcoin should be regulated in private law. As it may be inferred from many macro-economic tendencies, virtual currencies are getting more common in transaction processes as means of payment, and therefore it is appropriate to address these topics in private law as well.

## 3.2 *Bitcoin 2.0: Smart Contracts and Law of Contracts*

### 3.2.1 A Rise of Self-Enforcement, Representative Assets and Crypto-Equity

Rush around Bitcoin and its successors has led to so-called Bitcoin 2.0. This system incorporates more sophisticated forms of contracts, which have blockchain similar to Bitcoin, but allows complex contracts to be created and automatically enforced. Such self-enforcing contracts are called smart contracts, and the main structure is presented in Fig. 3. Within these, the traditional text of the contract is replaced with a code, but not only in the part which would be written in the traditional agreement—all acts and statements of intent are replaced with a code as well, sufficient for enforcing the contract (for example, a code is created which sends commands to the bank and Land Register, changing the balance of the seller's and the buyer's bank accounts and making the entry to the Land Register on a new owner and mortgage; parties sign it digitally and "trigger" the process).

In traditional contracts, each party is free to decide whether to fulfil the contract, whether to only partially implement the contract (by leaving out some obligations) or whether to breach the contract (and pay instead for damages or compensation). By contrast, in the case of smart contracts, parties have no choice but to implement the contract because the contract has been encoded, written into the code. It cannot be breached unless one actually manages to break into the code.[58]

Smart contracts are definitely great tools and make life in IT- and database-based world much easier and independent form trust. Smart contract are powerless when there is no technology behind them enabling the enforcement. This problem is solved by crypto-ledgers. Crypto-ledgers provide a novel way of issuing secure and

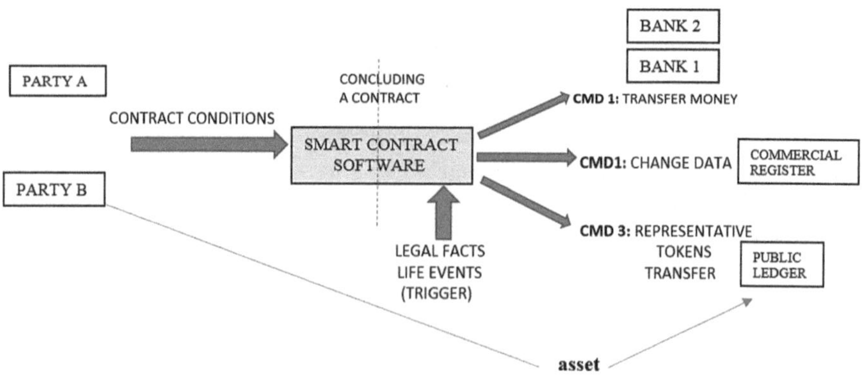


**Fig. 3** Smart contract structure

[58] de Filippi (2015).

tradable tokens via distributed networks. Although sometimes described as cryptocurrency, implying that the use value of the tokens is closest to currency, there are numerous other potential applications of these tokens that range from stock equivalents to previously unimaginable forms.[59] This has led to the development of crypto-equity, involving so-called representative assets. This instrument is very similar to representative money, being backed by certain asset.

Crypto-equity can be divided into four groups:

(1) shares in a project that serve a function similar to stock, allowing participation in the decision-making and participation in financial upside (i.e. BitShares);
(2) tokens which represent ownership in something other than a company, for example intellectual property (i.e. CommonAccord);
(3) product tokens which are redeemable for some product, perhaps one consumable in the context of a decentralised technology (i.e. Ethereum);
(4) access tokens which provide access to a particular set of benefits within a network, similar to a membership (i.e. Swarm).[60]

### 3.2.2 Regulatory Challenges

Smart contracts are undoubtedly the future of IT-based societies. From legal perspective, however, contract law meets great challenges to adapt itself with automatic enforcement. This seems to be the case. In the seminar which took place in Massachusetts Institute of Technology in January 2015 on cryptocurrencies and distributed ledgers, the theme question of the event was, "How can we design decentralized technologies that promote individual autonomy and fundamental rights (such as privacy and freedom of expression) while remaining compliant with the law?"[61]

Nick Szabo, developer of the smart contract idea, pointed out that most of the contractual dispute involves an unforeseen or unspecified eventuality. A common example of an unspecified eventuality is that the parties behind a pseudonym might change: corporate change of officers, sales of brand names and so on.[62] Indeed, smart contracts are, however, not designed to include all life events in the code which may influence the performance of contract and give just ground for refusal under the traditional contract law. We can add force majeure events; events where the circumstances under which a contract is entered into change after the entry into the contract, and this results in a material change in the balance of the obligations of

[59] Blockchain Workshops webpage. Berkman workshop (2014).
[60] Ibid.
[61] Blockchain Workshops webpage. MIT Workshop (2014).
[62] Szabo (1997).

the parties making it unreasonable[63]; etc. But we cannot write everything into code, which eventually creates conflict between law and automatic enforcement. This goes especially for consumer contracts, where one side is assumed to be in a weaker position and the idea of law is to prevent the consumer to be stuck in the complicated machinery created by the merchant. Smart contract may be something like this machinery, if wanted to be used for inappropriate purposes.

The solution for this problem requires the adaption of law on the principles' level, when it comes to activities taking place after the performance and upon the performance. The function of law is not to make things always easy but to ensure fair balance of interests in society. Evolution of smart contracts poses a question, whether we should give up some of those rights, give a green light to freedom of contract principle and start to minimise post-performance remedies. This question highlights two possible development scenarios for smart-contract-related laws.

## 4 Conclusion

The current approach towards the need to regulated Bitcoin is based on governments' needs. Applying anti-money laundering and tax regulations to Bitcoin gets most of the attention, as perpetrators have taken advantage of Bitcoin's confidential characteristics. Taxation issues are highlighted, as well as current system enables tax evasion schemes. The fundamental question—what Bitcoin is—remains unanswered. It definitely does not fall under the current definition of money and e-money, while it functions as money *de facto* regardless of its foundation of legitimacy. Its decentralised nature has prevented it from being classified as regulated means of payment. While the financial stability is being valued more and more and there is no overall public trust towards Bitcoin, it is not probable that such decentralised means of payment will be regulated as money.

P2P relations between the miners and users of Bitcoin system remain unregulated. Current private law and certain fields of contract law meet several problems related to Bitcoins used instead of money. Therefore, it would be reasonable for the legislators to classify it and recognise it as equal to either money or asset.

The main regulatory obstacles for smart contracts are different from Bitcoin's but remain in the field of private law. As the performance of contract takes place automatically under the code, the code must either regulate much more life events (e.g. force majeure events) to follow current contract law principles or leave a cap to the code, which makes it insufficient. Evolution of smart contracts leads us

[63] Under section 97 (1) of Estonian Law of Obligations Act, it may give a legal ground for terminating the contract. This clause was used in contracts a lot when Estonia changed Estonian kroons to euros and contracting parties were safeguarding themselves from unexpected exchange rate of EEK to EUR.

towards softer interpretation of freedom of agreement principle and development of the concept of representative assets. It probably reduces the power of consumer protection laws as well, as the code is not designed to be as flexible as the laws.

# References

## *Literature*

Bryans D (2014) Bitcoin and money laundering: mining for an effective solution. Indiana Law J 89 (1)

Buterin V (2014) DAOs are not scary, Part 1: self-enforcing contracts and factum law. Bitcoin Magazine, February 2014. Available online: https://bitcoinmagazine.com/10468/daos-scary-part-1-self-enforcing-contracts-factum-law/ (15.4.2015)

de Filippi P (2015) Smart contracts. Legal aspects. P2P Foundation. Available online: http://p2pfoundation.net/Smart_Contracts (25.4.2015)

Desjardins J (2014) Bitcoin: a modern gold rush? Visual Capitalist, 05.8.2014. Available online: http://www.visualcapitalist.com/bitcoin-modern-gold-rush/ (16.4.2015)

Eamets R (2005) Sissejuhatus majandusteooriasse. (Introduction to economic theory). University of Tartu

Elwell CK, Murphy MM, Seitzinger MV (2014) Bitcoin: questions, answers, and analysis of legal issues. Congressional Research Service, July 2014. Available online: https://fas.org/sgp/crs/misc/R43339.pdf (15.4.2015)

European Central Bank (2012) Virtual currency schemes. Frankfurt am Main. Available online: https://www.ecb.europa.eu/pub/pdf/other/virtualcurrencyschemes201210en.pdf (16.4.2015)

Friedman M (1991) The Island of Stone Money. Working Paper in Economics E-91-3. Stanford: February 1991

Gercais A, Karame KO, Capkun S (2014) Is Bitcoin a decentralized currency? IEEE Security and Privacy Magazine. Available online: http://www.syssec.ethz.ch/people/agervais.html (14.4.2015)

Kien-Meng Ly M (2014) Coining Bitcoin's "Legal-Bits": examining the regulatory framework for Bitcoin and virtual currencies. Harv J Law Technol 27(2)

Kleiman JA (2013) Beyond the silk road: unregulated decentralized virtual currencies continue to endanger US national security and welfare. American University National Security Law Brief, vol 4, issue 1

Lomas U (2014) Sweden calls for EU ruling on Bitcoin taxation. Tax-News, 22.7.2014. Available online: http://www.tax-news.com/news/Sweden_Calls_For_EU_Ruling_On_Bitcoin_Taxation____65303.html (15.4.2015)

Mirjanich N (2014) Digital money: Bitcoin's financial and tax future despite regulatory uncertainty. DePaul Law Rev 64(1)

Mishkin FS (2013) The economics of money, banking, and financial markets (alternate edition). Addison Wesley, Boston

Nakamoto S (2009) Bitcoin: a peer-to-peer electronic cash system. Available online: https://bitcoin.org.pdf (15.4.2015)

Omohundro S, Gregory G, Oezer T (2015) Smart contracts – from P2P foundation. Available online: http://p2pfoundation.net/Smart_Contracts (14.4.2015)

Sermet L (1998) The European Convention on Human Rights and property rights. Human rights files, No. 11 rev. Council of the Europe Publishing

Shcherbak S (2014) How should Bitcoin be regulated? Eur J Leg Stud 7(1)

Stanley-Smith J (2014) Finland recognises Bitcoin services as VAT exempt. International Tax Review, 14.11.2014. Available online: http://www.internationaltaxreview.com/Article/3400689/Finland-recognises-Bitcoin-services-as-VAT-exempt.html (25.4.2015)

Suede M (2012) Bitcoin: crypto-anarchism and the digital money revolution. Available online: http://mic.com/articles/4980/bitcoin-crypto-anarchism-and-the-digital-money-revolution (15.4.2015)

Szabo N (1997) Formalizing and securing relationships on public networks. First Monday, vol 2, no 9

Wolman D (2014) The end of money. Translation to Estonian. Äripäev

Woolsey WW (1991) Full privatization of currency in a nearly conventional money and banking system. Cato J 11(1):86–87

## Electronic Sources

*How does Bitcoin work?* – Bitcoin webpage, 2015. Available online: Bitcoin webpage https://bitcoin.org/en/how-it-works (24.4.2015).

*Berkman workshop: Crypto-equity & the Law. Questions To Be Addressed.* – Blockchain Workshops webpage, Blockchain Global Impact, 14.12.2014. Available online: http://crypto.sabir.cc/?p=147 (25.4.2015).

*MIT Workshop: Understanding Decentralization.* - Blockchain Workshops webpage, Blockchain Global Impact, 14.10.2014. Available online: http://crypto.sabir.cc/?p=62 (25.4.2015).

*Taxation of transactions with Bitcoins.* – Estonian Tax and Customs Board, march 2014. Available online: http://www.emta.ee/index.php?id=35227 (in Estonian, 15.4.2015).

*Revenue and Customs Brief 9 (2014): Bitcoin and other cryptocurrencies. Policy Paper.* –HM Revenue & Customs, 3.3.2014. Available online: https://www.gov.uk/government/publica tions (15.4.2015).

*Silk Road shutdown: how can the FBI seize Bitcoins? (2013)* - The Guardian, 3.10.2013. Available online: http://www.theguardian.com/technology/2013/oct/02/bitcoin-silk-road-how-to-seize (14.5.2015).

*Regulation of Bitcoin in Selected Jurisdictions.* – The Law Library of Congress, Global Legal Research Center, Global Legal Research Directorate Staff, Washington, 2014. Available online: http://www.loc.gov/law/help/current-topics.php (20.3.2015).

## Legal Acts

*Convention of Cybercrime.* – Budapest, 23.10.2001. Available online: https://www.riigiteataja.ee/akt/550359 (15.4.2015).

*The European Convention of the Human Rights.* – Rome, 4.11.1950. Available online: https://www.riigiteataja.ee/akt/78154 (14.5.2015).

Council directive no 2006/112/EC of 28.11.2006 *on the common system of value added tax,* article 135. - OJ L 347, 11.12.2006, p. 1–118.

Directive 2009/110/EC of the European Parliament and of the Council of 16 September 2009 *on the taking up, pursuit and prudential supervision of the business of electronic money institutions* amending Directives 2005/60/EC and 2006/48/EC and repealing Directive 2000/46/EC. - OJ L 267, 10.10.2009, p. 7–17.

Directive 2007/64/EC of the European Parliament and of the Council of 13.11.2007 *on payment services in the internal market* amending Directives 97/7/EC, 2002/65/EC, 2005/60/EC and 2006/48/EC and repealing Directive 97/5/EC. - OJ L 319, 5.12.2007, p. 1–36.

*Estonian Income Tax Act*. 15.12.1999. - RT I 1999, 101, 903; RT I, 19.03.2015, 2. English translation available online: https://www.riigiteataja.ee/en/eli/502042015008/consolide (15.4.2015)

*Estonian Law of Obligations Act*. 26.9.2001. - RT I 2001, 81, 487; RT I, 29.06.2014, 109. English translation available online: https://www.riigiteataja.ee/en/eli/516092014001/consolide (25.4.2015).

*Estonian Money Laundering and Terrorist Financing Prevention Act*. 19.12.2007. - RT I 2008, 3, 21; RT I, 19.3.2015, 4. English translation available online: https://www.riigiteataja.ee/en/eli/502042015014/consolide (15.4.2015).

*Estonian Taxation Act*. 20.2.2002. - RT I 2002, 26, 150; RT I, 17.03.2015, 3. English translation available online: https://www.riigiteataja.ee/en/eli/519032015001/consolide (14.5.2015).

*Estonian Value-Added Tax Act*. 10.12.2003. - RT I 2003, 82, 554; RT I, 30.12.2014, 4. English translation available online: https://www.riigiteataja.ee/en/eli/527012015016/consolide (15.4.2015).

*U.S. Internal Revenue Code*. Available online: https://www.law.cornell.edu/uscode/text/26 (14.5.2015).

## Court Practice

ECHR decision of 8.6.1976 *Engel and Others v The Netherlands*, application no 5100/71; 5101/71; 5102/71; 5354/72; 5370/7.

ECHR judgment of 23.9.1994 *Sporrong and Lönnroth v Sweden*. - Series A no. 52.

Tallinn Administrative Court ruling of 18.11.2014 no 3-14-50581 *Otto Albert de Voogd v Financial Intelligence Unit*. – Not available publicly.

# Smart Contracts

**Merit Kõlvart, Margus Poola, and Addi Rull**

**Abstract** There has been little discussion about smart contracts in relation to contract law. The concept of smart contracting has remained incomprehensible to most lawyers, and programmers tend to perceive it as a solution that replaces traditional contracts and contract law. The aim of this chapter is to clarify that, usually, a smart contract is a programmed functionality which executes some part of the legal contract. This may be an automated payment function that performs the payment obligation by contract law. Authors do not exclude the possibility that a contract shall be fully performed by a smart contracting solution in the future, but this depends on whether such a program can fulfil all requirements of contract law necessary for the execution of a specific transaction. This chapter provides an overview of the concept of smart contracting, e-contracts, smart property and contractual requirements necessary to conclude a contract.

## 1 Introduction

Nick Szabo believed as early as two decades ago that a variety of contractual clauses can be attached in the hardware and software in a manner to make the breach of contract expensive.[1] According to Nick Szabo, a smart contract is a computerised transaction protocol that implements the terms of the contract.[2] The

[1] Szabo (1997).

[2] Babbitt and Dietz (2014), p. 10.

M. Kõlvart (✉)
Estonian Ministry of Justice of Republic of Estonia, Tallinn, Estonia

Department of Informatics, Tallinn University of Technology, Akadeemia tee 3, 12618 Tallinn, Estonia
e-mail: merit.kolvart@just.ee

M. Poola • A. Rull
Tallinn Law School, Tallinn University of Technology, Akadeemia tee 3, 12618 Tallinn, Estonia
e-mail: margus.poola@ttu.ee; addi.rull@ttu.ee



T. Kerikmäe, A. Rull (eds.), *The Future of Law and eTechnologies*,
DOI 10.1007/978-3-319-26896-5_7

main advantages of using smart contracts besides traditional contracts is the efficiency of the contractual process, e.g. using smart contracts allows easily to maintain an overview of the past behaviour of contracting parties. Contract terms are self-enforceable and can include references to legal contracts. Smart contracting minimises the risk of malicious and accidental exceptions and the necessity for trusted intermediaries.[3]

A smart contract is an intelligent agent. In other words, it is a computer program capable of making decisions when certain preconditions are met. The intelligence of an agent depends on the complexity of a transaction it is programmed to perform. Contracts can be very simple transactions executed in seconds and minutes or relatively complex and lengthy transactions that involve negotiations and tens of pages of written text with specific rights and obligations which may take hours or months to complete. Today smart contracts fall into the category of relatively simple transactions.

Algorithmic trading in the financial sector is a good example of making use of smart transactions. It may account for more than 50 % of equity trades in the United States and European stock markets. Computer programs use complex mathematical methods to buy and sell financial instruments on behalf of traders behind investment banks and pension funds. Save the difference in the underlying technologies, this is very similar to what smart contracts as automated programs do by transferring digital property (cryptocurrency) in the blockchain after certain triggering conditions are met.[4]

Advocates of revolutionary technologies such as Ethereum or Codius suggest that there is a paradigm shift in the practice of smart contracting, triggered by technologies which enable transactions in a decentralised mode leaving different intermediaries and middlemen aside.[5] The possibility to avoid banks, lawyers, consultants and other intermediary service providers is certainly appealing, because it lowers the transaction costs and makes the whole contracting process more efficient. The vision is that a transaction is as simple and easy to handle as possible. A computer program takes care of the whole contracting cycle. It concludes a contract and then fulfils contractual terms automatically.

Electronic commerce offers many possibilities to develop smart solutions. For instance, a computer program can be programmed not to release payment before delivery of goods is made. This is not so complicated because smart delivery systems already exist. However, what if a wrong item is delivered, an ordered item is not delivered or quality problems occur? These are variables harder or impossible to check by a computer program as long as steps which may cause the

[3] Ibid.

[4] Fairfield (2014), p. 38.

[5] Babbitt and Dietz (2014), p. 11. Smart contracts can be used in the process of decentralised autonomous organisations (DAO) which are decentralised networks for narrow artificial intelligent autonomous agents which divide its processes into computationally intractable tasks and tasks which it performs itself. Computationally intractable tasks are such tasks that humans have to perform.

described misconduct are not fully supervised by automatic control systems. These elements form a crucial part of the substance of the same contract even if a part of that contract automatically checking the delivery and the payment is smart.

Usually, certain minimal preconditions necessary to conclude a contract are met once people engage in transactions. Then a myriad of different legal instruments from domestic, European or international domains apply depending on the type and the complexity of a transaction. If a computer program must take care of all the main contractual steps, including pre-contractual negotiations, formation and performance of the contract, dispute resolution, and take into account laws applicable to a particular transaction, then it requires the capability of a very advanced artificial intelligence.

Smart contracts are not so smart yet. Smart contracts perform a certain functionality in a legal contract, e.g. being an intelligent agent that fulfils a payment obligation, and as technology advances more contractual terms can be programmed to perform automatically.[6]

In the legal sense, a contract is an agreement between parties giving rise to a binding legal relationship or some other legal effect.[7] Smart contracts are seen as new forms of arrangements which are similar to contracts and which are written in source code. A program implements the terms of a contract.[8] Smart contracts do not substitute legal contracts but operate aside legal contracts and are used when legal contracts are not practical.[9] Therefore, smart contracts are used together with or aside legal contracts to provide automated arrangements for some parts or clauses of a contract. A smart contract by itself is not a legal contract. It may become a legal contract if it meets the requirements of contract law. Certain minimum criteria must be met to conclude a legal contract. A contract is concluded when parties intend to be legally bound and they reach a sufficient agreement without any further requirement.[10] To fulfil this criterion specific principles of contract law are considered. If smart contracts are capable to take into account the legal norms applied to contracts, then smart contracting can attain legal contracting effect.

## 2 E-Contracting

Various contracting methods are used to make the process of contracting more efficient. Legal contracts can be performed as traditional contracts, e-contracts and partly or fully automated e-contracts. Different contracting methods can be used at the same time. For example, a legal contract is formed electronically, signed

---

[6] Ibid., p. 10.

[7] DCFR (2009), p. 18.

[8] Miller et al. (2013), p. 1.

[9] Ibid.

[10] Art. 2:101 (1) PECL (2002).

digitally and some of the contract terms are enforced by a smart contracting process.

E-contracting is increasingly used to support the contracting process.[11] There are two kinds of e-contracts. A distinction is made between shallow e-contracting and deep e-contracting. The difference is whether the level of automation leads to a new business process or it does not. If the level of automation leads to a new business process, then it is deep e-contracting and when the level of automation does not lead to a new business process, then it is shallow e-contracting.[12]

One type of e-contracting is automated e-contracting where both parties operate through machines and the process has minimal or no human intervention.[13] In theory automated e-contracting can be carried out as deep e-contracting when the level of automation leads to new business process and as shallow e-contracting in case the level of automation does not lead to a new business process. A question arises is it technically possible to carry out automated e-contracting in such a way that it does not lead to a new business process?

From a legal point of view it is hard to see the difference between automated e-contracts and smart contracts. Smart contracts as well as automated e-contracts use automated arrangements and both can be seen operating aside legal contracts. It is being predicted that the usage of smart contracts starts to transform traditional business processes and to make new business structures and methods possible.[14] When the use of smart contracts leads to a new business process, smart contracting falls into the deep e-contracting category. Today due to the broad definition of smart contracting it cannot be categorised as shallow e-contracting or deep e-contracting. As long as there is no one definition of smart contracting, categorising is possible only on the level of a particular contracting process.

## 3 Different Understandings of Smart Contracting

The understanding of the concept of smart contracts seems to differ among representatives of different sciences. IT professionals consider smart contracts as automated jurisdiction-free arrangements.[15] For lawyers smart contracts are automated arrangements aside legal contracts because it is not possible to avoid jurisdiction. Jurisdiction guarantees access to justice, which is a fundamental right and the foundation of the rule of law.[16] It includes the right of an individual to submit a

[11] Angelov and Grefen (2003), p. 8.

[12] Ibid.

[13] ICC Guide for eContracting (2004), pp. 3–4.

[14] Szabo (used 28.07.2015). See more about formalising and securing relationships on public networks, available: http://szabo.best.vwh.net/formalize.html.

[15] Miller et al. (2013), p. 1.

[16] Francioni (2007), p. 1.

claim to court and have a court adjudicate it.[17] Access to justice is a key element in ensuring the rule of law. This right cannot be excluded even if more efficient contract enforcement procedures exist.

Perhaps the different points of view among professionals of IT and law are the consequence of several interpretations given to a contract. One definition of contract used in relation to smart contracts is that a contract is an agreement creating obligations enforceable by law.[18] Although this definition includes the enforceability of the agreement by law, it does not indicate that there cannot be other legal opportunities to enforce contract terms. Using smart contracting aside legal contracts to enforce contract terms is one legal opportunity to enforce contract terms provided that parties of the contract have agreed to use smart contracting. In most cases using smart contracting to enforce contract terms may exclude the need to enforce contract terms in court, but it does not set aside jurisdiction. There is and should always be an opportunity for the contracting party to protect his rights in court.

## 4 Smart Property

The main difference between using smart contracting process and traditional contracting process is that operating through smart contracting the property must be controlled by digital means, e.g. traded and loaned via block chain.[19] Property that is controlled by digital means is smart property.

Legally property consists of rights and obligations. One of the rights making up property is the ownership right which consists of the right to possess, use and dispose of property. Possession means the right to be in control of property. Usage is the ability to enjoy property in accordance with its purpose.[20] The right to dispose of property is an underlying aspect of the right of ownership since it is this aspect of ownership that enables the transfer of the property, thus making it merchantable and turning property into an asset.

The right of ownership in smart property is controlled by digital means. The usage and the disposal of property is carried out by digital means. Primitive forms of smart property are quite common already, e.g. immobilisers, key cards allowing access to property, etc. Primitive forms of smart property often lack reliability and

[17] Ibid.

[18] Legal Information Institute (used 3.8.2015).

[19] Szabo (used 28.07.2015). See more about formalising and securing relationships on public networks, available: http://szabo.best.vwh.net/formalize.html; Hearn (2015). See more about Smart property in relation to Bitcoin, available: https://en.bitcoin.it/wiki/Smart_Property.

[20] Council of Europe (1998), p. 17. See more about The European Convention on Human Rights and property rights: http://www.echr.coe.int/LibraryDocs/DG2/HRFILES/DG2-EN-HRFILES-11 (1998).pdf.

they are easy to manipulate because the private key is kept in a physical container.[21] The rule is that purely electronic assets are easier to control by digital means than physical assets. Physical assets require some kind of support to be controlled digitally.[22]

The ownership of Bitcoin as smart property is controlled via block chain, using contracts.[23] In the context of Bitcoin the blockchain is a ledger which is public and transparent and gives a chain of transactions that is secure and reliable.[24] Digital controllability is needed for monitoring and verifying contract performance. Opportunities for contracting parties to monitor one another's performance of the contract and verifying the fulfilment of the contract are two main objectives of smart contract design.[25] Therefore smart contracts provide better observation and verification where proactive measures run short.[26] It is believed that automated monitoring over the fulfilment of a contract is not possible with contemporary technologies because computer based technologies lack the understanding of the terms of an agreement and the accurate exchange of values.[27]

## 5 Smart Contracts as Legal Contracts

Smart contracts can be independently performed as legal contracts only if the contracting terms meet the principles of contract law. Section 9 (1) of the Estonian Law of Obligations Act (LOA) provides that a contract is entered into by an offer being made and accepted or by the mutual exchange of declarations of intent in any other manner if it is sufficiently clear that the parties have reached an agreement.[28] Similar provisions regulating the formation of contract are found in the United Nations Convention on Contracts for the International Sale of Goods (Vienna, 1980) (CISG)[29] as well as in more recent texts of UNIDROIT Principles of International Commercial Contracts (PICC),[30] Principles of European Contract

[21] Hope (2014).

[22] Ibid.

[23] Hearn (2015). See more about Smart property in relation with Bitcoin, available: https://en.bitcoin.it/wiki/Smart_Property.

[24] Garay et al. (2015), p. 1.

[25] Szabo (used 28.7.2015). See more about formalising and securing relationships on public networks, available: http://szabo.best.vwh.net/formalize.html.

[26] Ibid.

[27] Surdan (2012), p. 632.

[28] Estonian Law of Obligations Act (RT I 2001, 81, 487).

[29] Art. 14-24 CISG (1980).

[30] Art 2.1.1 UNIDROIT Principles 2010.

Law (PECL)[31] and Draft Common Frame of Reference (DCFR).[32] The above mentioned provision of Estonian LOA provides for the formation of the contract in the traditional way by the exchange of an offer and an acceptance, but also allows other ways of concluding a contract.

Several studies conducted at different points of time show the traditional model of offer and acceptance is known in the contract law of most legal systems.[33] It can be taken as the basis of this analysis. However, it has been noted that in practice there are several ways of reaching an agreement that do not fit into the model of offer and acceptance. Thus modern contract law must allow a contract to be formed in other ways than the traditional model.[34] In particular, it is said, the development of electronic commerce has brought out the need to recognise other ways of concluding a contract.

In the traditional model one party (the offeror) has to make an offer that is sufficiently definite and includes the intent of the offeror to be bound by a contract in case the other party (the offeree) accepts the offer. The contract will be concluded on the terms included in the offer, because in the traditional model the acceptance must correspond exactly to the offer, i.e. it must be a repetition of the terms of the offer without any significant changes. If the acceptance includes changes, it will be considered as a rejection of the original offer (i.e. no contract will be formed as a result) and at the same time as a new offer (a counter-offer) that will then require acceptance (i.e. an acceptance corresponding exactly to the counter-offer) from the original offeror in order to form a contract.[35]

According to Article 2:103 PECL agreement between contracting parties must be sufficient.[36] Article 2:103 (1) PECL provides that, agreement is are precise enough so that the contract can be enforced or the rights and obligations of the parties can be determined.[37] The general rule is that one of these requirements must be fulfilled to reach an agreement. There may, however, be additional requirements that need to be met before a contract is concluded. According to Article 2:103 (2) PECL, if one party refuses to conclude a contract unless a specific term is agreed upon, then a contract will not be concluded unless agreement about that term has been reached.[38] For example, in case one party refuses to conclude a contract unless the price of the goods for the entire contract period is fixed, there will be no contract until the parties reach an agreement about the price for the whole contract period. In this latter case, agreement is not sufficient on general terms stated in Article 2:103

[31] Art. 2:101 PECL (2002).

[32] Art. II 4:101 DCFR (2009).

[33] Schwenzer (2010), p. 233.

[34] Schwenzer (2010), p. 233; Von Bar et al. (2009), p. 290; UNIDROIT Principles (2010), p. 34.

[35] See, e.g., Art 14-24 of the CISG. The text of the United Nations Convention on Contracts for the International Sale of Goods (Vienna, 1980) (CISG).

[36] Art. 2:103. PECL (2002).

[37] Art. 2:103 (1), PECL (2002).

[38] Art. 2:103 (2), PECL (2002).

(1) PECL, but Article 2:103 (2) PECL is applicable instead. The offeree has a right to set further conditions for concluding a contract. In case the other party does not agree to further conditions, the offeree has the right to refuse to conclude a contract. In such case, there is no contract until further conditions have not been agreed by both or all contracting parties. Presenting additional conditions is a counter-offer of one party to another.[39]

According to PICC Article 2.1.13, a contracting party can insist during the negotiations that the contract is not concluded until there is agreement on specific matters or in a particular form.[40] Usually, the contract is concluded after the parties have reached an agreement on the terms essential to the type of transaction involved, while minor undetermined conditions of the contract are implied by the factual behaviour of parties or derived from law afterwards.[41]

Because the offer determines the conditions of the contract, it must be sufficiently definite. The basic terms of the contract must be contained in an offer in order to inform the offeree about the intent of the offeror.[42]

In case a smart contracting solution is used in a legal contract, the contracting requirements described above must be considered. Parties must agree to use the smart contracting solution to implement the contract terms; otherwise, smart contracting is not part of the legal contract and therefore not legally binding. Smart contracting is legally binding only if parties have agreed upon all essential requirements needed for the conclusion of the contract.

It is not entirely clear what must be included in the offer for it to be definite. The CISG requires to include the description of goods, the quantity and the price of goods, whereas the latter do not have to be expressly provided in the contract.[43] In case the quantity and the price are not mentioned, then there has to be a way to determine them. Some commentators share the opinion that the missing agreement on the price of goods does not bring a court to the conclusion that a contract is not formed under the CISG.[44]

The Estonian Law of Obligations Act, PICC, PECL and the DCFR do not expressly provide for any terms that need to be fixed in the offer for it to be sufficiently definite. Commentators explain that the essential terms of the contract such as the description of goods and services, the quantity, the price, the time and the place of performance, etc. must be fixed in the offer, but in case some or all of these elements are missing, it does not automatically mean that the offer is not sufficiently definite. Ultimately, the formation of the contract depends on whether the offeror and the offeree intended to enter into a binding agreement by one

[39] Art. 2.1.1 (1) UNIDROIT Principles (2010).

[40] Art. 2.1.13 UNIDROIT Principles (2010).

[41] UNIDROIT Principles (2010), pp. 54–56.

[42] Schwenzer and Mohs (2006).

[43] The text of the CISG does not require that the price must be fixed as a certain number. It is also possible to agree on a formula that allows the calculation of the price.

[44] Huber and Mullis (2007), p. 77.

making an offer and the other accepting it, and conclusion of the contract does not depend on missing elements. Undetermined conditions can be clarified by interpreting the agreement on the bases of the implied intentions of parties and the applicable law. In other words, sufficient content is needed to give effect to the contract.[45] Authors of this chapter are of the opinion that it is difficult to imagine a contract without any indication of the kind of goods or services. Thus, at least a very general description of goods or services must be apparent from the offer. This does not mean that all aspects of the quality and the full description of goods or services must be fixed in the contract, but it must be possible to determine what kind of goods or services are provided. Also, it is questionable that a contract has sufficient content if the quantity of goods or services is not specified, or if not described, then it must be possible to derive it.

The most important requirement for the formation of the contract is, however, the parties' intent to enter into a legally binding relationship[46] or bring about some other legal effect.[47] The idea of this requirement is to distinguish contracts from agreements that include merely social engagements or that include only provisional understandings in the course of negotiations.[48] The parties' intent is assessed according to how their statements or conduct are reasonably understood by a reasonable person in the same situation as the other party.[49] In other words, the intent of the party is assessed objectively based on his statements or conduct.

Intent to be legally bound may be found in different statements or acts of a party. Most commonly, that intent is found from the acceptance of an offer. It may, however, be determined from any other conduct of a party which shows he wanted to be bound by the agreement (e.g. shipping of goods, payment of price, etc.).[50] Due to a broad use of language, the provisions of the DCFR and PICC cover a contracting where automated arrangements for performing a contracting process are used, i.e. where contracting parties have agreed on using a system or platform for self-executing electronic or automated actions without the intervention of a natural person to perform the conclusion of a contract.[51] The concept of acceptance of an offer is used to ascertain whether, and if so when, the parties have reached an agreement.[52]

It is, however, difficult to bring out specific statements or conducts that prove that a party's intent was to enter into a legally binding relationship. Because situations that may arise are very different, it ultimately depends on how in the particular context a statement or conduct appeared to a reasonable person. It can,

---

[45] Art. 14 (1) CISG (1980).

[46] DCFR (2009), pp. 289–290; UNIDROIT Principles (2010), p. 33.

[47] DCFR (2009), pp. 289–290.

[48] Ibid.

[49] DCFR (2009), p. 298.

[50] Art 2.1.1 UNIDROIT Principles (2010) and Art II. – 4:101 DCFR.

[51] UNIDROIT Principles (2010), p. 36.

[52] Art 2.1.1 UNIDROIT Principles (2010).

however, be held that the clearer and more honest the parties are about their intentions and the more specific they are in their agreements, the easier it is to find that intent.

The concept of the conduct of the parties as required under PICC Article 2.1.1 and DCFR Article II. – 4:101 is necessary on the occasions where the moment of the contract formation cannot be determined; e.g., contracts are often concluded after prolonged negotiations without an identifiable sequence of offer and acceptance; therefore, it could be difficult to determine if and when a contractual agreement has been reached.[53] According to PICC Article 2.1.1 and DCFR Article II. – 4:101, a contract may be held to be concluded even though the moment of its formation cannot be determined, provided that the conduct of the parties is sufficient to show agreement.[54]

The general rule as stated, for example, in Article 2.101 (2) PECL[55] and in Article 1.2 of PICC[56] is that a contract does not need to be concluded or evidenced in writing, nor is it subject to any other requirement as to form. This means that a contract may be concluded and later proved by any means, including e-mails, witnesses, Skype conversations, etc. There may of course be exceptions as sometimes certain mandatory requirements are set for the contract form by the applicable national law.[57] But even if the law does not set any requirements, it may often be desirable to conclude a contract in a specific form in order to ensure that the intent of the party can be easily proven. The parties have an opportunity to agree on a specific form for the contract, and this is often done in practice. Usually, the purpose of contractual form requirements is to exclude the possibility of accidental statements to be given legal effect. However, the parties may also agree to conclude the contract in an automated system and may agree on more specific technical requirements that need to be met for there to be an agreement. They may also make the validity of the contract or amendment to the contract dependent on the form requirements. In such case, only those contracts or amendments that meet the agreed formal requirements will have legal effect.

It is also important that difference is made between the offer for opening negotiations and offer for the conclusion of a contract.[58] The offer or proposal to make offers is not an offer for concluding a contract.[59] It is merely an offer or proposal for opening negotiations, where agreement could or could not be reached. It is suggested that one way of making a difference between an offer and an invitation to make an offer is to ask whether a potential contracting party may agree to it by just saying yes. If this is the case, it is an offer. If additional

[53] Ibid.

[54] Ibid.

[55] Art. 2:101 (2), PECL (2002).

[56] Art. 1.2 UNIDROIT Principles (2010).

[57] Art. 1.4 UNIDROIT Principles (2010).

[58] UNIDROIT Principles (2010), p. 37.

[59] Schwenzer and Mohs (2006).

negotiations are required, it is probably not an offer but an invitation to make an offer.[60]

There is, however, one specific situation that should perhaps be mentioned in the context of smart contracts. Sometimes statements or acts are made that are very similar to offers but are not considered to be offers. The reason for this is that there is a principle that an offer has to be made to a specific person. A statement made to the public rather than a specific person (e.g. an advertisement) is not considered to be an offer unless the statement clearly states that it is one.[61] Instead, such a statement is considered to be an invitation to make an offer. So if a person goes to a store and asks to buy advertised goods, it is this person who makes the offer and not the store that made the advertisement. In the context of smart contracts, application of this principle may bring questions of who is making an offer and who is accepting it in case a description of goods, price, possible delivery terms and storage amount is communicated from one party to another. It is probable that with this information available it is not the person communicating the information that is making the offer but rather the person who makes an order. Or on the other hand, if someone states that he is willing to buy certain goods from anyone offering them, it is again probably not the person who communicates this that is making the offer but rather the person who acts on this information.

When using smart contracts as legal contracts, in other words conducting the whole contracting process as smart contracting, determining the intent of the contracting parties is complicated. The use of International Chamber of Commerce (ICC) eTerms 2004[62] might to some extent help bring clarity to the question of intent of the parties. ICC eTerms 2004 is a self-regulatory instrument for providing legal certainty in electronic contracts.[63] ICC eTerms 2004 are used to make the intent to be in a contractual relationship clear through electronic messages or through other automated processes. Using ICC eTerms 2004 as part of their contract, parties agree that an automatically concluded contract is binding on them.[64] ICC eTerms 2004 deals with issues about contacting parties, timing and place of contract and how the contract is concluded.[65] It is important to notice that ICC eTerms 2004 does not deal with the substance of the contract. Nevertheless, it may prove a useful tool as it covers the possibilities on how a contract is concluded using electronic means, e.g. automatically (using smart contracting), electronically (using e-mail), etc. The aim of the ICC eTerms 2004 is to exclude the possibility of dispute over the technical means used to transmit an offer and/or an acceptance that show the intention to be in a contractual relationship for concluding a contract.

---

[60] UNIDROIT Principles 2010, p. 37.

[61] See, e.g., Art 14 (2) CISG (1980).

[62] ICC Guide for eContracting (2004). E.g., see more about ICC eTerms2004: http://www.iccwbo.org/products-and-services/trade-facilitation/tools-for-e-business/.

[63] Ravindra (2004).

[64] ICC Guide for eContracting (2004).

[65] Ravindra (2004).

## 6 Smart Contracting Technologies

Bitcoin is the best known community initiative that uses a smart contracting technology. It has triggered the development of new business models around crypto-currencies and trust-less technologies.[66] There are more open-source projects that use smart contracting. One of these is Ethereum with an objective to provide a blockchain with a built-in fully fledged Turing-complete programming language.[67]

Ethereum smart contacts are written in a low-level, stack-based bytecode programming language which consists of a series of bytes, and each byte represents an operation.[68] A practical use of the Ethereum smart contracts is that it provides an ecosystem for the development of decentralised file storage where users can rent out their own hard drives to earn money.[69] Ethereum allows implementing the on-blockchain token systems like individual tokens, e.g. representing smart property used as point systems for incentivization. Token systems are databases with one operation: "Subtract X units from A and give X units to B, with the proviso that (1) A had at least X units before the transaction and (2) the transaction is approved by A," and to implement a token system is necessary to implement the operation logic into a smart contract.[70] Ethereum uses smart contracts which unlock contained value if specific conditions are met, and smart contracts can be built on top of the platform with added powers of Turing completeness, value awareness, blockchain awareness and state.[71]

The aim of the Ethereum blockchain is to create smart contracts which can be used to encode random transaction functions and other functions that are needed.[72] Blockchain is seen as a distributed database for independently verifying the chain of ownership of artefacts.[73] Originally, blockchain is the main technological innovation of Bitcoin.[74] Block as a linear and chronological recording which is part of the blockchain records some or all recent transactions, and when the recording is completed the block goes into the blockchain as a permanent database.[75] When one block is completed, a new block is generated and linked with the previous block in certain linear, chronological order while containing a hash of the previous block,

---

[66] Fairfield (2014), p. 38.

[67] Ethereum/wiki (2015).

[68] Ibid.

[69] E.g., see more about "decentralized Dropbox contract": Ethereum/wiki (2015). White Paper: A next-Generation Smart Contract and Decentralized Application Platform. Available: https://github.com/ethereum/wiki/wiki/White-Paper.

[70] Ethereum/wiki (2015).

[71] Ibid.

[72] Ibid.

[73] Norta (2015).

[74] Investopedia (used 6.8.2015).

[75] Ibid.

and therefore there are innumerable blocks in the blockchain.[76] Ethereum blockchain architecture contains a copy of transaction list and the most recent state and the block number stored in the block, while Bitcoin blockchain architecture does not contain a copy of both the transaction list and the most recent state.[77]

There are several Markup Language projects aimed at using smart contracting. One of the recent projects initiated by Norta et al. is called eSourcing Markup Language (eSML).[78] The underlying idea of the language is to facilitate a collaborative B2B business model where parties can easily join to transact with each other.

## 7 Conclusion

Smart contracts are automated computer agents that fulfil certain tasks, for instance, transferring digital property. Smart property is a property which right of ownership is performed and controlled by digital meas. Smart contracts are used aside legal contracts to automatically implement the terms of legal contracts. Smart contract is not a legal contract by itself. Using smart contracting without considering contract law may not guarantee the sufficient protection of contracting parties. To perform smart contracting as legal contracting, the underlying intention of the parties to be in a legally binding contractual relationship has to be determined. The intention of the parties is determined by the offer and the acceptance. New smart contracting solutions are emerging as technologies advance, and lawyers have to be prepared to look for matching legal solutions.

## References

### *Literature*

Angelov S, Grefen P (2003) An analysis of the B2B E-contracting domain – paradigms and required technology. Available online: http://cms.ieis.tue.nl/Beta/Files/WorkingPapers/Beta_wp102.pdf (29.6.2015)

Council of Europe (1998) The European Convention on Human Rights and property rights, Council of European Publishing 1998. Available online: http://www.echr.coe.int/LibraryDocs/DG2/HRFILES/DG2-EN-HRFILES-11(1998).pdf (25.7.2015)

Fairfield J (2014) Smart contracts, Bitcoin bots, and consumer protection. Wash Lee Law Rev Online 71

[76] Ibid.

[77] Ethereum/wiki (2015).

[78] Norta et al. (2015), p. 5.

Francioni F (2007) Access to justice as a Human Right: the rights of access to justice under customary international law. Oxford University Press

Garay JA, Kiayias A, Leonardos N (2015) The Bitcoin backbone protocol: analysis and applications. Cryptology ePrint Archive. Available: https://eprint.iacr.org/2014/765.pdf (used 1.9.2015)

Huber P, Mullis A (2007) The CISG. A new textbook for students and practitioners. Sellier

Miller MS, Van Cutsem T, Tulloh B (2013) Distributed electronic rights in JavaScript. Springer-Verlag, Berlin Heidelberg. Available online: https://static.googleusercontent.com/media/research.google.com/et//pubs/archive/40673.pdf (13.8.2015)

Norta A (2015) Creation of smart-contracting collaborations for decentralized autonomous organizations. Research Gate. Available online: http://www.researchgate.net/publication/277034537_Creation_of_Smart-Contracting_Collaborations_for_Decentralized_Autonomous_Organizations (13.8.2015)

Norta A, Dua Y, Ma L, Rull A, Kõlvart M, Taveter K (2015) eContractual choreography-language properties towards cross-organizational business collaboration. J Internet Serv Appl 6(8):1–23

Ravindra P (2004) Byte- International Chamber of Commerce to release model E-terms. Internet Law Bull 7(6). Available online: http://www.galexia.com/public/research/articles/research_articles-byte01.html (13.8.2015)

Schwenzer I (2010) Commentary on the UN Convention on the International Sale of Goods (CISG), 3rd edn. Oxford University Press

Schwenzer I, Mohs F (2006) Old habits die hard: traditional contract formation in a modern world. Sellier, European Law Publishers, vol 6, pp 239–246. Available online: http://www.cisg.law.pace.edu/cisg/biblio/schwenzer-mohs.html (13.8.2015)

Surdan H (2012) Computable contracts. UC Davis Law Rev 46(2):629–700

Von Bar C, Clive E, Schulte-Nölke H, Beale H, Herre J, Huet J, Storme M, Swann S, Varul P, Veneziano A, Zoll F (2009) Principles, definitions and model rules of European Private Law: Draft Common Frame of Reference (DCFR). Sellier. European Law Publishers GmbH. Available online: http://ec.europa.eu/justice/policies/civil/docs/dcfr_outline_edition_en.pdf (13.8.2015)

## *Electronic Sources*

Babbitt, D.; Dietz, J. (2014). *Crypto-Economic Design: A Proposed Agent-Based Modeling Effort.* Swarmfest 2014. Available online: http://www3.nd.edu/~swarm06/SwarmFest2014/Crypto-economicDesignBabbit.pdf (13.7.2015).

Ethereum/Wiki. *White Paper: A Next-Generation Smart Contract and Decentralized Application Platform.* Available online: https://github.com/ethereum/wiki/wiki/White-Paper (3.8.2015).

Hope. J. (2014). *Introduction to Smart Contracts.* Amsterdam Ethereum Meetup, 2014. Available online: https://www.youtube.com/watch?v=AHAAktdxSOE (13.8.2015).

Hearn, M. (2015). *Smart Property.* Bitcoinwiki. Available: https://en.bitcoin.it/wiki/Smart_Property

ICC Guide for eContracting (2004). Available online: http://www.iccwbo.org/products-and-services/trade-facilitation/tools-for-e-business/ (13.8.2015).

Investopedia. *Blockchain.* Available online: http://www.investopedia.com/terms/b/blockchain.asp (13.8.2015).

Legal Information Institute. *Contract.* Cornell University Law School. Available online: https://www.law.cornell.edu/wex/contract (13.8.2015).

Szabo, N. (1997) *The Idea of Smart Contracts*. Nick Szabo's Essays, Papers, and Concise Tutorials 1997. Available online: http://szabo.best.vwh.net/smart_contracts_idea.html (13.8.2015).
Szabo, N. *Formalizing and Securing Relationships on Public Networks*. Szabo's Essays, Papers, and Concise Tutorials. Available online: http://szabo.best.vwh.net/formalize.html (3.8.2015).

## Legal Acts

Estonian Law of Obligations Act, Available online: https://www.riigiteataja.ee/en/eli/516062015006/consolide (13.8.2015).
International Institute for Unification of Private Law. UNIDROIT Principles of international commercial contracts. 2010. Available online: http://www.unidroit.org/english/principles/contracts/principles2010/integralversionprinciples2010-e.pdf (13.8.2015).
Principles of European Contract Law (PECL) 2002, Available online: http://www.trans-lex.org/400200/ (13.8.2015).

# Usability Factors in Transactional Design and Smart Contracting

**Maria Claudia Solarte-Vasquez, Natalia Järv, and Katrin Nyman-Metcalf**

**Abstract** This book chapter contextualizes the origins of the proactive law movement to explain its current developments and advance its conceptual underpinnings towards applications of the perspective closest to the digital economy and electronic trade with regard to transactions and contracts. It aims at proposing transactional design as an expression of smart contracting practices, explaining its scope within the principled conflict management and dispute resolution collaborative culture. Additionally, standards of efficiency, effectiveness, and satisfaction are taken from within the computer sciences and the law to present an integrated taxonomy of usability parameters for the planning and assessment of sustainable business and other human transactions consigned in electronic texts mediated by technology. It is argued that the applicability of such integrated cross-disciplinary models is ensured given the growing reach and range of digital services and also because their formulation reflects the interconnected society principles, needs, and capacities. While featuring innovative aspects in alternative contracting practices, it refrains from addressing visualization in depth. However, the complexity of engaging with semiotic analysis of visualization techniques in legal interface design is signalled as an especially worthy field for further research.

M.C. Solarte-Vasquez (✉)
World Mediation Organization in Estonia, Tallinn, Estonia

Tallinn School of Economics and Business Administration of Tallinn University of Technology, Akadeemia tee 3, 12618 Tallinn, Estonia
e-mail: mcsolartev@gmail.com

N. Järv
Department of Informatics, Tallinn University of Technology, Akadeemia tee 15a, 12618 Tallinn, Estonia
e-mail: natalia.jarv@gmail.com

K. Nyman-Metcalf
Tallinn Law School, Tallinn University of Technology, Akadeemia tee 3, 12618 Tallinn, Estonia
e-mail: katrin.nyman-metcalf@ttu.ee



T. Kerikmäe, A. Rull (eds.), *The Future of Law and eTechnologies*,
DOI 10.1007/978-3-319-26896-5_8

# 1 Introduction

Private transactions and contracts are among the most important governance expressions of the interconnected society and possess bonding, not merely binding, power across all forms of social organizations while giving structure to the digital economy. The dynamics of the networks have determined the future of contracting and transacting. Security and efficacy concerns give rise to two chief subfields steaming from the opportunities and challenges that technology mediation and mediatization pose, partially being addressed by research on smart contracts and proactive contracting and design, respectively.[1] This book chapter focuses on the second area because of its humanist dimension with transformative potential and integrative cross-disciplinary origins.

The digital economy promise realizes slowly. Within the European Union, practical, sociocultural, and regulatory barriers to cross-border e-trade fragment the pan-European market.[2] For instance, consumer protection, redress mechanisms, and dispute resolution schemes are not unified or effectively implemented.[3] The segmentation of the existing methods may impose higher costs to business transactions, but harmonization by formal regulatory means has not proven efficient.[4] The frequent deployment of innovative technology solutions and continuous upgrading of the laws and public policies may play an important role enabling social development, but social institutions will adjust at their own pace, gradually. To facilitate the adoption and exploitation of new technologies once the initial enthusiasm has passed requires readiness, awareness, understanding, capacities, trust, practice, and time.

---

[1] Mediated and mediatized are terms referring to the use of devices as intermediaries between agents/users, and in electronic exchange that fills content online (public or accessible), respectively. Digital, self-enforcing "smart contracts" were proposed by Nick Szabo in 1993, when the economic and communications infrastructure were unfit to support them (Szabo 1997). Technical and economic conditions are now available, but the issue of trust in fully automated services and artificial intelligence is not well resolved yet. Trust is of fundamental importance for the accomplishment of any e-strategy such as e-health, e-finances, e-government, and the expansion of the Internet of Things. Legal systems can easily adapt to smart contracting practices, whereas as for now, smart contracts could impose insurmountable ethical, legal, and safety constraints as they demand a very significant allegiance from the human to automated agents.

[2] One could interpret the *regulatory or social evolution* lag as an opportunity for iteration, revision, and adaptation. If the digital market was to deliver too fast the economic growth it is expected to produce, exhaustion would follow, together with the depletion of all of resources available to maintain social and economic organizations afloat. Mismatch between formal regulations and the so-called slow-moving institutions embedded in social practices and cultures is common.

[3] See the study report on Cross-Border Alternative Dispute Resolution in the European Union online at: http://www.europarl.europa.eu/meetdocs/2009_2014/documents/imco/dv/adr_study_/adr_study_en.pdf.

[4] Solarte-Vasquez (2014).

For the networked economy, connections and relationships matter as much as the exchanged goods are the object of transactions, or at least become intertwined with these. The sustainability culture where collaboration takes precedence over competition and exclusion emerges then, as a self-preservation mechanism, preventive and proactive. Smart contracting becomes a feature of the business and legal world that contributes with more than effectivizing and securing pacts and dispensing self-executing clauses like smart contracts could do.[5] A transaction well designed is also smart when it does not only seek at establishing rights and duties but also procures a satisfying contractual experience that precedes the agreement and engages the parties for compliance. It departs from looking at contracts as relational tools (technologies) and functional products that the legal services could "produce." All other regulations could also be seen from this utilitarian point of view where optimality is a serious concern to determine the ease of use or utility of any object.

The transformation power of the networked age has also begun to be embedded into the legal practice, products, and services, incorporating its main governance principle: collaboration.[6] Many are the arguments that favor this transition. Collaboration is an inexorable phenomenon of the times as emphasized in the works of Castells and Fuchs, just to cite two examples by sociology experts of recognized influence.[7] The networked society is empowered to exercise freedoms that formerly existed only on paper, or were long forgotten. It is the effect of increased political engagement, less restricted self-organization power, growing interest in cocreation an innovation, and the reactivation of self-regulatory competences, all enabled and supported by technological solutions. In trade, now more than ever, collaboration is essential for growth and key for value creation.

A notable shift towards sustainable goals (both ecological and corporate) inspires the business models and strategies' collaborative trend, which in turn has questioned the capacities of organizations that hold a single focus on profitability, normally associated with short-term business agendas. Underlying the problem of sustainability is the precarious balance between profit goals and mission. Companies are now expected to help maintain the availability of resources in the interest of their own continuity and committed to ethical and social development goals. Information and communication technology (ICT) development relies on the

[5] Norta et al. (2015).

[6] Collaboration is a human competence, an asset that amounts to social capital; it is necessary to achieve corporate and social missions and determine the sustainability of the organization in itself (long-term operations) and its activities (impact). Social capital is generally understood as the economic value of networks and social cohesion. The concept is much better explained by Portes (2000, p. 45).

[7] Read Castells in general and: "The rise of the network society: The information age: Economy, society, and culture," in particular (Castells 2011); and Fuchs' contributions in: "Internet and society: Social theory in the information age" (Fuchs 2007).

stability of both layers of the networks, their structural composition, and their social dimension as well.

In the following, two sections will explain the ontological and epistemological dimensions of the transactional design proposal. The first will focus on its contextualization as an interdisciplinary concept and its origins in the conflict management and dispute resolution field. The second will explain the combined criteria of usability and the parameters applicable to prescriptive electronic texts such as contracts or administrative regulations in online repositories. The chapter ends with concluding remarks that include reflections on the challenges and opportunities that this line of research reveals.

## 2 Smart Contracting in Transactional Design

### *2.1 Antecedents and Background*

In transactions of the traditional type people are "bound" to do, to refrain, or to transfer things of value. For the networked society and in the digital age, it can be said that transactions create not merely a binding link but also a complex bond or several, some of which may refer to rights and duties. On a more practical account, the creation of rules nowadays needs to focus on the protection of immaterial things of value and control the actions of people and noncorporeal entities in an environment that is basically borderless. Tangible goods and manufactured products are no longer the most valuable; instead, more worth is being assigned to intangibles or things intimately linked to nonphysical processes, relationships, networks, information, and knowledge.[8] A most critical legal challenge is then to determine to which extent the traditional theory can explain regulatory coverage to entities that are composed by bits, not atoms, and to those that did not qualify as resources earlier but emerge in the aftermath of shifting global governance, social and trade patterns.[9]

The laws of obligations and contracts have not cared for relationships beyond those that create, modify, or extinguish rights and duties. No traditional rule seeks to maximize anyone's ends in particular and much less to campaign for attitudes or promote any sort of behavior in the field of commerce and trade where competition has been a key driver. Sharing, cooperation, and collaboration have in times even been associated with extreme ideologies and stigmatized as if in contrast with the

---

[8] The rules of the analogous world, specially procedural ones, are limited to some extent because they predicate on physicality and jurisdictional borders. The substantial laws on the links between persons and between goods and persons (natural or legal entities but not artificial intelligence agents) are well developed and refined but revolve around one chief goal: the creation of enforceable catalogues of rights and obligations.

[9] Conte et al. (2012).

liberal ideals. The interconnected society self-organized around an ample spectrum of values, old and new in an environment where the roles of parties are expanded and dynamic as they can be global consumers, technology users, network stakeholders, global citizens, and so on.

In scenarios of the past, because the doctrine of equality prevents states from formulating rules for or against any agent, and the jurisdictional system can only guarantee procedural justice, avenues for the satisfaction of individual and collective interest and the reduction of adversarial interaction were proposed.[10] The alternative dispute resolution (ADR) movement awoke in the second half of the past century, and a whole culture of less antagonistic and self-sufficient governance models began forming.[11] ADR methods were the most used to prevent and administer employment- and commerce-related conflicts in the beginning, but soon they were extended to all private affairs and later even applied to the public sphere within the public administration and in criminal law.[12] Academics and practitioners pushed long and somewhat successfully for reforms in the legal profession, but the prevalence of traditional formalities, formats, and mediums for transacting did not clearly concede to legal innovation until the advent of the ICTs when the interconnected society imposed it. Only then did arguments for preventive and collaborative legal services as the ADR culture promoted for nearly half a century become of widespread concern for the legal profession and the legislator. Legal systems struggle to preserve their internal consistency while becoming responsive to the needs of other systems that are more dynamic, less formal, and human centered.[13] The proactive law approach, which evolved from its origins within the conflict management and dispute resolution, has contributed to the unification of collaborative models.[14] This includes considering all the stakeholders (situational),

[10] Political economy considerations are not legal enunciates or necessarily have to conform with the pure theory of law. Policy makers create exceptions and use other governance strategies but cannot act upon ideological and other priorities by affecting core propositions deriving from the rule of law.

[11] *-Indigenous-* Conflict prevention and resolution mechanisms have been historically in use by every society long before the contemporary methods where introduced. Even more broadly exercised, freedom of contracting has been a practical (rather than moral) principle inspiring constructive action for centuries, as it is intrinsically related to free will that can be put to the service of any purpose.

[12] The ombudsman's role is that of a dispute manager/administrator. Depending on the context and the level of institutionalization of the figure, it can intervene to a different degree. Mediation in criminal matters intends to implement restitution and reconciliation processes from the conflict and peace studies in the criminal system. See Lahti (2000).

[13] Consult, for instance, the latest EU Initiatives on ADR and online dispute resolution (ODR) and related documents regarding consumer disputes at: http://ec.europa.eu/consumers/solving_consumer_disputes/non-judicial_redress/adr-odr/index_en.htm#related_documents, and the Opinion of the European Economic and Social Committee on The proactive law approach from 2009 available online at: http://eur-lex.europa.eu/legal-content/EN/TXT/HTML/?uri=CELEX:52008IE1905&from=EN.

[14] Groton and Haapio (2007). Proactive law has grown from its therapeutic beginnings into a philosophy for better private and public regulations and still can be placed into a conflict management and dispute prevention continuum.

their relations, and human interaction as the direct object of any given transaction, focusing on shared benefits and collaboration and encouraging empowerment and self-regulation. These ideas are consistent with the principles and values of the networked society.[15]

## 2.2 *Evolution of the Conflict Management Concept. The Context*

The evolution of recent thoughts on conflict can be explained as a continuum that reveals a gradual transition to a responsive and engaging legal practice, like the proactive law movement.[16] All alternative proposals (to traditional methods) of the past 60 years have to do with ways to minimize the impact of crisis, resolve, transform, or prevent conflicts and disputes. The most influential recent peace and conflict theory born in the years after the second World War can be described as liberal, rational, and humanistic and has been applied to the practice of private law and used to develop lawyering and negotiation methods and techniques for inside and outside courtrooms with growing sophistication.[17] Figure 1 illustrates the process and suggest interconnections that link the specialization areas within the conflict management and dispute prevention domains, as well as the place where to fit a novel proposal on transactional design.[18] The scheme below covers only the most general denominations and trends of practices of the past 60 years.

The figure begins with the emergence of conflict resolution as an object of research coinciding with the post-World War II period when the era of human rights and the relevance of individuals and groups over states began to outline democratic activism. People and states were to be protected from the horrors of violent conflict and the economic catastrophe that wars create. At the same time,

[15] The proactive proposal spoke of legal knowledge as a competitive advantage although the result of an associative work during the planning stages of commercial contractual relationships. See *infra*, notes 22 and 46 and Rekola and Haapio (2011).

[16] Pohjonen (2010), among other publications of the same author, provides an excellent explanation on the origins and fundamentals of the proactive law movement with implications on her research in the field of collaborative contracts.

[17] The humanist life stance trusts the cognitive and emotional capacities of the human being to preserve views in which the human dignity, interests, and values predominate and to solve their problems with epistemological (rational in the sense of systematic) proficiency. It is liberal in that it endorses autonomy and promotes self-determination.

[18] On the original proposal on the preventive law practice, read Brown (1951); on proactive law as first conceived, read Siedel and Haapio (2010); on ADR, find distinguishable stands in Barrett and Barrett (2004), Schneider (1999), Henry (2000), and Lieberman and Henry (1986) and an overview in Sander (1985). Daicoff (2005) speaks of a comprehensive law practice. An interest study by Jasperson et al. (2002) reviews power, one of the main elements in conflict studies and its relationship with technology, and on general conflict and peace studies read "The Handbook of Peace and Conflict Studies," edited by Webel and Galtung (2007).

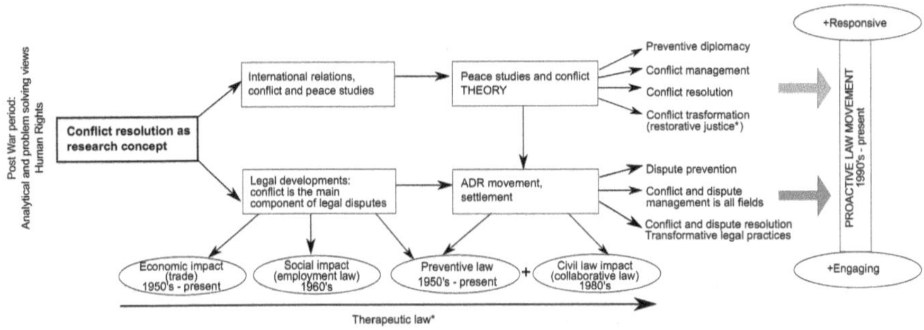


**Fig. 1** From conflict resolution studies to the proactive law movement

analytical problem-solving methods were applied to conflict analysis focusing on human motives and relationships (and soon were seen to apply at all social and political levels).

The appeal of the ideals of peace, justice, and dispute prevention was obvious to two general lines of research, public affairs, and political studies on one hand and law on the other. International relations took over the field of conflict and peace studies and by the 80s had developed theory with application not only to the international sphere. In the practice of law, it meant that the conflict underlying legal disputes began to be addressed as the core component of any relationship with legal relevance and most clearly in the case of structural social conflicts such as employment relationships. The study of conflict had an enormous social and economic impact that caused a revival of ADR and the emergence of new views on the role of law and legal experts in the administration of disputes.[19]

Steadily, the roots of a postgenocidal humane consciousness, combined with a practical approach to managing social vindication movements, created new schools of thought and therapeutic legal practice.[20] This amounts to a value revolution as explained by the main proponents of all movements, the most inspiring of which continues to be Brown with his preventive law philosophy.[21] By the beginning of the 90s, ADR and the field of conflict studies were already developing sophisticated techniques or creative self-determination for a peaceful management of conflicts, the prevention of disputes, and reparation and reconciliation. Access to justice did no longer rely exclusively on legal procedures and court rulings. Collaborative, principled, and integrative strategies were found to produce more than settlements do; increasing the rate of efficient, durable, and amicable resolution of disputes adapted to the need of their users/parties. The theory of interests and needs has been in fact the most influential in altering the political, social, and legal philosophies linked to conflict, on all expressions that try to modify traditional adversarial institutions.[22] At the end of the spectrum in the chart belongs the proactive law

---

[19] Menkel-Meadow (1985).

[20] Stolle and Wexler (1997).

[21] Brown (1951, 1956).

[22] For a complete overview, consult Burton (1985), and Burton and Sandole (1987).

movement that draws from those techniques, links them to the institutional shifts that society experienced with the influence of ICTs, and places a renewed therapeutic law practice on the spot for lawyers and policy makers.[23] The fundamentals of the line of research on conflict and peace make proactive law more responsive, while ADR resources and techniques make the proactive law practice more collaborative and, therefore, engaging.

As unusual as it may seem to define the scope of these reflections on improved transactional competences and better contracts from the perspective of conflict management, it is a fresh view that seems appropriate to underline its foundational discipline. Collaborative Transactional Design is a function within the proactive law practice, whereas the proactive law movement is an advanced conflict management development or a subfield that also holds nontraditional power views and uses analytical interdisciplinary tools to balance adversarial political, legal, and industrial institutions (which remain a challenge despite the advent of the ICTs). Charting the conflict resolution continuum is neutral to legal traditions; conflict management and resolution skills are highly transferable, always relevant and applicable to all domains that share concern for transactional efficiency and effectiveness, as well as for the vitality of organizations and relationships that transactions govern. In addition, conflict is pervasive and may afflict any level of social interaction regardless of its format, and/or if they rise to become a legal dispute.

The intermediation of technology (software in computers and mobile applications, for example) characterizing social interaction and the digital economy does not promise to improve transactions by itself, but it does prompt the consideration of arguments long brought forward in the social sciences and the humanities regarding the way in which humans relate to one another. Technology has exposed the strengths and flaws of human nature (and legal systems) in ways no social movement or school of thought before could do with critical discourses, research, publications, and campaigns. Human nature, relationships, and interaction are the core objects of conflict studies. Conflict management competences are fundamental to assess and influence the structural bonding of society and its parallel constructs with legal relevance and of economic value. Conflict has been a topic of undiminished relevance and growing popularity for many decades now, which has allowed the accumulation of vast amounts of knowledge from a diversity of disciplines, and now is applicable to digital human interaction. Platforms staging transactions proliferate (computer, mobile devices and with the Internet of Things, everything), becoming crucial factors in all communication processes. Conflict management considerations are the unexplored path in design thinking and systems planning. If *dispute prevention and conflict management principles* were premises of consideration for engineering and design, in law making and practicing, and in organizational development and management, better products and services could be

[23] On the past and future of proactive law, read, for instance, Berger-Walliser (2012).

offered: software, applications, interfaces, laws, regulations, contracts, business strategies, etc.

The proactive law approach was first proposed as a preventive law derivative that combined legal expertise with a promotive business orientation and focused on contracts. The main proponents sought to capture value from an association of fields long distanced by the adversariness of stagnant legal systems (law and business). Proactive law thinks of conflict management and preventive law and also incorporates the principles of interest-based negotiation and other alternative dispute resolution methods developed in the past 50 years. Proactivity closely connects with the collaborative law practice as well. In general, it could be seen as the summary of all the "alternative" wisdom developed on transactions, aligned with legal substantive and procedural rules and with economic relevance and a humanistic glow. Collaborative transactional design steams for the proactive law movement and seeks to engage in further interdisciplinary dialog.

In sum, *conflict management and dispute prevention* is an all-encompassing notion that should be preferred as the general classification or mother discipline for the proactive law. The understanding of conflict "management" is not misleading when it is clear that this denomination does not exclude the transformation, resolution, and proactivity functions or any technique of the therapeutic kind.[24] Moreover, proactive law is not a theory but a number of quality attributes translated into methods and techniques that draw from conflict management theories, as well as from others, and therefore continues to be a school of thought. Lawyers have administered and sought to remedy controversies from ancient times by applying legal standards and mastering the handling of legal disputes with focus on their settlement. Other professionals, often more concerned with resolution, address controversies using organization development techniques, management strategies, psychological tools, expertise, and criteria that are more flexible and are not constrained by authoritative rule. Transactional design is a proactive collaborative practice that smarts up the lawyering practice of contract management and can update the interfaces of legal texts.

[24] The literature on conflict management and resolution is vast, discussing expressions that were commonplace already in the 1970s, each referring to different frameworks, skills, and interests on the administration of disputes and heuristics to lessen the damaging impact of crisis. Any expression could be said to fall short of the possible applications of the understanding of conflict as a phenomenon, inherent to human association and a recognized catalyst of change as Galtung (1996) has explained. Most descriptions fail to explicitly include a preventive dimension. However, any functional approach can become useful to designate the many possible interventions that in different moments could be aiming at various effects as conflicts may long remain latent or extend over long periods of time.

## 2.3 Collaborative Transactional Design

The latest proactive initiatives use advanced facilitation techniques to turn regulations and business transactions into user-friendly texts and begin to explore knowledge visualization techniques from the design and management engineering field to enhance legal documents.[25] These human-centered considerations, uses, techniques and in general the heuristics of smart contracting practices such as usability checks, which will be enunciated later, are what transactional design is all about. According to Ramadier, creating seamless conceptual transitions across disciplines is first initiated with the use of dialects and the creation of communities of speech.[26] Transactional design accurately describes the incorporation of usability and contract drafting principles into the creation of extended schemes of collaborative contractual relationships, aimed at minimizing frictions and preventing disputes while aiding compliance.

Transaction is a legal category, generally understood as an exchange of things of value, material or immaterial.[27] The format could be any (unambiguous) conventional shape: a pact, contract, clause or a provision, an agreement, etc. More than one text may be involved in digital transactions.[28] One is of the essence where rights and duties formalize/enact, and the other could be a layer or several of the same text made available in interactive environments when transactions are mediated by technology.[29] These can be called interfaces. Traditional contracts can be assigned new "interfaces," one on its content, and when displayed on a screen device (mediated by technology) placed or not online (mediatized), another. In the design of legal interfaces, three special kinds of knowledge are required: on the technology (contracting); on human aspects, including some principles of communication, basic interaction, and mental computation; and about the goals to be accomplished. Because transactional design recognizes that relationships develop in time, the "coverage of service" is extended and transactions become much larger that the expression that embodies them. Design can be a rational engineering process that results in the creation of functional and ergonomic products, the realization of conceptual model that could be tasked with the humanization of

[25] Rekola and Haapio (2011).

[26] On articulation of new languages, see Ramadier (2004). The proactive movement has opened the space for interdisciplinary research and intellectual engagement by working very hard on terminological choices, resorting to metaphoric arguments and the careful articulation of shared renewed meanings.

[27] Domestic legal systems, statutes, codes, or legal acts define terms such as transactions, obligations, and contracts.

[28] In communication theory, text can be content or outcome of an interaction, no matter what format. Consult the Encyclopaedia of communication theory (Vol. 1), p. 148.

[29] In texts with augmented reality (the indirect view of a real world environment, like a sound and a shape, superposed on images for a composited view of displays), textured contracts (in layers), and so on.

technologies.[30] Consequently, when the contact between the parties to a transaction is indirect, their contact sporadic or very short, the "provider" of the legal service commits to design and stage a memorable (positive) transactional experience for the client/user that is efficient, effective, and satisfying.

Macneil and Paul Gudel saw contracts also for what they are, of a very limiting access to what they actually register about the humans that subscribe them.[31] On the importance of and extended view of transactions, Haapio also spoke, pointing out a vision not new but never made available as a pedagogical resource to managers and other business specialists, certainly not in terms of a mission. Three stages are of the interest of a transactional: the precontractual stage of planning and negotiation of the terms of the agreement, the enactment and formalization that must observe the requirements established by the laws for the creation of valid and enforceable contracts, and the postcontractual stage when the parties perform their dues. The collaborative nature of transactional design stems from the proactive thoughts on early engagement and teamwork but most importantly from principled negotiation techniques and conflict management theory developed by the Harvard Negotiation Project.[32] Collaborative transactional design is a novel legal practice that similarly to other types of social innovation could be hard to introduce but could reach sufficient dissemination levels if helped to institutionalize with practice and continuous research. In support of informal institutionalization via self-regulation mechanisms, it could be argued that transactions are guided by the principle of freedom of contracting and the context where this proposal belongs seeks to empower the private regulatory capacity of the networked society, rather than encouraging further state intervention on its affairs.

The transactional outcome should be binding if valid, and a bonding if a solution that can reach beyond the mere establishment of rights and duties onto mutually beneficial exchange.[33] Satisfaction can be perceived as a sense of control, accomplishment, and engagement strengthening the bonding factor. In the interest of compliance, the bonding aspects of the transaction should prevail.

There are no modifications to the contract theory in this transactional design proposal. From a legal standpoint, and to the extent explained, contracts for the digital market are not fundamentally different from analogous world agreements, but their interfaces might be. Validity is a precondition of existence and

---

[30] Verganti (2011). On ethics and sustainability of design see: Felton, Zelenko, Vaughan (Eds.) (2013).

[31] Macneil and Gudel (2001).

[32] Haapio presents the principled negotiation essentials in her publication with Groton, *ibid.* 30. Further references are available at the source of the Harvard Negotiation Project at: http://www.pon.harvard.edu/category/research_projects/harvard-negotiation-project/.

[33] Valid contracts submit to the requirements of the law as the civil theory of contracts summarizes at least the existence of elements of a contract, namely licit object and cause, capacity, formalities, and the meeting of the minds. These elements coincide in all civil codes of the civil law tradition. More on the Roman Tradition of contract formation in Cohen (1933) and Ghirardi and Crespo (1996).

enforceability but does not imply usability. Usability is a design question apart, closely related with information and communication technologies, and in the past years correlated with visual displays. Usability is achieved through better communication and also has a collaborative dimension in that to maximize clarity and understanding, the message has to appeal to an audience that can be reached in as much as needs and interest of people are taken into consideration.

## 2.4 *Contracts in Global Trade*

Global trade continues to rest on the assumption that exchange is secured by valid and enforceable agreements, but subscribed not only by well-established traditional agents such as transnational corporations and states. Cross-border trade relations now involve all kinds of entities and organizations of different sizes and nature, as well as individuals. With the boundaries of markets being open to such a large exchange, traditional, predictable, and well-studied contracting models, business operations, and strategies in human interaction/association have undergone a profound revision. The legal environment of business as for now appears to be more defined by digital means than by domestic laws. National borders, which traditionally have determined jurisdiction, do not matter much in the digital world where the ease of communication multiplies the amount of transactions across legal systems, and with it the complexity of conflicts and chances of disputes. Attempts to determine how to deal with jurisdictional matters in the cyberworld are still inconclusive, compromising access to justice and diminishing, in turn, consumer confidence in markets. These problems could be overcome with good smart contracting practices as transactional design and ADR that is recognized to improve market performance when schemes are well established.[34]

The study of transactions in the digital age suggests a return to basics. Empowered consumers need no more than a lean institutional framework with broad classic principles and fundamental general rules. The updates to harmonize contracting with the technoeconomic paradigm of the times need not be of legal kind. Peeling off the layers of excessive regulatory constraints allows focus on the essential elements of transactions and clarity on how to deal with human exchange in digital formats with no intrusion to actively promote what is considered good at a given moment in time. What it is that actually needs regulation? How could legal frameworks enable the realization of the will of self-regulatory entities?[35] Better transactions and better regulations are the product of smarter regulatory practices,

[34] On the role of formal and informal, legislative and nonlegislative measures to strengthen the culture of ADR within the EU and a discussion on ADR as an empowering self-regulatory solutions contributing to the success of cross-border and electronic trade, read further in Solarte-Vasquez (2014).

[35] See Teubner (1983) on reflexive law.

private and public, respectively.[36] Many are the concepts that have to be addressed to convey the imperative need for a renewed logic on the role of law in society, particularly in regard to the handling of human exchange and transactions and contracts to increase business and organizational capabilities. To illustrate, in favor of consumers only, European policy and regulations have issued communications, recommendations, regulations, and directives concerning transactions in access to justice (legal redress and settlement of disputes), e-commerce, and consumer contracts, among others. In the European Union law database on this particular group, it is hard to find documents that could not be linked to an exchange of goods, information, and/or transactions.[37] A well-functioning digital market is expected to result in a boost of economic growth of the region, but according to Eurostat data, the increase of transactions online concerns mainly purchases within countries. Only 15 % of the population engages in cross-border commerce.[38] Increasing the trust in digital services, including transactions themselves, could contribute to a better market performance, and much more.[39]

## 3 Usability Parameters Applicable to Legal Transactions

### *3.1 A Combined Taxonomy of Usability for Transactional Design*

Usability, a concept borrowed from Human Computer Interaction (HCI), well known in the ICT studies, has recently been added to the pool of traditional criteria to measure the quality of legal products. An overall purpose of the recent interest in usability applied to legal documents and regulations could be said to minimize their

[36] "Better Regulation" means, within the EU, good design of measures, formal and informal, that can be effective. More rules do not mean better regulatory environment but might mean the opposite. Consult more at: http://ec.europa.eu/smart-regulation/better_regulation/key_docs_en.htm REFIT (the European Commission's Regulatory Fitness and Performance programme) takes action to simplify the laws and reduce regulatory costs and is part of the EU governance innovation actions.

[37] Consult the EU directory/database on consumer legislation at: http://eur-lex.europa.eu/summary/chapter/consumers.html?root_default=SUM_1_CODED%3D09.

[38] The report and data source can be read in the European Commission ICT survey of Households and Individuals report of 2014. At http://ec.europa.eu/eurostat/statistics-explained/index.php/Information_society_statistics_-_households_and_individuals.

[39] The importance of this proposal on smart contracting and better transactions transcends economic considerations. Transactional design that could result in an improved contractual experience prevents disputes and reduces social and institutional tensions. For an introduction on the different costs of conflicts, disputes, and litigation in general, find: "Economic analysis of legal disputes and their resolution" by Cooter and Rubinfeld (1989), and "The intersection of therapeutic jurisprudence, preventive law, and alternative dispute resolution" by Schneider (1999).

complexity with the use of information knowledge management and visualization techniques. This chapter recognizes the importance of bringing into the legal informatics innovative conceptualizations of traditional notions, and schemes institutionalized usability standards in combination with parameters applicable in transactional design. A marginal reference to visualization is noted as a technique. Principled conflict management and dispute resolution techniques share most of their propositions with the human-centered design postulates.[40]

### 3.1.1 Quality Attributes of Legal Texts

The concern for the improvement of legal text is not new. Politicians and legal experts, practitioners or scholars, have always been preoccupied with the quality and efficacy of regulations. Normative components and concepts such as validity, enforceability, and legitimacy refer to rules that have been issued according to precise requirements or recognized by a system of very strict substantial and procedural standards. All prescriptions with regulatory power, including private contracts, are endowed with narrow "usability" properties (validity and enforceability). They can be made compulsory, grant certain allowances to the parties, support policy making, be traced to specific ideologies, promote doctrine, realize governance principles, etc. The legal system supplies its rules with deontological and teleological value in a way that their implementation always pursues the realization of ends higher than the rules themselves, but these are checks that a transactional designer should not be concerned with. Aesthetic values are not chief in law, so no methodologies are available to ensure that appearance will not distort the meanings of the law. The representation of nonpictorial concepts (like a precise causation and logic) and the introduction of new modalities of communication can be restricted by fundamental constraints that are not simple to overcome.[41] Usability, thus, appears to raise no complications in its applicability to legal "products," except from its visualization techniques.[42] These might not only involve matters of design but also call for proper expertise in the legal semiotics domain.

---

[40] Principled negotiation is the name assigned to the method developed by Fisher, Ury, and Patton and popularized in their book of tactics Getting to Yes and developed under the auspices of the Harvard Law School. See a recent application of the perspective in Lens (2004). A complete explanation on human-centered design principles is available by Norman (1883) and discussed in Norman (2005).

[41] Clarity and consistency of regulatory frameworks are requirements of predictable legal systems, owing to the observations of the rule of law principles (strongly committed to rule out arbitrary decision making and interpretation). Graphics and visual elements that are not conventions cannot be interpreted with certainty.

[42] Reimann and Kay (2010). Research and knowledge on mediated trust and persuasive technologies from the legal perspective are still insufficient. For an introductory reflection on the impact of visual technologies in the law, read Sherwin (2011).

Forshey, Kimble, and Phelps represent thoughts of the many that have spoken on improving legal writing and contract drafting in particular[43]; Seidel and Haapio, on providing a more comprehensive legal service when managing business transactions[44]; and Passera and Haapio, on turning contract drafting into a collaborative process to produce tools for understanding, consensus, and compliance.[45] These last introduced the analogy of usability and explored the effect of visualization in regard to documents with legal relevance and most particularly in the field of business transactions and administrative law.[46]

Most notably, these authors have campaigned against scientific compartmentalization. Their activism, bridging disciplinary divides with the use of language, has been validated and recognized as most influential, creating a wide interdisciplinary community of speech. Their major breakthrough has been connecting discipline-specific knowledge from different domains and formulating a dialect of shared meaning, using simple and heuristic metaphors to simplify communication across different areas of expertise and suggest thinking in a new direction such as the use of the design thinking approach to drafting contracts.[47] Despite their growing popularity in recent years, the topics of usability and information visualization have yet to fully make an incursion into the legal sphere and establish a cogent theoretical framework.

Usability and visualization are no commensurable categories, but they are closely interrelated when linked to learning and comprehension. Whereas usability is a field of interdisciplinary studies backed up by the cognitive sciences, visualization is a technique that reinforces communication and cognition within the information technologies and the computer sciences, but not exclusive to that area. Graphic representations of complex numerical or conceptual information can affect the data usability and discernibility, and usability standards apply to graphic interfaces. Design principles that emerge from the study of both will continue to develop for the creation of improved human-system and human-artifact interactions, but caution is recommended. Within the proactive law initiatives, the power of constitutive metaphors is being explored, and scholars are slowly moving to a more interpretative terrain for the creation of new meanings. Icons, images, and drawings in place of calligraphic formats refer to the articulation of a new language, and to law it may lead to substantial affectation of legal categories and the very ontology of the legal science, in a way adding vulnerabilities to the contractual

---

[43] Forshey (1978); Kimble (1996); and Phelps (1986). Look also into a psychological perspective in: Comprehension of legal contracts by non-experts: Effectiveness of plain language redrafting by Masson and Waldron (1994).

[44] Siedel and Haapio (2010a); Haapio (2010); and, Passera and Haapio (2011a, b).

[45] Passera and Haapio (2011b). See also Berger-Walliser et al. (2011).

[46] Passera et al. (2013a, b).

[47] For instance, in the ongoing Fimecc UXUS and completed PRO2ACT – projects. More information on these is available in their webpages: http://www.mindspace.fi/en/uxus/ and http://tuta.aalto.fi/en/research/operations_and_service_management/simlab/projects/pro2act/in_finnish/, respectively.

practice and uncertainty and "flawed usability" attributes. The stakes for accuracy are too high in law, and the usability heuristics affecting decision making may misguide despite the best intentions. The articulation process of deconstructing specific knowledge and reconstructing understanding is possible but requires a profound grasp of legal semiotics. As said, while visualization seems a very complex process when applied to prescriptive and authoritative texts, usability analysis does not. Usability tools can improve the communication power of meanings that do not necessarily degrade by way of reinterpretation.

With more relationships being mediated by technology, the need for a coherent body of knowledge in respect of regulatory interfaces is necessary. Regulations will increasingly be defined by their usability and accessibility of users to information with legal relevance. Self-regulatory competences, empowerment, and autonomy are put to the test already, for example, in the context of e-governance solutions provided by the state. A remarkable progress has taken place in the past two decades in furthering accessibility to laws. Their readability is the first aspect that public and private legal formulations intend to improve. The visual interfaces of texts with legal relevance, especially in the field of business, have timidly identified a domain open to innovation and exploration.

The classification below stems from the concept of transactional design to encompass activities that precede and follow the act of contracting in an extended relational process that could be studied also as a series of experiences. When mediated by technology, two transactional layers and one or several interfaces should be considered, the interface text in view on a device and the underlying relationship on text.[48] The agreement is treated as a technology embodied as manual of behavior and the result of collaborative work and a legal service design but not necessarily a collaboration inducing text in itself.[49] The persuasive power of these documents must be much further explored: on one hand, the semiotic value resulting from visualization and other alternative techniques can fail or mislead (misrepresentation), and on the other, persuasion would require a much deeper revision regarding the responsibilities associated with the message and the recommendations it may contain.[50] A legitimacy assessment of the source of information and authorship, not only of the content, would also be required because of their accuracy and efficacy first and also to ensure accountability.

[48] Text in here is any message on any medium which includes imagery, film, pictures, words, and sound. Various interfaces can be designed to increment choices, for instance creating different layers and textures, as well as modules for selecting and mixing. On modularity, find: Smith (2006).

[49] Persuasive technologies are designed to modify human attitudes and conducts. Read more in Fogg (2002).

[50] That contracts are created for information and persuasion is assumed in this section, but only the cognitive enhancement is being discussed. Another important assumption is that in simplifying a legal text, adding more than what seeks to inform and persuade would be superfluous and add noise to the text.

## 3.2 Usability Taxonomies

For the effects of the unified classification below, the legal term "parties" (to an agreement) and the business management equivalent "agents" (in transactions and operations) are equaled with the word "user"; the objects to be tested are the texts or interfaces representing and featuring a contractual relationship (an interface or two when mediated by technology). Consequently, texts can be static such as a plain document, even when posted online or dynamic when interactive and/or textured. Usability, according to Nielsen, is a quality attribute defined by the ease of use of any artifact and refers to methods that improve the design of interfaces so they become more than utility objects.[51] Usability in HCI is also about simplicity of the systems of interaction and experiencing, analogous to the user-centered design. Usability does not look at acceptability out of this realm or in law where such considerations would be adjectival to the validity and legality of the contracts and regulations themselves. The slogans and heuristics of usability are founded on ergonomics and notably very similar to those of conflict management studies: knowing the user, allowing participation, association and collaboration, control of the processes or codesign, iterative processes, saving of transaction and other costs, friendly and satisfactory outcomes that match the expectations of the users, etc.[52] The institutionalization of usability standards has been progressing for the past 30 years, particularly by way of the establishment of principles and best practices that the literature discusses extensively.[53] Table 1 presents a basic HCT taxonomy of usability with parameters applicable to graphic user interfaces.

The primary level of usability consists of three traditional quality attributes in most system assessments no matter the field: Effectiveness, Efficiency, and Satisfaction. Each general attribute results from the verification of several components or factors, corresponding to a secondary level of specifications that are compiled from the well-known literature on usability engineering and HCI.[54] The components of attribution are or denote qualities too and are measurable according to defined (or definable) parameters. Effectiveness in this context refers to the degree to which goals or tasks could be completed or the intended results of an action achieved. It is placed first on the table because its components are themselves functional needs that have to be present. An operative even if not an optimally accomplished working interaction system, so-to-say, should preexist an evaluation.

[51] Nielsen (1994).

[52] About the Harvard negotiation project find more at: http://www.pon.harvard.edu/category/research_projects/harvard-negotiation-project/.

[53] The International Organisation for Standardisation (ISO) and the International Electrotechnical Commission (IEC) have issued numerous materials that can be the reference for the development of usable products. Search on the database: http://www.iso.org/iso/catalogue_ics and refer in particular to ISO 9241. On a categorization of usability standards and a brief discussion on their applicability problems, consult Bevan (2006).

[54] Pearrow (2006) and Brinck et al. (2002).

**Table 1** Taxonomy of usability components in HCI

| Taxonomy of usability components for HCI | | |
|---|---|---|
| Effectiveness | Efficiency | Satisfaction |
| • Relevant & up-to-date content<br>• Clear information architecture<br>• Completeness<br>• Visibility<br>• Understandability<br>• Mapping with real-world conventions<br>• Communication through design<br>• Error prevention[a]<br>• Navigation[a] | • Readability<br>• Consistency<br>• Information visualization<br>• Learnability<br>• Flexibility<br>• Facilitating user control[a] | • Minimalistic design<br>• Aesthetically pleasant design<br>• Overall satisfaction |

[a]Applicable to interactive formats only

Efficiency is related to the costs and efforts required for task completion or the relationship between inputs and outputs. Satisfaction includes user engagement with the overall design, agreeability, and acceptability of the interface. All the components in this taxonomy are included in reference text on HCI, but the measuring parameters are not absolute and can be adjusted according to the assessment requirements, the type of users, and other variables affecting context. A classification was made and presented in Table 2 to connect plain language criteria for contracts and lean contracting with general principles of contract theory and a preventive/proactive lawyering orientation.[55] The table proposes a basic taxonomy of criteria for good drafting and contracting practices with parameters applicable to all three transactional stages.[56]

In the case of transactions, usability would be a novel term assigned to long-standing negotiation techniques and quality contracting standards. What is added is the focus on collaboration for an experience that should satisfy all users, and the visual elements.[57] On the primary level of usability, the only difference is the order

[55] Language is believed to be the main cause of contractual inefficiencies, particularly in consumer protection advocacy circles where the plain language movement is rooted. "Plain" when applied to a written document could be understood in three ways: the text is legible, meaning that it can be perceived and then read; it has unity, that is coherency and consistency in all language arrangements; and it is clear, meaning intelligible and with semantic precision. These three main characteristics determine the degree to which readers can comprehend text. On lean contracting, read Siedel and Haapio (2010), p. 26.

[56] Looking at the whole relational context (Braucher 1990), contracts acquire a new meaning. Braucher speaks of the dangers of contractarianism and recommends more sustainable and productive contractual relations not to sacrifice factors such as fairness and sense of community.

[57] Criteria for effective contract drafting combine linguistic technical skills with being able to identify the building blocks of a relationship and producing a strategic document for compliance, as well as a positive transactional experience. The same, one could argue, applies to other types of text consigning the creations of rights and duties. Criteria for good regulation have always been discussed in the literature; see, for instance, on boiler plate and standardized formats Stark (2003); Hillman and Rachlinski (2002) about standard-form electronic contracting; Tan and Thoen (2003)

**Table 2** Taxonomy of quality standards in contract drafting

| Taxonomy of quality contract drafting standards | | |
|---|---|---|
| Efficiency | Effectiveness | Satisfaction |
| • Readability;<br>Standards of plain language, information visualization, information processing, and standardized terms. (The language used in contracts and regulations is used to inform and persuade (Phelps 1986). However, legal witting and communication is described as unintelligible, wordy, and abstruse.)<br>• Consistency:<br>Clarity and standard formats<br>• Organization:<br>Systematic placement of information, hierarchy, and flow | • Completeness<br>• Collaborative<br>• Communication effect for consensus<br>• Pleasantly memorable | • Awareness (taking notice)<br>• Understanding (knowing)<br>• Consensus (engagement)<br>• Compliance (action) |

of the traditional attributes. The reason is for assessments to follow an inductive flow. Because the intrinsic functionality of an agreement would be a matter of enforceability, this feature does not need to be enhanced by design, if anything, just communicated more effectively. In short, by applying efficiency standards first, effectiveness is facilitated.

On the secondary level of specifications for transactional design, salient concerns on contracting capabilities according to scholars and practitioners are summarized under 10 components describing measurable qualities, characteristics, and results. The parameters that would apply to the factors grouped under satisfaction could be proposed in general terms for now while the practice evolves and a stable set of assessment criteria emerges. Experimental research could explore more precisely how to learn about more satisfying contractual relations depending on sectors, types of businesses, and the kind of users in question. This would be the link between transactional design, service development, and marketing, bringing into the picture the cognitive sciences and psychology in the development of products and services that enhance the user experience.[58]

on a risk/trust model for preparing the contract; and the concept on contract as a technology explained by Davis (2013), among the many authors with similar concerns. Some initiatives of a much wider range have derived from the plain language movement that in the 1970s is consumer protection activism inspired; find, for example, in www.plainlanguagenetwork.org and in www.clarity-international.net for more resources. Some of the traditional principles combined with the selection of usability parameters in this chapter compose a practical checklist to be used in transactional design.

[58] As if coinciding with Susskind on his assessments about today's legal landscape and his predictions about the future of legal services (Susskind 2008), the proposals by Passera and Haapio (2011a, b) unpack the possibilities of at least three of the categories that Susskind describes: the legal "knowledge engineer," the legal "risk manager," and the legal "hybrid." (Susskind 2008, pp. 272–273).

The factors or components of attribution of the second level in Table 1 may be detailed and technical, whereas in the second the degree of abstraction is higher. Still, some of the factors are shared and can be grouped under similar categories and researched using similar methodologies. The most contrasting mainly under the attribute of satisfaction could be explored with subsidiary interdisciplinary techniques. That the interface design in itself is the efficiency factor number one in the usability of transactions could argue against a combined taxonomy at first. But this can be solved when separating the layers of the text from its display, emphasizing the role of visualization and formulating a selective roadmap of checks.[59]

Under Effectiveness usability standards in HCI, the factors listed are *relevant and up to date information* first; in contracts, documents are expected to be comprehensive, *complete*. The existence requirements of legal transactions and basic formalities are determined by the law, and the interface should represent the essentials such as the rights and obligations of the parties. The second factor listed is *clear information architecture* to mean that all contents must be arranged in a clear, understandable, and intuitive manner; *Completeness* refers to the integrity and wholeness of the content provided; *Visibility* is about accessibility of content and commands. If it is not in the display upfront, then it should be at reach, without undue restrictions. Visibility enhances usability.[60] In interactive interfaces, the user should know what is happening at any moment of use. *Understandability* implies that even a novice user can navigate the text and grasp the information it contains. *Mapping* with real-world conventions is defined by the way in which the display matches the users' world knowledge making navigation intuitive and effortless. The design gains when it is "metaphoric." Some aspects of this can differ from culture to culture, i.e. reading from left to right or the other way around. In legal texts, this characteristic belongs within "plain language" and organization and could be achieved by phrasing the text naturally, using everyday words arranged in an order that could seem the most logical. *Communication through design* would be to rely on data enrichment techniques like layering information graphically, with color, shape, textures, etc. *Error prevention* in interactive design is achieved through engineering and practice. By minimizing the possibility of mistakes with proper guidance, users do not need to solve any problem, or if they should, then feedback would be provided containing the error description and

[59] This argument becomes especially relevant in the case of Passera's work, which uses boundary object theory in her contracting enhancement proposal (2012). An "easy" way to skip the complex conceptual articulation phase when attempting these classifications could be to leave conflict theory and proactive and collaborative principles aside and concentrate on the fact that the illustration of transactions is preventive and promotive enough, requiring no evaluation on their own.

[60] The field of usability is replete with advice on characteristics that can be categorized (read, for example, in Lidwell et al. (2010)), but few are the principles that sufficiently guide a proper research design to improve the interaction experience such as the focus on user needs, choosing an experimental approach, and design thinking engineering tools. In this section, the usability factors included in the taxonomy can be said to be the basic and most widely applicable in the practice of usability testing as for now.

instructions on how to solve it. The last factor, *Clear navigation*, also applicable to interactive interfaces, can be comparable to mapping and making all functions visible with regard to dynamic content. For instance, clickable elements should be distinguishable from static content.

The first factor under Efficiency on the usability standards in HCI and most important in the improvement of contract drafting practices is *readability*, present when the content and system are intelligible. Techniques can be implemented to increase the *readability* on aspects of the use of language (plain, simple, and when needed explained), formatting (types and consistency, proper labeling, headings, and so on), layout (flow of information is facilitated, for instance, by the strategic use of spaces), and size and appearance (all features concerning the text, including color, can help in conveying meaning). *Readability* is also the first factor under the attributes of efficiency in contract drafting, for it is the chief condition for understanding the ultimate goal of any communication process. It can be explained as the degree to which users can identify information contained in texts or images and usually rests on conventions contained in the language. The law is a language with its own categories, which inevitably decreases the usability of legal documents by default, particularly because there are not many visual legal categories codified and/or widely accepted so far.[61] *Readability* for contracts suggests techniques of plain language (also lean contracting), information visualization, and information processing. *Consistency* is the second efficiency component in both tables. In HCI it bears on language, structure, navigation, layout, and design and translates well to contract drafting techniques to achieve clarity through the organization of concepts, ideas, and considerations of structure when composing texts and presenting information. *Information visualization* is a component apart in the HCT taxonomy, whereas within the taxonomy for contract drafting is nested within *readability*. This placement also shows that visualization is being ranked here at least a layer beneath in the design of legal texts because the theory that could support its relevance has yet to be developed. The incipient knowledge on the field of legal visualization has captured the attention of researchers and scholars, but that so far focuses on experimental design initiatives.[62] By *information visualization* is not meant the visual display of precise data only but any kind of graphic support regardless of precision or recall and tactics of composition involving pictures, icons, timelines, and flowcharts.[63] *Learnability* is related to the subtle acquisition

[61] Traffic signs and logos of the creative commons are some of the very few (search them on http://creativecommons.org/).

[62] Look at an experimental evaluation report in Passera (2012).

[63] Precision and recall are characteristics that are commonplace in information visualization and data representation in regard to information retrieval to indicate correctness and completeness. They could also apply to semantics, but the tensions between the degree of exactitude needed and the benefits of clarity in HCI and plain language in transactional design could detriment communication and raise more questions about the visualization of concepts. Whether the need for metrics in visual information analysis would be applicable to the visualization of the law cannot be ascertained in these few pages.

of the logic of the design. It rests on the familiarity that is crated with use or the ability to complete a task in one attempt.[64] The last for static text on the table is *flexibility*, which is attributed to a system that accommodates the users and not the other way around. The interface should be usable for any kind of user. For experts, the experience could be enhanced by modifying affordances and adding functionalities. Adding layers of information or options with differing complexity levels for novice and experienced users is also an option. *Facilitating the user's control* in interactive systems allows a sense of freedom and competence, so the system does not take over and users can correct mistakes or change their mind (undo function). Except some minor differences and the order of the quality attributes discussed, the two sets of factors determining effectiveness and efficiency are comparable. The same cannot be said on the components of satisfaction, given that traditionally the ultimate goal of an agreement is to ensure enforceability or create incentives for compliance based on the assumption that promises are kept mainly because sanctions are ensued.

Satisfaction is about the user experience in HCI, and partly in contracting, if collaboration (teamwork, association, and mutual gain) has been part of the negotiation strategy. HCI factors that could increase satisfaction are *minimalistic design* and *pleasant aesthetics*. The first consolidates a logic that considers content more important than style, tends to be lean and simple, and discourages distractions. Tufte's principle of data-ink ratio identifies with this.[65] Eliminating distractions does not mean depriving the interface from being attractive, agreeable, and if possible promotive of positive emotions while in use. *The overall satisfaction* with a graphic user interface can be measured by a mixed research methodology using the parameters that the discipline already recommends.[66] In contrast, the law practically assigns no validity to aggregates and being a closed system in times even disallows their use during interpretative assessment of concrete cases. In transactions, the fit of legal acts to the needs and interests of the parties makes all tasks associated human centered such as in the drafting of a good contract (except in the case of standard format[67]). The satisfaction that transactional design seeks to accomplish with its collaborative and proactive approach should result from a text that can raise *awareness*, *understanding*, *consensus*, and *compliance*. Effective information increases understanding of the terms of agreements and with it the trust in the transactional process, and the own competences in decision making. This in turn can persuade on the merits of a collaborative and principled transaction and engagement on the basis of authentic consensus, winning the parties with no need

---

[64] For a review of this feature in context, read Ziefle (2002).

[65] Data-ink is the nonerasable ink. If removed from the image, the graphic would lose the content. Non-Data-Ink is, accordingly, the ink that does not transport necessary information but creates noise Tufte and Graves-Morris (1983).

[66] Introduction to Human Factors Engineering by Wickens et al. (1998), and Interaction Design-beyond human–computer interaction by Preece et al. (2015) are recommended texts on research methods in HCI.

[67] Read further in Hillman and Rachlinski (2002).

for further prescriptive incentives. To comply with mutually beneficial terms of agreements is also a question of self-interest and can be expected in the frame of at least cordial business relationships or to consolidate them so. The *overall satisfaction* of the users will always be determined by the user's perceptions on how the system or the text is furthering their satisfaction of needs and interests. This evaluation should include qualitative research methodologies, using interviews and self-reported narratives on the experience of use of the product.

Table 3 regroups and combines the standards or principles listed above. It is to be expected that the significant improvement of efficiency factors of the legal interface facilitates working on effectiveness components, to produce an improved transac-

**Table 3** Combined taxonomy of usability components applicable to transactions

| Taxonomy of usability components for transactional design | | |
|---|---|---|
| Efficiency | Effectiveness | Satisfaction |
| • Readability (perception, attention, memory, and mental models): Standards of plain language, information visualization, information technology, and standard terms<br><br>• Consistency (pattern recognition): Clarity and standard formats<br>• Organization: Systematic placement of information, hierarchy, and flow<br>• Information visualization (mental models, affordances (Affordances are the allowances of action and manipulation of an object, which in contracting could be said to be analogous to the range of actions that a regulatory tool allows, including non-compliance. A designer of interfaces thinks in advance of these affordances, how to enable as well as how to disable users on particular actions. Sometimes the tools lend themselves for certain actions irrespectively of the designer's intervention, and these should too be detected; in legal relationships this is supposed to be analyzed during the stage of contract planning and risk | • Completeness (mental models)<br>• Collaborative (emotions): Mutual gain as incentive enough of performance<br>• Communication effect for consensus (perception, attention, memory, pattern recognition, mental models, and affordances)<br>• Pleasantly memorable (attention, memory, and emotions)<br>• Sustainability | • Awareness (taking notice)<br>• Understanding (knowing)<br>• Consensus (willful participation, engagement)<br>• Compliance (action)<br>• Overall satisfaction with the transacting experience and the sustainability of the agreement |

(continued)

**Table 3** (continued)

| Taxonomy of usability components for transactional design | | |
|---|---|---|
| Efficiency | Effectiveness | Satisfaction |
| evaluation. On affordances and control read, Turvey (1992), who also explains Gibson's original proposal.), emotions)<br>• Learnability (memory, mental models, emotions)<br>• Flexibility (emotions)<br>• User control (perception, attention, memory, mental models, and emotions)[a] | | |

[a]Applicable to interactive formats only

tional experience and higher satisfaction levels. Indications are given as to what cognitive functions can affect or could be affected by HCI or usability engineering interventions. The study of human information processing and cognition aspects supply with valuable knowledge as to how to design optimal operational systems in technical fields. In the law, where a more intelligent and convivial flow of legal processes is badly needed, these considerations should not continue to remain neglected.

# 4 Concluding Remarks and Future Research

Collaborative transactional design and other smart contracting methodologies have the potential to influence the future of the theory and the practice of mediated contracts in the terms of conflict management and human-centered design. Proactive contracting and usability could be expected to correlate in the improvement of business and other human interaction also regardless of the use or not of devices and software applications. It is easy to envisage more visual contracts; after all, the inspiration for the articulation of this interdisciplinary proposal comes from the field of graphic user interface design. However, on visualization this chapter has urged caution. The normative ontologies of the legal system combine with common sense knowledge of the real world in very specialized epistemological structures. The articulation of visual legal categories requires therefore a very specialized combination of skills, expertise, competences, and preparatory research on disciplines such as legal theory and semiotics. This venture warrants a separate assessment and is beyond the scope of this chapter.

Transactional design practices can conveniently smooth the transition in the direction of smart contracts, and other systems of automated agency that cannot be ignored. In this interlude, the popularity of the proactive law discourse and the general enthusiasm for human-centered design could help the institutionalization of collaboration in stagnant social structures such as the legal systems or within very competitive environments such as business and trade. Transactional design practices could convince business to transcend the competitive advantage fixation by formulating strategies with collaborative components that can contribute to the organization's sustainability. Based on usability slogans, a multitude of other innovative possibilities can be anticipated like the creation of multifunctional contracts of escalating levels of difficulty, different versions for different people with all tools and interface apart adaptable on its own but under the control of the users, the generation of functionalities, affordances, and visuals that would explain and clarify transactions automatically, generated not merely upon request but also because the system perceives the need. Could more sustainable transactional capacities be trusted to artificial intelligence agents when technologies are mature enough on the basis of efficiency considerations alone? To which extent should human interaction rely mainly on growingly smarter contract solutions? Could smart contracts render human agents superfluous in some or all fields of social organizations? Answers to these questions cannot be found in specialized fields through individual disciplinary lenses. Even if research and development work in the computer sciences includes the issue of how to understand the human role in a technologically driven world, answering needs input from other disciplines.

As contracts are important legal tools and different contract-related questions form a significant part of the work of many lawyers, the willingness of the legal profession to embrace smart contracts and the understanding legal research has of the issue are essential. ICT applications work for and against social interaction, so powerful tools are devised to understand the complexities of the current socioeconomic system. One of them is agentification, agent-base modeling methods with people and technology both in focus. Nevertheless, future research directions on the topic of transactional design should begin at the simplest and most basic level of technology-mediated interaction (individuals–individuals and individuals–entities) to understand what creates preferences and fosters effectiveness and satisfaction. It could continue with observations onto how interaction at other levels forms. Additionally, empirical tests can analyze ways in which transactional design may create or maintain collaborative features across cultures in self-organizing, collective, global, and subtle institutionalization patterns. The interdisciplinary view of proactive transactions and transactional design as presented in this text could fit into the computational social sciences, economics, and the digital humanities that assess these issues in respect to governance, legitimacy, legality, trust, privacy, ethics, development, contextual knowledge, and human ecology.

The whole spectrum of disciplines researching the digital phenomena converge at the issue of social interaction and, more particularly, electronic transactions. This chapter explained the impact of some of the ICTs and HCI principles and capacities onto the legal sciences and specifically in what regards contracts and obligations linking it, on one hand, with the evolution of the field of conflict management and dispute prevention and, on the other, with the principles and imperatives of the interconnected society. Further, the chapter reflected on the speedy shift in legal practice paradigms towards a preventive proactivity in all legal services and how technology diffusion expedited the process. Definitional aspects were given chief importance to bridge disciplinary boundaries and represent the necessary theoretical crossovers. Usability (UX) was used as the reference term in good transaction design, UX parameters applicable to transactions were identified and conceptualized, and the visual law approach was presented as an efficient tool for enhancing the user/consumer experience and speedy institutionalization of the new transactional models. Better contracts and smooth interaction could be determined by the degree to which they reduce transaction costs, fostering compliance and satisfaction and diminishing the registration of disputes and/or increasing the resolution rate of disputes that have already been registered.

## References


Barrett JT, Barrett J (2004) A history of alternative dispute resolution: the story of a political, social, and cultural movement. John Wiley & Sons

Berger-Walliser G (2012) The past and future of proactive law: an overview of the development of the proactive law movement. In: Berger-Walliser G, Østergaard K (eds) Proactive law in a business environment. DJØF Publishing, pp 13–31

Berger-Walliser G, Bird RC, Haapio H (2011) Promoting business success through contract visualization. J Bus Ethics 17:55

Bevan N (2006). International standards for HCI. Encyclopedia of Human Computer Interaction, p 362

Braucher J (1990) Contract versus contractarianism: the regulatory role of contract law. Wash Lee Law Rev 47:697

Brinck T, Gergle D, Wood SD (2002) Designing Web sites that work: usability for the Web. Morgan Kaufmann

Brown LM (1951) Practice of preventive law. J Am Jud Soc 35:45

Brown LM (1956) The law office. A preventive law laboratory. Univ Pa Law Rev 940–953

Burton JW (1985) The history of international conflict resolution. Int Interact 12(1):45–57

Burton JW, Sandole DJ (1987) Expanding the debate on generic theory of conflict resolution: a response to a critique. Negot J 3(1):97–100

Castells M (2011) The rise of the network society: the information age: economy, society, and culture, vol 1. John Wiley & Sons

Cohen MR (1933) The basis of contract. Harv Law Rev 553–592

Conte R, Gilbert N, Bonelli G, Cioffi-Revilla C, Deffuant G, Kertesz J, ... Helbing D (2012) Manifesto of computational social science. Eur Phys J Spec Top 214(1):325–346

Cooter RD, Rubinfeld DL (1989) Economic analysis of legal disputes and their resolution. J Econ Lit 1067–1097

Daicoff SS (2005) Law as a healing profession: the comprehensive law movement. Pepperdine Dispute Resolution Law J, Fall, 06-12

Davis KE (2013) Contracts as technology. NYUL Rev 88:83

Fogg BJ (2002) Persuasive technology: using computers to change what we think and do. Ubiquity, 2002(December), 5

Forshey JR (1978) Plain English Contracts: the Demise of Legalese. Baylor Law Rev 30:765

Fuchs C (2007) Internet and society: social theory in the information age. Routledge

Galtung J (1996) Peace by peaceful means: peace and conflict, development and civilization, vol 14. Sage

Ghirardi JC, Crespo JJA (1996) Derecho romano. Eudecor

Groton J, Haapio H (2007, October) From reaction to proactive action: dispute prevention processes in business agreements. In: IACCM EMEA Academic Symposium, London, vol 9

Haapio H (2010) Business success and problem prevention through proactive contracting. Stockholm Institute for Scandinavian Law, 1999

Henry JF (2000) Some reflections on ADR. J Disp Resol 63

Hillman RA, Rachlinski JJ (2002) Standard-form contracting in the electronic age. NYUL Rev 77:429

Jasperson JS, Carte TA, Saunders CS, Butler BS, Croes HJ, Zheng W (2002) Review: power and information technology research: a metatriangulation review. MIS Q 26(4):397–459

Kimble J (1996) Writing for dollars, writing to please. Scribes J Leg Writ 6:1

Lahti R (2000) Towards a rational and humane criminal policy? Trends in Scandinavian penal thinking. J Scand Stud Criminol Crime Prev 1(2):141–155

Lidwell W, Holden K, Butler J (2010) Universal principles of design, revised and updated: 125 ways to enhance usability, influence perception, increase appeal, make better design decisions, and teach through design. Rockport Pub

Lieberman JK, Henry JF (1986) Lessons from the alternative dispute resolution movement. Univ Chicago Law Rev 424–439

Macneil IR, Gudel PJ (2001) Contracts: exchange transactions and relations: cases and materials. Foundation Press

Masson ME, Waldron MA (1994) Comprehension of legal contracts by non-experts: effectiveness of plain language redrafting. Appl Cogn Psychol 8(1):67–85

Menkel-Meadow C (1985) Transformation of disputes by lawyers: what the dispute paradigm does and does not tell us. Mo J Disp Resol 25

Nielsen J (1994) Usability engineering. Elsevier

Norta A, Dua Y, Ma L, Rull A, Kolvart M, Taveter K (2015) eContractual choreography-language properties towards cross-organizational business collaboration. J Internet Serv Appl 6(8):1–23

Passera S (2012, July) Enhancing contract usability and user experience through visualization-an experimental evaluation. In: 16th International Conference on Information Visualisation (IV). IEEE, pp 376–382

Passera S, Haapio H (2011a) Facilitating collaboration through contract visualization and modularization. In: Proceedings of the 29th Annual European Conference on Cognitive Ergonomics. ACM, pp 57–60

Passera S, Haapio H (2011b) User-centered contract design: new directions in the quest for simpler contracting. In: Bringing together academics and practitioners to promote research and best practice in Contracts and Commercial Management, Academic Forum for Innovative Research and Practice, International Association for Contract and Commercial Management (IACCM), Ridgefield, pp 80–97

Passera S, Pohjonen S, Koskelainen K, Anttila S (2013a) User-friendly contracting tools–a visual guide to facilitate public procurement contracting. In: Proceedings of the IACCM Academic Forum

Passera S, Haapio H, Barton TD (2013b) Innovating contract practices: merging contract design with information design

Pearrow M (2006) Web site usability handbook (internet series). Charles River Media, Inc

Phelps TG (1986) New legal rhetoric. SW Law J 40:1089

Pohjonen S (2010) Proactive law in the field of law. In: Wahlgren P (ed) A proactive approach, Scandinavian studies in law, vol 49. Stockholm Institute for Scandinavian Law, pp 53–70

Portes A (2000) Social capital: its origins and applications in modern sociology. In: Lesser EL (ed) Knowledge and social capital. Butterworth-Heinemann, Boston, pp 43–67

Preece J, Sharp H, Rogers Y (2015) Interaction design-beyond human-computer interaction. John Wiley & Sons

Ramadier T (2004) Transdisciplinarity and its challenges: the case of urban studies. Futures 36 (4):423–439

Reimann P, Kay J (2010) Learning to learn and work in net-based teams: supporting emergent collaboration with visualization tools. Designs for learning environment of the future. New York: Springer, pp 143–188
Rekola K, Haapio H (2011) Proactive contracting+ service design= success! Int J Serv Econ Manage 3(4):376–392
Sander FE (1985) Alternative methods of dispute resolution: an overview. Univ Fla Law Rev 37:1
Schneider AK (1999) The intersection of therapeutic jurisprudence, preventive law, and alternative dispute resolution. Psychol Public Policy Law 5(4):1084
Sherwin RK (2011) Visualizing law in the age of the digital baroque: Arabesques and entanglements. Routledge
Siedel G, Haapio H (2010) Proactive law for managers. A hidden source of competitive advantage. Gower
Smith HE (2006) Modularity in contracts: boilerplate and information flow. Mich Law Rev 1175–1222
Solarte-Vasquez MC (2014) Reflections on the concrete application of principles of internet governance and the networked information society in the European Union institutionalization process of Alternative Dispute Resolution methods. Tanel kerikmäe (Toim.). Regulating eTechnologies in the European Union. Springer Verlag, 251–283
Stark TL (2003) Negotiating and drafting contract boilerplate. ALM Publishing
Stolle DP, Wexler DB (1997) Therapeutic jurisprudence and preventive law: a combined concentration to invigorate the everyday practice of law. Ariz Law Rev 39:25
Susskind R (2008) The end of lawyers. Rethink Nat Leg Serv 32:50
Szabo N (1997) Formalizing and securing relationships on public networks. First Monday 2(9)
Tan YH, Thoen W (2003) Electronic contract drafting based on risk and trust assessment. Int J Electron Commer 7(4):55–71
Teubner G (1983) Substantive and reflexive elements in modern law. Law Soc Rev 239–285
Tufte ER, Graves-Morris PR (1983) The visual display of quantitative information, vol 2, no 9. Graphics Press, Cheshire, CT
Turvey MT (1992) Affordances and prospective control: an outline of the ontology. Ecol Psychol 4 (3):173–187
Verganti R (2011) Designing breakthrough products. Harv Bus Rev
Webel C, Galtung J (eds) (2007) Handbook of peace and conflict studies. Routledge
Wickens CD, Lee JD, Liu Y, Gordon-Becker S (1998) Introduction to human factors engineering
Ziefle M (2002) The influence of user expertise and phone complexity on performance, ease of use and learnability of different mobile phones. Behav Inf Technol 21(5):303–311

# Digital Marriage and Divorce: Legality Versus Digital Solutions

**Kristi Joamets**

**Abstract** Rapid developments in several relations between a citizen and a state have raised a question about the possibility to apply the whole digitalised system to administrative deeds, including contracting marriage and confirming divorce. Technology must be in conformity with law, not only with procedural law but also with substantial law. On the other hand, society must be open to innovations, including to the new values and traditions influencing the attitudes related to family matters. Society's reluctance to accept new ideas can lead to a situation in which a digital solution is not applicable because of an outdated substantive law. The article analyses which legal problems can arise in the digitalisation of marriage and divorce and discusses if those problems would be the impediments to ensuring the legality of the procedure. By this analysis, many questions can arise and would need an answer; for example, is it possible to control certain data, wills and conditions? How does one give explanations and avoid fraud? Are marriage and divorce deeds with similar legal and social meaning to put them into the digital form? Should the traditional marriage and divorce models be replaced by the digital one, or should they exist concurrently? How ready is society in such a novel digital thought at all?

## 1 Introduction

Increase of cross-border family relations and hence the strong mutual impact of traditions of different nations, globalisation and tolerance to multiculturalism has changed the nature of family law.[1] More and more prevailing is the understanding that it is too complicated to relate family law to a certain closed region or tie it up with one certain tradition. It is hard to determine a tradition or culture as well. For

[1] See, e.g., Macedo (1998); Bradley (2003); Garrison and Scott (2012); Lifshitz (2012).

K. Joamets (✉)
Tallinn Law School, Tallinn University of Technology, Akadeemia tee 3, 12618 Tallinn, Estonia
e-mail: kristi.joamets@ttu.ee



T. Kerikmäe, A. Rull (eds.), *The Future of Law and eTechnologies*,
DOI 10.1007/978-3-319-26896-5_9

example, in Europe, the family laws of member states which have been described as a "closed" branch of law, because they are based on the different cultures of the member states, have lost their "singularity". Instead of diversity, the similarity is gradually more often emphasised and in this respect the understanding about one single European culture too.[2] The truth is that cross-border family relations cannot be managed in such an inflexible diversity. Avoiding conflicts needs some tolerance from member states. This all shows the evolution of family law and justifies a question whether it is time to overlook this branch of law in whole—how much of the values expressed in a legal norm are contemporary, and how many of them are outdated? Additionally, can those changes develop the substantive law and lead to the changes in procedural law as well?

As family law is so close to the people, it is vulnerable in its nature to the changes in society. Changes take some time, but often one can predict that the amendments come anyway. This can be proved, for example, by the changes in divorce law, legitimation of children born outside the marriage, spread of cohabitation, gender-neutral marriages, etc.[3] One can notice that family law has become more tolerant. However, such indulgence should be reflected also in a procedure of family event. Nevertheless, one can assume that emerged new family relations should maybe reduce the responsibility of a state in protecting the "something" or the "somebody" and leave more responsibility to the citizens.

This article aims to break the current understandings about how family events should be registered by the state. The given analysis leads to the substantial questions about the essence or nature of certain phenomenon in family law: marriage and divorce. All this is useful for the discussion about the possibility of applying digital means to a registration process, bearing in mind that digital system must be in accordance with the principles provided by substantive law. As long as substantial law is too rigid, many digital solutions cannot be applied in the procedure; still, in some cases it is additionally justified to suggest changes in substantive law to liberalise the deed. The truth is that, on the one hand, family relations and their regulations have become more complicated; on the other hand, it is bolder to interfere with the relations and suggest new more simplified regulations.

The given article can be rather referred to as an imagination than an evaluated and controlled proof. Nevertheless, it is a trendsetter and a set of ideas about the possible developments of the administrative procedures related to the family event. The article bases on Estonian[4] example and practice: its digital system and legal regulations have been discussed based on the general principles and concepts of family law in general.

---

[2] See Peters (2013), p. 676; Detloff (2003), p. 61; Stark (2013), p. 690.

[3] See, e.g., Needham (2014); Willekens (2003); Mason et al. (2001); D'Angelo (2014); Sörgjerd (2012); Antokolskaia (2003).

[4] Estonian legal acts in English are available on the website www.riigiteataja.ee/en/. As the article bases mainly on Estonian Family Law Act and Estonian Vital Statistics Procedure Act, then references to certain paragraphs are made only when they have a certain importance or the norm is difficult to find.

Gurtin states that "In the 21st century, variously called the Digital Century, the Information Age, or even the Postinformation Age, the Networked Society, and numerous other tech-hopeful names, publicly accessible data and information technologies will be critical to the success of international, national, regional, and local policies".[5]

Digitalisation always raises a question about the readiness and capability of society[6] to use digital solutions. Pan Suk Kim has noted that governments around the world have been eager to seise upon the massive potential of the Internet as a means of initiating public sector reform and to find new paradigms to overcome the inefficiencies of previous governments. According to a United Nations report, the majority of UN members have embarked upon some form of e-government as a universal strategy for government renovation.[7]

Digitalisation in family matters is nothing new; related to the "free movement of civil status data"[8] and creating one common pan-European civil status data register, it is a part of the EU policy today. Anyway, the idea that marriage or divorce could be registered online is a novel one. The author of given article believes that the main reason in postponing this development by the state is a fear that such digital solution could lead to the fraud and insufficient protection of the weaker party of the relationship. Anyhow, the following questions will additionally accompany the discussion about digitalising marriage and divorce: does digital marriage and divorce cause more fraud than a traditional one? Is it possible to control certain data, wills and conditions? Are marriage and divorce the deeds with similar legal and social meaning to put them into the digital form? Should the traditional marriage and divorce models be replaced by the digital one, or should they exist concurrently? How ready is society in such a novel digital thought? These questions can be answered and can lead to the conclusion that the apparent fears are not reasoned.

Based on the analysis of the United Nations E-Government Survey 2014,[9] in 2013 75 % of the Estonian population used the Internet.[10] Nevertheless, the same

[5] Gurtin (2010), p. 309.

[6] New information and communication technologies have been described additionally as the new smart community movement (see Coe et al. (2001), pp. 81 and 82).

[7] Kim (2005), p. 100.

[8] See European Commission. Green Paper to Promote Free Movement of Public Documents and Recognition of the Effects of Civil Status Records. COM(2010) 747 final, 14. December 2010; Proposal of the Regulation of the European Parliament and of the Council on promoting the free movement of citizens and businesses by simplifying the acceptance of certain public documents in the European Union and amending Regulation (EU) No 1024/2012, COM(2013) 228 final 2013/0119 (COD).

[9] United Nations E-Government Survey 2014, E-Government for the Future We Want. New York: United Nations. 2014, Bridging a digital divide (Chapter 6), p. 125.

[10] Only Sweden had a bigger percentage—94 %. That is, Estonia was on second place. Nevertheless, based on Digital Economy and Society Index 2015, Estonia is characterised as a medium-performance group, together with the United Kingdom, Luxembourg, Ireland, Germany, Lithuania, Spain, Austria, France, Malta, Portugal and the Czech Republic. They are doing well in certain

study shows that in 2012 Estonia was on the 10th place of the OECD countries in citizens using the FAikins in their interactions with public authorities.[11] Anyhow, today there are more than 3000 digital services in Estonia, and this area is developing continuously.

Digital solution of using an e-ID[12] and digital signature facilitates the development of e-governance, including the registration of family events. Digitally connected registers allow the X-use of the data in different databases.

The Estonian Information Society Policy emphasises the need to revise the current law to evaluate its contents related to the possible digital solutions as well.[13] This guideline supports the idea to further analyse substantive law in order to find out the outdated rules in the context of digital society.

## 2 Administrative Procedure of Marriage and Divorce (on the Estonian Example)

According to the Estonian Family Law Act,[14] marriage is contracted in the presence of a registry official of a vital statistics office (registrar[15]).[16] Procedure begins by the presentation of the application to the official by both future spouses. Applicants

---

areas but still need to progress in others (http://ec.europa.eu/digital-agenda/en/digital-economy-and-society-index-desi (25.02.2015)). Estonia's digital development has been described by the Digital Agenda Scoreboard as follows: Estonia is at the forefront in the supply and use of digital public services, which are the second best in Europe. Estonia remains the leader in the comprehensiveness of pre-filled online forms and the use of ePrescriptions by general practitioners (100 %). Estonians are well-skilled in the use of digital technologies (their digital skill levels are above those of the average EU user) and keen users of a variety of Internet activities. 22 % of Estonians shop cross border, a higher rate than the European average (https://ec.europa.eu/digital-agenda/en/scoreboard/estonia (25.02.2015)).

[11] United Nations E-Government Survey 2014, E-Government for the Future We Want. New York: United Nations. 2014, Bridging a digital divide (Chapter 6), p. 142.

[12] Card enables electronic authentication and serves as a digital signature to allow Estonians to sign contracts, vote, submit their tax declarations, etc.

[13] Estonian Information Society Policy 2013, p. 24.

[14] State Gazette (in Estonian Riigi Teataja (RT)) I 2009, 60, 395 (29.06.2014, 104).

[15] The Estonian Family Law Act uses the term "vital statistics official", but in most legal literature the word "registrar" is commonly used. For this reason, in the article the word "registrar" is used and means an official with the authority provided for a vital statistics official by the Family Law Act, the Vital Statistics Registration Act and other acts regulating the registration of vital statistics acts. Additionally, the term "official" has been used to refer to the state representative in an administrative deed—it covers vital statistic official, notary and clergyman.

[16] In Estonia, vital statistics procedures are carried out by the county governments and rural municipalities or city governments. Moreover, marriages are contracted and divorces confirmed only by the county governments. Notaries have been given the authority to contract marriages and confirm divorces since 2010. Clergymen have been contracting marriages since 2001. Not all clergymen have such right, only those who have taken an exam on the rules of marriage regulation

have to be both present when fulfilling the application, and the procedure consists of the explanation by the official about the property regimes that future spouses have to choose when marrying. After the waiting period (from 1 to 6 months), the prospective spouses express their will to contract marriage before a registrar, notary or clergyman, both being present in person at the same time. Procedure consists of the question by the official to both prospective spouses whether they want to contract marriage with the other party. Marriage is contracted after the answer "yes" by both prospective spouses. After that, an official[17] enters the contraction of marriage into the Population Register.[18] Anyway, it is important to consider that marriage has a legal effect already from the moment of answering "yes" by the prospective spouses. For this reason, in the procedure the time of answering "yes" is registered as a legal fact. From the moment of saying "yes", the legal rights and obligations begin from the marriage.

Divorce is one of the grounds for the termination of marriage. When both spouses agree with divorce, they can get divorced at the registrar or at a notary's office by a joint written petition.[19] When one of the spouses disagrees with the divorce, the marriage must be terminated in a court. Since 2010, the law has separated the disputes related to divorce, marriage property and custody.[20] This means that when spouses do not have disagreements related to the mere fact of divorce, they can terminate their marriage at the registrar or notary and after that turn to a court with a dispute over the marriage property or over the custody of their children. When marriage is terminated at the registrar or notary, the spouses are

provided by law, including procedure, and have got a special right from the Minister of Interior. Further, they are under the supervision of county governments, which advise them on the one hand, and on the other hand they supervise clergymen in charge of handling administrative deeds concerning marriage. In Estonia, the religious wedding ceremony (religious marriage) and the civil marriage are separate. Only civil marriage has legal meaning, but the law allows those two procedures to be officiated at the same time in a church. The expansion of the authority of the vital statistics procedures derives from the need to facilitate the life of citizens. Still, Estonian Embassies do not have the right to contract marriages or confirm divorces, but they do other registrar's obligations that the digital system of Population Register allows (see, e.g., Consular Act RT I 2008, 29,175. 30.10.2013).

[17] The notary has the right to enter the data related to those procedures into the Population Register; the clergyman accomplishes the needed documents on paper, and the data are entered into the register by the registrar of the county government.

[18] Population Register (see Population Register Act RT I 2000, 50, 317. 18.06.2014) is a base register for the national public administration containing the basic data of individuals (citizens and residents), which is updated continuously. As it consists of civil status data, it is the main database where other registers get their basic data about individuals. Anyway, not all public registers are yet connected to the Population Register, but this goal is the policy of Estonian digital development. This would ensure a similar civil status data in every register (see more about this policy in Joamets (2014), p. 147). Civil data in the Population Register have legal meaning, and the public sector must use the civil status and other data of this register in their administrative deeds.

[19] Estonia differs from many EU member states in terms of the possibility to divorce outside of court.

[20] See Family Law Act par 65 (2).

divorced from the moment the data about the divorce are entered into the Population Register.

There is a difference compared to the moment marriage or divorce is enforced. The reason for the difference is caused by the fact that marriage can be contracted outside the registrar's office[21] while divorce is always confirmed in an office with an access[22] to the system of the Population Register. Therefore, there is a space of time between saying "yes" and entering the data about this marriage into the Population Register. Spouses must know from which moment they are married because their property relations and inheritance rights depend on it.

At a first glance, the procedures of these administrative deeds seem simple and thus a question can be raised: why not do them online? But going deeper into the content of the procedure, it can be understood that only some single deeds in the procedure can be fulfilled via the Internet, while others cannot, or at least their possibility to carry out specific acts online is questionable. In order to evaluate the possibility of digital marriage and divorce, one should first understand the legal essence of those procedures from the scope of a state. That is, all single obligations provided by the law protect one of the applicants or other individuals. Nevertheless, related to the procedure it needs to be discussed if such protection can be guaranteed via online too.

In Estonia, the whole administrative procedure of registering family events has become digital from 2010 by the entering into force of the Vital Statistics Registration Act.[23] Since 2002, the family data have been collected and recorded in the Population Register. However, this digital registering does not mean registration online without being present at the registrar's office but rather indicates that an official does not fulfill the paper(s) in the procedure but enters all the data into the civil register. The civil register as a digital environment for the procedure of registering the family event is a section of the Population Register—in this respect, a registrar (also notary) enters the data and performs all the administrative deed procedures directly onto the Population Register.

Marriage and divorce are vital statistics procedures, which means that they are simultaneously administrative deeds with participation of the state. This deed consists of several independent but still related procedures ending with the contraction of marriage or confirmation of divorce. When the Estonian Family Law Act provides substantive rules, the Estonian Vital Statistics Registration Act consists of the rules of procedure—in this respect, the rules of the Family Law Act are ensured by the procedural rules provided in the Vital Statistics Registration Act.

Even though today the civil status data of persons are in the Population Register and not only available but additionally obligatory to use for the state officials and

[21] Notaries have the right to contract marriages outside their offices; ceremonies take place in masons, seashore, farm; clergymen in their churches or elsewhere.

[22] When there is no access to the system, then the entry about the divorce on paper has legal meaning; divorce enters into force from the signature of the registrar of a written entry.

[23] RT I 2009, 30, 177. 29.06.2014, 6.

the administrative procedure itself is digital, there are still many procedures the applicant must undergo, such as being physically present before the official.

As mentioned above, the procedure of marriage begins with presenting a joint written application of the future spouses. Applicants have to go together to the registrar, notary or clergyman[24] and provide the following data:

names and identity code (or date of birth) and place of birth; this is to identify a person, and in case a person's data are not in the Population Register, create a subject[25] with all the needed data provided by the Population Register Act. Date of birth allows to check the age of prospective spouses as adolescents have additional conditions to marry.[26]

Residency provides different rules related to marriage capacity—marriage impediments are controlled by the law of the residence of prospective spouses.[27] In addition, a person's data allow to check from the Population Register whether there are any impediments related to marriage, such as consanguineous marriages between a parent and child, brother and sister, other close kinship, adopter and adopted, etc. A residency other than in Estonia can lead to the requirement of additional documents: marriage impediment certificate or confirmation of legal bases of stay.[28]

Contact details are required in case the official needs to contact the applicants concerning certain data. Having Estonian citizenship can change the rule regarding marriage impediments being controlled by the state of residence replacing it with the state of citizenship.[29]

Marital status must be single. When a person has been married and this marriage is terminated, then he/she must provide a document confirming the termination of this marriage. Additional confirming documents are needed when the data in the Population Register are insufficient. Furthermore, as the data related to civil status acts made abroad can be transferred to the Population Register also by the Estonian Embassies, it is complicated to hide a vital statistics event abroad today.

Prospective spouses have to express their wish to contract the marriage with each other. They confirm that there are no circumstances hindering the contraction

[24] As the clergyman has usually no access to the Population Register, the data are controlled later by the county government to which the clergyman co-operates.

[25] The subject of the Population Register is an Estonian citizen; a citizen of the European Union, Member State of the European Economic Area or the Swiss Confederation who has registered his or her residence in Estonia; or an alien who has been granted a residence permit or right of residence in Estonia (Population Register Act par 4).

[26] The court gives consent to marry after evaluating the capability of an adolescent to understand the legal consequences derived from marriage.

[27] International Private Law Act (RT I 2002, 35, 2017) par 56.

[28] See Vital Statistics Registration Act par 38 (3).

[29] This can derive from the international agreements which are applicable instead of national law because of their supranational nature.

of marriage. Besides, they confirm whether one of them chooses a surname of the other prospective spouse.[30] Applicants have to choose a time for contraction of the marriage.[31]

The number of marriages to be contracted is, on the one hand, statistical data; on the other hand, this confirmation allows the state to ensure that all the marriages contracted are in the Population Register in order to fix up the data in the register and to check whether the previous marriages are terminated. The personal names and personal identification codes of the joint children to be living with the prospective spouses after the contraction of marriage are also considered statistical data. Includingly, nationality, mother tongue, education and area of activity are data collected for statistical reasons. Providing all the statistical data is voluntary.

From the legal aspect, the proprietary relationship the prospective spouses must choose is important: jointness of property, set-off of assets increment or separateness of property. Law provides an obligation of an official to explain to future spouses the difference between the aforementioned three proprietary relationships.

Divorce is actually an easier deed than marriage. As explained above, marriage can be terminated at the registrar's office or at the notary only in case there is no dispute concerning the fact of divorce. This does not comprise custody over children and marital property questions.

In order to file a divorce, spouses must personally submit a joint written application to the registrar's office or notary. In the application, the spouses express their wish to divorce and confirm that they have no disputes concerning the circumstances relating to the divorce.

An application must further contain the time and place of contraction of the marriage being dissolved, the surname after the divorce (if a spouse wishes to restore the surname which was last borne before the marriage being dissolved or the surname which was last borne before the first marriage) and, as statistical data, the number of the marriage being dissolved and the number of joint children.

In case the marriage to be divorced has not yet been entered into the Population Register, a document certifying the contraction of marriage should be appended to the application. The latter mainly concerns marriages contracted abroad, since all Estonian marriages are in the Population Register.

Differently from marriage applications, an application for divorce can be submitted by only one of the spouses being present before the official. However, this is allowed only in case the other spouse cannot appear with a good reason and the spouse present brings along a separate notarised application of the absent spouse. Even though in general an official can grant a divorce in the presence of both spouses, there is in fact a possibility that only one of the spouses comes to the office on the day of divorce. Nonetheless, the divorce may be granted without the presence of one spouse only if the other spouse cannot appear with good reason

[30] The choice of surname is regulated by the Estonian Name Law Act (RT 2005, 1, 1).

[31] In general not earlier than 1 month and not later than 3 months from the application. There can be an exception with good reason for shortening or extending the term.

and the consent of the spouse to the divorce without the presence of the spouse which is notarised or certified by a consular officer is submitted.

Furthermore, divorce has a special reconsideration term—a divorce will not be granted earlier than 1 month and later than 3 months from the date of submission of the application. If the spouses cannot appear at the vital statistics office on the determined date with good reason, they shall notify the vital statistics office thereof and the vital statistics office shall determine a new date for divorce. But if the spouses fail to appear at the vital statistics office on the determined date to get a divorce without giving a reason for the failure to appear, they shall be deemed not to have submitted the application for divorce.

Procedure itself consists of presenting a pre-completed form of divorce entry to the divorcing spouses for signing, and after their signature, the official will immediately register a divorce in the Population Register.

For registration of the divorce, the following data will be entered in the Population Register: the personal name, personal identification code and residence of both spouses; the pre-marital surname if a spouse wishes to restore the surname which was last borne before the marriage or the surname which was last borne before the first marriage; the time and place of the divorce; and the name of the office which granted the divorce.

## 3 Digital Applicability

Currently, the widespread statement is that marriage and divorce are too complicated legal procedures to provide them as an online service. Anyhow, analysing each single activity in these procedures can lead to another understanding.

Every single deed in the procedure has a special role, including presenting a lot of data in every one of them. However, why should prospective spouses give all the aforementioned data in a written form on an application? What if the data are given via the Internet with two digital signatures? In addition, some of the data are possible to transform from the Population Register to the digital application: e.g., name and identity code, date and place of birth, residence and citizenship. In this respect, there could be a partly refilled application. Should a person want to change some data, this can be done through this deed or with another separate specific action through *eesti.ee*.[32]

When additional obligations derive from the residency, these obligations can be explained by the pop-up windows with a link to send to an official a certain certificate or document. In this respect, there are two types of documents. One type is the documents proving the data enterable into the Population Register as civil status data, e.g. birth, previous marriages and their termination, residency and residence permit. Another type of documents is the ones the official needs for

[32] See www.eesti.ee.

evaluating their content, e.g. marriage impediment certificate, an application to shorten or extend the time of marriage or divorce.

For example, when an applicant needs to prove his/her marriage capacity and has to submit a marriage impediment certificate issued by another state, the content of this certificate plays a role. As family law differs from state to state, there can be cases in which certain legal facts (e.g., valid previous marriage, gender, age) are not impediments in a state issuing the marriage impediment certificate but may be regarded as impediments according to Estonian law. Is such a situation, the Estonian law will be applied. In this respect, a mere fact that there is no impediment according to the law of the state issuing the marriage impediment certificate is not sufficient. An official has to evaluate its content. The author sees no solution for leaving an official aside in the deeds in which the evaluation of the content of the document is needed.

As every person must guarantee that all his/her civil status data are in the Population Register, the obligation to enter the data can be considered separately from marriage or divorce. Anyway, all the needed data must be available from the register. To enter the data into the Population Register needs again the participation of the registrar because entering the data from certain documents, e.g. via *eesti.ee*, does not confirm the authenticity of the document. Besides, sending a document by e-mail using a certain digital solution to the official seems not to be sufficient.

This is a question of possible fraud and the first weakness in the whole digital procedure. The question "is a picture of the original enough to control the authenticity of the document?" can be raised. To support the idea of digitalisation, one can ask whether it is impossible or considerably harder to falsify a paper document. It is very well known that paper documents are falsified as well. Anyhow, in relation to the digital procedure, there are two possible solutions to avoid falsification: first, to bring the original document to the registrar before the day of marriage celebration or divorce or, second, to allow digital marriage only for those whose civil data are in a Population Register and whose residence is Estonia.[33] The first solution does not support the whole digital system; the other restricts the circle of persons who can use digital marriage. Still, such restriction is justified as long as there is no idea on how to control the picture of the document. Actually, this all could partly be solved by the digital co-operation of states. For example, a state which issued a document sends a digital confirmation with certain data to the official.[34] This takes an obligation from the Estonian official for the further evaluation of the authenticity of a document.

However, an evaluation of the content of the certificate related to the conformity of Estonian substantive law needs an activity of an official. In this regard, a formal

[33] See Vital Statistics Registration Act par 39 and 40.

[34] See Proposal of the Regulation of the European Parliament and of the Council on promoting the free movement of citizens and businesses by simplifying the acceptance of certain public documents in the European Union and amending Regulation (EU) No 1024/2012, COM(2013) 228 final 2013/0119 (COD).

and substantive recognition should be distinguished. Although there could be analysed a possibility to fulfil certain boxes in sending the document into the Population Register, e.g. "Are you married?" "What is your gender?" etc., the computer can read and select those with the problems and send them to the registrar to evaluate the content of the document providing certain legal fact.

Statistics given through the Internet is not less correct than given directly to the official. In the eyes of the author, the data submitted via the Internet can be even more accurate, considering that a person has more time to think about the questions and consequently understand them better. Likewise, a pop-up window with an explanation on the role of statistics for a state or regarding its use will serve an explanation function well. Facing the official, an applicant may not even understand the reason for asking such data; especially as statistics consist of special terms and classifications, their verbal quick reading can easier lead to misunderstandings than reading them in a written form.

The Estonian Name Law Act provides that a change of name needs an explanation about the alternatives. Though the general rules for this can be given by a text in a pop-up window, there can still be obstacles for quick procedure when prospective spouses are related to the name tradition different from Estonian. In such cases, there is a need to discuss the alternatives with an official. Includingly, in some cases a registrar or notary will need to consult a linguist or an Embassy of the specific state. Certainly, this can also be done through the mailbox in an opening window. But the problem will be that the answer can come some or many days later. Anyhow, as certain data in an application can be changed until the day of contracting the marriage, the application can be signed and changed later.[35] Besides, as shown in some cases, the communication with an official is needed; the solution by providing 24/7/365[36] access to the deed will still take some time.

When submitting an application, future spouses need to choose a date for their marriage. This is an easy digital solution, includingly, the change of the date when necessary.

Nevertheless, when spouses want to shorten or extend[37] the date of marriage, they have to add an explanation and, in most cases, a document proving a reason to change the marriage date. Estonian law does not determine the specific reasons applicable. It uses a concept of "good reason". Whether a reason is a "good reason" is decided by an official by using his/her discretion.[38] A digital solution for this can be complicated. One way out can be again involvement of an official, but this will take time, and this will be only partly digital solution. Furthermore, citizens cannot

[35] Moreover, in today's practice when an application is accomplished before an official, the future name of one spouse can be changed later but before the day of marriage.

[36] Lal and Haleem (2002), p. 101.

[37] This means that less than 1 month and later than 3 months.

[38] In Estonian practice, the shortening of the marriage date is seldom. Officials know very well their responsibility to ground the exception and understand that the shortening of the term for no reason leads to nullity of the marriage.

maybe explain sufficiently why they need to shorten or extend the date. As computers cannot read or understand[39] the meaning of the sentences, there could be choices of reasons, e.g. probable death of one prospective spouse, birth of the child before the marriage, going to war, etc. But this list must be an open list as the law leaves the reasons open and by this again raises the question how to read the reasons and proves the need for an official.

Changing the law and leaving out the possibility to shorten or extend the date of marriage would restrict the rights of an individual and will not be proportional. However, there is a possibility not to allow such marriage via the Internet.

Another point in this respect is to specify the concept of "good reason". When analysing the role it plays, it becomes evident that abolishing the 1-month waiting period can lead to the weakening of the concept of marriage as many of the "quick-emotional" marriages would probably soon be divorced. Anyway, is it the state's responsibility at all to avoid emotional decisions of its citizens? From theoretical perspective, one can doubt the need for a waiting period; it seems to be a custom instead of carrying clear legal premises. Why does the state demand people to rethink if they want to marry? Only people with active legal capacity can marry. Besides, why does the state presume in this contract that prospective spouses have not thought about the legal consequences marriage brings along? Or conversely, how many married couples have discussed the legal consequences before they get married? Furthermore, is the meaning of the waiting period to rethink about the emotional readiness to marry? Then again, can the state interfere with the emotions of an individual at all? The Estonian Family Law Act does not define "love" but only defines the "mutual proprietal obligations" and "respect" and "support" (not clear if emotional or financial). This will give rise to a question, what is marriage in the first place? The author has analysed the meaning of marriage in a changing society[40] and states that the concept of marriage in today's society is not the same we have used to know as traditional marriage. Change in the concept of marriage further determines discussions about the meaning of the waiting period in a marriage process and can lead to the understanding that it is an outdated obligation.

Even more, compared to the ordinary transaction, only some transactions have a certain right for withdrawal in transaction during a certain period of time—marriage cannot be withdrawn, only nullified on certain legal bases[41]; as a matter of fact, feeling that love has been ended is not included into those bases. Moreover, considering that marriage is not the only recognised type of family life in Estonia, then why does marriage need more protection than other relations? Actually, practicians state that only few marriages are not contracted because of the waiver

[39] Hamelink has said: "Computers cannot understand information in the form of pictures or words, but only when it is broken down into binary digits or bits: "zero" or "one", "yes" or "no", "on" or "off"" (Hamelink 1997, p. 4).

[40] See Joamets (2012, 2013).

[41] See Marriage Law Act par 9.

of one spouse to marry during the waiting period. In this respect, the legal meaning of the waiting period is truly questionable.

Divorce does not consist of too many deeds requiring the participation of an official. The law does not provide an explanation in the procedure. In principle, there can be a need to explain that in the registrar's office or at a notary's office, a divorce can be confirmed only when spouses have no disputes related to the divorce and that this dispute does not cover custody or marital property as already mentioned above and that by the divorce a spouse who took in the marriage a surname of his/her spouse does not have an obligation to relinquish it.[42] Besides, these both are explanations that could possibly be provided in a pop-up window. Differently from marriage, which requires the presence of both applicants on the day of marriage, divorce can be confirmed only by one of the spouses being present. In this respect, the author sees no legal obstacles for allowing a digital divorce.

Every digital solution raises a question regarding "cultural effects".[43] This is certainly one of the essential questions similarly related to marriage and divorce. As Estonian tradition does not have a special celebration of marriage or divorce, then there is no fear to dispute with the "civic ritual", as Oostveen describes in relation to e-voting.[44]

Besides, in digitalising the whole world we cannot forget that the Internet is only an instrument and not an end in itself. That is, first comes the deed and then its digitalisation. But it will not be correct to protest digitalisation by the reasoning that "it has always been like this"—besides, customs are changing. The reason to avoid digitalisation must be a more serious matter than a reference to the previous practice.

Aikins and Krane refer in their research to the communication between an official and a citizen. They discuss that "[c]ommunication between citizens and officials is a two-way street in which both parties send and receive messages, and, as has long been understood, the quality of communication is a function not only of the message (content) but of the mode of communication as well. Different modes of communication are characterized by differential benefits and costs to public officials, and officials will exhibit preferences for particular means of communication over others, depending on the audience and the situation."[45] When an official is replaced by a computer or when communication with an official is digital, the direct "face to face" contact is missed out. Still, as society is used to it, this can be called a "new culture of our society".

As long as marriage means a celebration, alternative digital solution can only cover the first part of the deed: fulfilling and presenting an application which will then reach the desktop of an official. After evaluating the presented data and

[42] In practice, when a spouse takes the surname of another spouse, by divorce this spouse loses a right for this surname.

[43] See, e.g., Oostveen and van den Besselaar (2007), p. 3.

[44] See Oostveen and van den Besselaar (2007), p. 3.

[45] Aikins and Krane (2010), p. 91.

documents, asking additional data and/or documents, including the documents on paper, an official prepares the data for a marriage. On the wedding day, the prospective spouses will come to the contraction of the marriage. This part of the marriage will remain unchanged compared to today's practice.

The entire process of digital marriage can take place when the data needed for contracting a marriage is in the Population Register and there is no need to present additional documents, e.g. marriage impediment certificate. After submitting an application, the future spouses log into the certain Internet site on a day they choose to marry and confirm their consent to marry by the digital signature. Pessimists will refer to the fact that ID card and passwords can be stolen. Well, of course such things can happen but additionally in every other deed we do today with e-signature as well. So this is not a profound reason to deny digital marriage.

In Estonian practice, a paper certificate proving the marriage has played an emotional role. However, despite many performances in media regarding how the solution to give up paper certificates[46] will harm and offend citizens who will not receive anything from the state on this special day, one must understand that digital solutions are paper-free solutions. Certainly, a solution would be to build in a deed an appliance to print out the document about the data of marriage, but such document cannot[47] have a legal meaning.

One is sure, digital marriage and divorce cannot replace the traditional deed of marriage and divorce as long as people need a "celebrated marriage" and lack digital skills and access to the Internet. Nevertheless, offering such a solution would be especially comfortable for divorce as divorcing people often would not like to meet each other anymore after the decision to live their lives separately. In today's practice, it is common that divorcing people ask officials about the possibility to divorce without meeting the other spouse.

In point of fact, there are, in practice, cases where prospective spouses cannot find a mutually suitable time to present an application in an office because their working times do not correspond to the opening times of the registrar's or notary's or clergyman's office. In such cases, a suitable solution would be presenting an application online.

How willing is society to adapt such a novel digital solution? When a new Family Law Act was passed in 2010, there was feedback from the citizens published in media. Many of them suggested digital marriage and believed that the percentage of marriages would grow if people could marry without leaving their homes. Unfortunately, there do not exist social analyses on the readiness of Estonian society about digital marriage and divorce, but based on a fact that digital

[46] Public sector has to use the data in the Population Register. See fn. 18.

[47] And does not have to as well because in Estonian public sector, the data of this marriage are taken from the Population Register; using a document abroad needs a special confirmation anyway, and according to the state a document should be presented; the form of the document differs based on several international agreements regulating the recognition of family event documents.

solution will not replace but support current deed, then this could bring a lot of gain to the society.

# 4 Conclusion

Kim has stated that "Participation in the 21st century revolution requires much more than the application of technology—it requires new ways of thinking and acting. In the future, we may be talking about 'u-governance' (network free, device free, time free and relationship free) since various countries are drawing up a future strategy for ubiquitous government beyond e-government. A ubiquitous society enables all national resources to be intellectualized and networked and provides daily services to citizens anywhere and anytime. No matter what it is called, in the future, businesses and government will adopt the ubiquitous paradigm. As such, online services and computerization will be more closely intertwined into the daily lives of people."[48] Estonia is a state which promotes all kinds of digital solutions. In most cases society accepts them.

In principle, it would be possible to work out a digital solution for marriage and divorce as well. Furthermore, based on the analysis of the article, there can be two possible solutions. First, all the data needed in a procedure of marriage or divorce should be available in the Population Register. This will mainly cover Estonian residents with active legal capacity with no relation to the name tradition of another state; second, there is a need for a partly digital solution in which an official is involved, entering the data of foreign documents into the register and confirming a right to use a special surname derived from the name tradition of another state. The main obstacle for digital marriage and divorce is entering the data of foreign documents presented in the process as there does not exist a good solution to evaluate the validity of the document by merely looking at the picture. The waiting period between the application and marriage or divorce does not serve the purpose for which it has been provided and can be an outdated measure in this process.

Statements that digital marriage promotes people to marry are doubtful; the author believes that digital marriage will not guarantee this. Additionally, this solution does not solve the so-called social problem—more and more children are born outside marriage. Those people who have decided not to marry and live in cohabitation will not marry even when the procedure is made more comfortable. But for those who do want to marry, the digital solution could facilitate the procedure.

In relation to divorce, the author believes that the divorce rate will rise. But this cannot be seen as an "enemy" to Estonian family life, and vice versa, it is welcomed that people put in order their relations in legal meaning and, by this, avoid future problems related to their property.

[48] Kim (2005), p. 105.

At any event, digital marriage and divorce need support. There are not-so-serious legal obstacles in these deeds to exclude this solution, especially related to divorce. Furthermore, this solution will make the deed more flexible and will promote correctly registered family relations.

# References

## *Books and articles*

Aikins SK, Krane D (2010) Are public officials obstacles to citizen-centered E-government? An examination of municipal administrators' motivations and actions. State Local Gov Rev 42 (2):87–103

Antokolskaia MV (2003) Developments of family law in Western and Eastern Europe: common origins, common driving forces, common tendencies. J Fam Hist 28:52–69

Bradley D (2003) Comparative law, family law and common law. Oxf J Leg Stud 23(1):127–146

Coe A, Paquet G, Roy J (2001) E-governance and smart communities. A social learning challenge. Soc Sci Comput Rev 19(1):80–93

D'Angelo A (2014) Re-thinking family law: a new legal paradigm for stepfamilies? In: Boele-Woelki K, Detloff N, Gephart W (eds) Family law and culture in Europe. Developments, challenges and opportunities. Intersentia, pp 217–227

Detloff N (2003) Arguments for the unification and harmonisation of family law in Europe. In: Boele-Woelki K (ed) Perspectives for the unification and harmonisation of family law in Europe. Intersentia, Antwerp-Oxford-New York, pp 37–64

Garrison M, Scott ES (2012) Legal regulation of twenty-first-century families. In: Garrison M, Scott ES (eds) Marriage at the crossroads. Law, policy, and the brave new world of twenty-first-century families. Cambridge University Press, Cambridge, pp 303–326

Gurtin GG (2010) Free the data!: E-governance for megaregions. Public Works Manage Policy 14 (3):307–326

Hamelink CJ (1997) New information-communication technologies, social development and cultural change, UNRISD Discussion Paper No. 86

Joamets K (2012) Marriage capacity, social values and law-making process. Int Comp Law Rev 12:97–115. Palackŷ University

Joamets K (2013) Gender as an impediment of marriage, free movement of citizens, and EU charter of fundamental rights. In: Kerikmäe T (ed) Protecting human rights in the EU. Controversies and challenges of the charter of fundamental rights. Springer, pp 91–106

Joamets K (2014) Civil status registration – more than data collection: EU digital development in promoting the free movement of civil status document. In: Kerikmäe T (ed) Regulating eTechnologies in the European Union. Normative realities and trends. Springer, Cham-Heidelberg-New York-Dordrecht-London, pp 141–156

Kim PS (2005) Introduction: challenges and opportunities for democracy, administration and law. Int Rev Adm Sci 71(1):99–108

Lal R, Haleem A (2002) E-governance: an emerging paradigm. J Bus Perspect 99–109

Lifshitz S (2012) The pluralistic vision of marriage. In: Garrison M, Scott ES (eds) Marriage at the crossroads. Law, policy, and the brave new world of twenty-first-century families. Cambridge University Press, Cambridge, pp 260–286

Macedo S (1998) Sexuality and liberty: making room for nature and tradition? In: Estlund DM, Nussbaum C (eds) Sex, preference and family: essays on law and nature. Oxford University Press, New York, 86-10

Mason MA, Fine MA, Carnochan S (2001) Family law in the new millennium: for whose families? J Fam Issues 22(859):859–888
Needham C (2014) The difficult relationship between family law and families. North East Law Rev 2:37–44
Oostveen AM, van den Besselaar P (2007) Non-technical risks of remote electronic voting. Idea Group Inc., Amsterdam
Peters M (2013) The democratic function of the public sphere in Europe. German Law J 14 (5):673–694
Sörgjerd C (2012) The European Union's Council of Europe's and human rights' perspectives on changing cohabitation models. Reconstructuring marriage. The legal status of relationships in a changing society. Intersentia, Cambridge, Antwerp, Portland, pp 275–311
Stark B (2013) International law from the bottom up: fragmentation and transformation. Univ Pa J Int Law 34(4):687–742
Willekens H (2003) Is contemporary western family law historically unique? J Fam Hist 28 (70):70–107

## *List of other documents*

Proposal of the Regulation of the European Parliament and of the Council on promoting the free movement of citizens and businesses by simplifying the acceptance of certain public documents in the European Union and amending Regulation (EU) No 1024/2012, COM(2013) 228 final 2013/0119 (COD).
European Commission. Green Paper to Promote Free Movement of Public Documents and Recognition of the Effects of Civil Status Records. COM(2010) 747 final, 14. December 2010.
United Nations E-Government Survey 2014, E-Government for the Future We Want. New York: United Nations. 2014, Bridging a digital divide (Chapter 6).
Digital Agenda Scoreboard. Available at: http://ec.europa.eu/digital-agenda/en/digital-economy-and-society-index-desi (25.02.2015).
Estonian Information Society Policy 2013.

## *Legal acts*

Estonian Name Law Act RT 2005, 1, 1.
Estonian Consular Act RT I 2008, 29,175. 30.10.2013.
Estonian Population Register Act RT I 2000, 50, 317. 18.06.2014.
Estonian International Private Law Act RT I 2002, 35, 2017.
Estonian Family Law RT I 2009, 60, 395. 29.06.2014, 104.
Estonian Vital Statistics Registration Act RT I 2009, 30, 177. 29.06.2014, 6.

# Challenges in Collecting Digital Evidence: A Legal Perspective

**Agnes Kasper and Eneli Laurits**

**Abstract** Collection of digital evidence is relevant in the majority legal proceedings in some way. In criminal proceedings, the public authorities have powerful legal measures at their disposal that allow collection of evidence, but often these measures are not specifically designed to deal with digital evidence. Besides the problem of suitability of traditional evidence rules, law enforcement also has to deal with higher legal standards and often work together with the private sector. Moreover, the practical use of existing special powers addressing digital evidence (like the ones set forth in the CoE Cybercrime Convention) still needs a lot of encouragement. On the other hand, collection of digital evidence in a civil law suit follows different principles; parties have less control over the process but have more flexibility, and following the "meet and confer" principle can establish better tailored rules for their case. However, failure to properly manage preservation and collection of digital evidence may lead to unfavourable outcomes in legal proceedings and end up in getting fines or disruption of business functions and processes. This article discusses issues relating to collection of digital evidence in criminal proceedings, civil cases, arbitration and other legal purposes in order to identify areas where private sector actions can inform law enforcement efforts and vice versa while outlining a model for legal requirements of digital forensic readiness.

## 1 Introduction

In our information societies we use less and less information that is not digital. Virtually, all aspects of life are manifested in a digital form in one way or another; therefore, it is not surprising that digital evidence is the dominant form of evidence in legal proceedings as well. Digital evidence may have relevance in criminal, civil

A. Kasper (✉)
Tallinn Law School, Tallinn University of Technology, Akadeemia tee 3, 12618 Tallinn, Estonia
e-mail: agnes.kasper@mail.ee

E. Laurits
Criminal Policy Department, Ministry of Justice, Tõnismägi 5a, 15191 Tallinn, Estonia
e-mail: eneli.laurits@just.ee



T. Kerikmäe, A. Rull (eds.), *The Future of Law and eTechnologies*,
DOI 10.1007/978-3-319-26896-5_10

and out-of-court dispute resolutions, as well as in administrative processes and in negotiations. Moreover, digital evidence may be used for investigating security breaches and for the purposes of enhancing information security by deterrence or other non-judicial ends. Despite the clear need for rules on transborder dealing with digital evidence, it appears that in reality the existing legal frameworks are often inflexible or ineffective to address several aspects of digital evidence.

Incompetent or improper management of digital information and potential evidence may have a serious impact on the performance of organisations' functions and processes. Organisations, including law enforcement agencies, courts and enterprises, may severely be hampered in the performance of their functions and processes if they do not possess capabilities to deal with digital evidence. This problem has been addressed in organisational studies from a proactive perspective suggesting that organisations should implement "digital forensic readiness"—that is, they should have comprehensive plans for dealing with digital evidence. Rowlingson defined digital forensic readiness "as the ability of an organization to maximize it's potential to use digital evidence whilst minimising the costs of investigation",[1] which in essence is a resource optimisation exercise. Pooe and Labuschagne's general conceptual model identified four main factors that impact digital forensic readiness of organisations: people, processes, technology and policy.[2] Policy factor included legal requirements—without elaborating on its content.

People, processes and technology aspects have been widely discussed and addressed both in practice and academic literature. However, legal issues are addressed at best in a very superficial manner in international or transnational context due to the diversity and complexity of regulation applicable to it. This article discusses issues relating to collection of digital evidence in criminal proceedings, civil cases, arbitration and other legal purposes in order to identify areas where private sector actions can inform law enforcement efforts and vice versa while outlining a general model for legal requirements of digital forensic readiness.

## 2 What Is Digital Evidence and What Is the Problem with it?

Potential sources of digital evidence can include financial and business records, e-mails, individual smartphones and computers, access control logs, configuration event information, intrusion detection logs, anti-virus logs, Internet activity logs, backup media or even remnants of deleted files, etc.

[1] See Rowlingson (2004), p. 5.

[2] People category included CIRT (computer incident response team) formation and skills management, security awareness; process category contains incident response plans and investigation methodology; technology category covers proactive and reactive tools, security-/forensic-oriented network design; policy category incorporates both organisational and legal requirements.

Most types of crime now also involve computers in one way or the other, either in that computer data and systems are the target of the offence or in that the offence is committed through computers or in that electronic evidence on a computer may be important in relation to an offence that otherwise is un-related to computer systems.[3] Any offence may involve important evidence located on a computer (including mobile devices), even if this offence is otherwise un-related to computer systems. While this is not cybercrime, the criminal justice system nevertheless needs to be able to recognise and handle electronic evidence.[4] Therefore, in a family violence case important evidence can be an e-mail or deleted photograph recorded on the suspect's device. However, in those criminal cases, when we can talk about a digital crime scene, so crimes where the prohibited conduct takes place mainly in the virtual world, it is clear that more attention must be paid to the improvement of investigators' skills.

While technological development increases economic efficiency and convenience on the one hand, it carries risks to rule of law and human rights on the other. Such risks have been identified—among others—by the Council of Europe, which has long ago recognised that "while the threat and complexity of cybercrime and challenges related to electronic evidence are increasing, the authority of criminal justice institutions to investigate and prosecute cybercrime and to obtain and share electronic evidence appears to be diminishing".[5]

Digital investigations involve transborder elements more than ever, and the global reach of social media networks pose some serious challenges to the traditional, territorially based approaches to evidence, because the Internet is created by everyone and things of everyone—everywhere. Furthermore, the volume of data that is produced and consumed by an exponentially increasing speed may render a number of legal principles practically counterproductive.[6]

Serious international efforts are under way to establish standards that can assist both law enforcement and businesses but also can serve as guidelines for judges or policymakers to find reliable methods and good practices.[7] In order to narrow the very broad scope of this topic, the authors decided to focus on what they believe is one of the most critical moments in the management of digital evidence: collection. Identification and appropriate collection of digital evidence is key to legal disputes; however, the diversity in procedural and privacy approaches among different jurisdictions is a minefield for regulatory compliance, cross-border dispute resolution or criminal investigations. Academic research dwells into the details of one or

---

[3] See CyberCrime@IPA (2011), p. 10.

[4] Ibid., p. 4.

[5] A restatement of the problem can be found in the Cybercrime Convention Committee's report. 12th Plenary Meeting Report, 2–3 December 2014, Strasbourg, nr T-CY(2014)22.

[6] "Data on the internet more than doubles every two years"—See Turner et al. (2014), p. 2.

[7] ISO/IEC 27037, ISO/IEC 27041 (draft), ISO/IEC 27042 (draft), ISI/IEC 27043 (draft), ISO 27050 (draft).

another but rarely approaches the process relating to digital evidence from a cross-cutting perspective.

Although there are number of problems in criminal proceedings that connect to digital evidence collecting, within the frames of this article, the analysis from law enforcement perspective would concentrate on a quite common situation in a search and seizure. As a rule, search and seizure is inevitable for collecting digital evidence. The discussion from civil law and private dispute resolution perspective will focus on a variety of practices in different legal traditions and the obstacles that arise from such diversity. The aim is to identify the common traits of legal requirements for collection of digital evidence in all legal contexts and consider issues for improvement.

Despite the lack of harmonisation in legal matters governing the collection of digital evidence across borders, it is conceivable to establish a general model of legal requirements of digital forensic readiness.

## 3 Methodology

The present chapter is partially based on professional experience and the challenges identified in practice by the authors, especially the parts related to criminal offences. The practical perspectives are integrated with systematic literature analysis that was conducted to identify the main scientific contributions and legal problem areas relating to collecting digital evidence. Based on the findings and overview of each area, a practical framework is proposed to address the most common issues in collecting digital evidence and the systemic approach is used to draw up a model for the planning and assessment of digital forensic readiness in organisations from legal perspective.

In literature review process, the EBSCO academic and business collections were searched, on 9 May 2015. The search used the keyword "digital evidence" OR "electronic evidence", applying filters of full text, peer-reviewed journal items since 2000, and produced in 296 unique results. The titles and abstracts of the 296 items were reviewed and categorised according to six main focus areas. Duplicates, book reviews, articles where the electronic evidence is a tool and not the focus of discussion were excluded. Articles from each category were selected for detailed analysis according to their quality and relevance to the collection phase of digital evidence. The authors of this chapter also added to the analysis a number of policy documents, legislation, guidance material, project reports from international organisations and local judicial authorities based on their own experience and knowledge of the field.

# 4 Focus Areas Related to Digital Evidence

In this chapter, what follows is the review of literature and guidance material relevant to dealing with electronic evidence both in criminal context and in the context of private dispute settlement and investigations both in court and outside courts. This category-by-category overview is augmented by personal experience and expertise. These categories also reveal the major legal problem areas in handling complex cross-border issues.

## *4.1 Universal Legal Principles*

The first category covers articles attempting to explain overarching problems of digital evidence without having specific regard to location and jurisdictions. The general approach is to discuss the general principles of trust, authenticity reliability,[8] proportionality and reasonableness[9] and to provide analysis of principles and methodologies applicable in all tactical, operational and strategic levels.

### 4.1.1 Nature of Digital Evidence: Trustworthiness and Credibility

Majority of authors focus on just a handful of basic principles relating to the very nature of digital evidence. Although some of the qualities (and terminologies used) by different authors may have somewhat different contents depending on the field, they tend to refer to credibility and trustworthiness of records each time. Special attention is paid to social media evidence authentication.[10]

The simple fact that technology separated data from the media on which it is stored has a great consequence. This means that digital data depends on and can be easily altered by the system in which it is stored, while a paper record exists without its management system and its integrity is not affected by that.[11] The evidence that is recorded by an analogue device is capable of being manipulated, but it takes great skill to alter the negative of a photographic film, but alternations can be detected. However, in comparison, digital images can be altered with ease.[12] Stephen Mason has argued: "The essential point about digital evidence, which is not readily understood by many judges and lawyers, is the complexity of the topic and the nature of the characteristics of digital evidence". By failing to have even a basic knowledge of the subject, lawyers and digital evidence specialists responsible for

[8] See Grimm et al. (2012); McDonald (2014), pp. 40–50; Hannon (2014), pp. 314–323.

[9] See Bennett (2013), p. 433. Seventh Circuit Electronic Discovery Pilot Program report (2010).

[10] See Democko (2012); Grimm et al. (2012).

[11] See Chasse (2012), p. 18.

[12] See Mason (2008a, b), p. xxxv.

investigating a case and deciding whether to initiate criminal action against an individual are in danger of committing grave errors.[13]

These intrinsic qualities of digital data make it difficult to establish trust as the basis for recognition of legal value of computer records in any context, criminal, commercial or private. Duranti and Rogers explain the shift in establishing trust relationships on the Internet and in assessing the trustworthiness of documentary evidence and draw up a conceptual framework of trust for digital forensic and archival data. Trustworthiness therefore encompasses qualities of reliability, accuracy and authenticity (sub-qualities of which are identity and integrity), but distinction must be made between human-generated computer records, computer-generated records and the combination of these.

Mason discusses the issues of reliability and quality of digital evidence and states that the nature of it is often misunderstood. There is a tendency that evidence put forward by a bank or insurer is believed without challenge as opposed to evidence put forward by an individual claimant, which points to the inequality of parties. Technology can be easily bypassed, and it can be difficult to obtain proof (of, for example, signs of unauthorised entry)[14]; nevertheless, the systems integrity that produced the particular evidence often remains unquestioned. There is a similar problem with presumptions of reliability of digital systems. Reliability can be verified by analysing the source code—which is often a trade secret and therefore inaccessible—which makes the presumption of reliability effectively irrebuttable.[15] This results in the absurd situation where the laws are dictating what the nature of electronic records are, although the nature of electronic records should be reflected in the rules.

The trustworthiness and credibility aspects play a major role in admissibility of digital evidence in legal proceedings. Components of admissibility in common law countries include aspects of authenticity, best evidence and hearsay,[16] some of which have no equivalent civil law traditions. Several authors have emphasised the problems that the inconsistent understanding of the nature of digital materials poses to the application of the admissibility principles.[17] One of the main concerns is about the originality requirement (best evidence rule is interpreted as a general requirement for the original), which is practically rendered meaningless in case of digital records[18] and can be replaced by the "functional equivalence" principle.[19]

Although certainly pertaining to the admissibility assessment, requirements of relevance and legality are seldom discussed in general context. Illegally obtained

---

[13] Ibid.

[14] See Mason (2012), p. 199.

[15] See Mason (2012), p. 200.

[16] See Goode (2009), pp. 1–64; Duranti and Rogers (2012), pp. 522–531.

[17] See Duranti and Rogers (2012), pp. 522–531; Mason (2008a, b), pp. 48–54; Atkinson (2014), p. 245; Alba (2014), pp. 384–421; O'Toole (2008), pp. 3–17.

[18] See Mason (2008a, b), p. 1.

[19] See Alba (2014), p. 392.

evidence may be automatically excluded in one jurisdiction while may be admitted in another. However, relevance of evidence, along with questions on proportionality of the e-discovery, was in the focus of a US landmark case, where judge Peck acknowledged the importance of technology-assisted relevance determination and ordered the use of a technique called "predictive coding" in the *Da Silva Moore, et al. vs Publicis Group* case.[20]

While techniques of digital forensics aid in preserving and locating potential evidence from a crime scene or elsewhere, the extent to which this may be trusted and used as evidence in a particular legal argument still needs to be determined. We suggest that validation of digital evidence, a difficult task for the investigator, poses an even greater challenge to legal practitioners when constructing legal arguments. Legal practitioners may be unaware of the full nature and significance of digital evidence that is more technically complex compared to conventional forms of evidence.

### 4.1.2 Processing of Digital Evidence: Proportionality and Reasonableness

Principles of proportionality, cooperation and reasonableness form a distinct group that relates to management and processing of digital evidence. Performance of such activities and processes seem to depend on the external circumstances of digital evidence rather than its intrinsic nature. Both proportionality and reasonableness[21] principles have been addressed mostly in the context of pre-trial discovery and e-disclosure in common law traditions, and authors stressed the requirement of cooperation and possible agreement (meet-and-confer principle) in this respect.[22] The determining factors have been the relations between the resource intensity of production and nature and value of claims, complexity of case, conduct of the party.[23] Resource intensity in most cases depends on the technologies necessary for producing data, which in turn depends on type, format and medium of data storage, but to certain extent on the volume of data as well.[24]

[20] Da Silva Moore v. Publicis Groupe et al, No. 1:2011cv01279 – Document 175 (S.D.N.Y 2012).

[21] On the issue of reasonable search, see, for example, Digicel (St. Lucia) Ltd & Ors v Cable & Wireless Plc & Ors [2008] EWHC 2522 (Ch) (23 October 2008) [2008] EWHC 2522 (Ch), [2009] 2 All ER 1094; Zubulake v. UBS Warburg LLC, 217 F.R.D. 309, 2003 U.S. Dist. LEXIS 7939 (S.D.N.Y. 2003) ("Zubulake I"); Al-Sweady & Ors, R (on the application of) v Secretary of State for the Defence [2009] EWHC 2387 (Admin) (02 October 2009) [2010] UKHRR 300, [2010] HRLR 2, [2009] EWHC 2387 (Admin).

[22] See Bennett (2013), pp. 433–464.

[23] US Federal Rules of Civil Procedure; General Provisions Governing Discovery – Rule 26. See also Notes of Advisory Committee on Rules – 1983 Amendment; UK Civil Procedure Rules 44(3)5.

[24] Rowe Entertainment, Inc. v. The William Morris Agency, Inc. 205 F.R.D. 421 (S.D.N.Y. 2002).

For questions of proportionality in e-discovery, the Sedona Conference's work in this regard deserves special mentioning as it provides a "discusses the origins of the doctrine of proportionality, provides examples of its application, and proposes principles to guide courts, attorneys, and parties".[25] Establishing general principles governing e-discovery was the apparent objective of the Seventh Circuit Electronic Discovery Pilot Programme, which has provided significant guidance to practitioners and addresses cooperation[26] and proportionality[27] in the first and the second place, respectively.[28]

## 4.2 General Procedural Diversity

One of the broadest approaches that can be identified deals with the context where digital evidence is used. Obvious differences exist between evidence rules in criminal and civil legal proceedings. Besides this, authors emphasise the lack of harmonisation in rules of evidence and procedural diversity between jurisdictions, and the main theme is the lack of interoperability between systems, such as arbitration and court procedures or common law e-discovery and civil law jurisdictions. These authors also provide comparative analysis, and typically some tactical advice on how to cope with problems arising from the general procedural diversity.[29]

### 4.2.1 Criminal Proceedings

In criminal proceedings, the burden of proof is on the state, and on many occasions the investigative organs find themselves in a situation where it is necessary to collect evidence from another state. It is necessary to combat, on the one hand, with international crime in the traditional sense where criminals act on different physical

---

[25] See The Sedona Conference (2010), p. 292.

[26] Principle 1.02 (Cooperation)
An attorney's zealous representation of a client is not compromised by conducting discovery in a cooperative manner. The failure of counsel or the parties to litigation to cooperate in facilitating and reasonably limiting discovery requests and responses raises litigation costs and contributes to the risk of sanctions.

[27] Principle 1.03 (Discovery Proportionality)
The proportionality standard set forth in Fed. R. Civ. P. 26(b)(2)(C) should be applied in each case when formulating a discovery plan. To further the application of the proportionality standard in discovery, requests for production of ESI and related responses should be reasonably targeted, clear, and as specific as practicable.

[28] Seventh Circuit Electronic Discovery Pilot Program, Interim Report of Phase Three May 2012–May 2013, www.discoverypilot.com. Accessed 25.05.2015.

[29] Dodson and Klebba (2011); Bolt and Wheatley (2006).

grounds and, on the other hand, with such international crime that is committed with info technology. In the majority of cases, there is a need to collect digital evidence. The questions that raise are as follows: are these evidence accepted in another jurisdiction; are there any common rules for collecting digital evidence; how can we ensure admissibility of collected digital evidence in any court?

Already in 2005, Orin S. Kerr stressed the need for special regulation over the collection of digital evidence: "Digital evidence is collected in different ways than eyewitness testimony or physical evidence. The new ways of collecting evidence are so different than the rules developed for the old investigations often no longer make sense for the new."[30] Moreover, continuously many authors have stressed the need for "new regulations". "The Internet has removed the geographical dimension in terms of the borders of sovereign nations, and correspondingly, criminals have become much more difficult to identify and apprehend. With the rapid advancements in computer technology over the past few years, there has been increasing concern of the need to develop laws in order to take full advantage of technological improvements, and also to ensure that states can respond to computer crime and related criminal law issues."[31]

The onus is on the prosecution to show to the court that the evidence produced is no more and no less now than when it was first taken into the possession of law enforcement.[32] Moreover, developing legal arguments can be frustrated if unskilled use is made of the digital evidence, with unanticipated and often detrimental outcomes. For example, when presenting a legal case based on what appears to be convincing digital evidence, the case can collapse if the defence can show that the security integrity of the network is defective and shows contamination or alteration of the digital evidence it is supposed to protect. Consequently, if the validity of the evidence can be established, its weight in legal argument is enhanced; however, if its validity is uncertain or invalidated, then weight of the evidence is diminished or negated.

Another problem arises in cases of live acquisition, where it is impossible to compare the original with the copy since there is no original anymore. Incident-handling teams should have robust forensic capabilities. More than one team member should be able to perform each typical forensic activity. Hands-on exercises and IT and forensic training courses can be helpful in building and maintaining skills, as can demonstrations of new tools and technologies.[33]

---

[30] See Kerr (2005a, b), p. 280.

[31] See Lazetik and Koshevaliska (2014), p. 63.

[32] Good Practice Guide for Computer-Based Electronic Evidence, Association of Chief Police Officers, (ACPO), UK, p. 7. Available at http://www.cps.gov.uk/legal/assets/uploads/files/ACPO_guidelines_computer_evidence[1].pdf. Accessed 30.05.2015.

[33] See Kent et al. (2006), p. 22.

### 4.2.2 Private Disputes

Since the use of information and communication technologies has penetrated into most fields of life, it is perhaps not surprising that digital evidence can be relevant for virtually all types of civil or administrative disputes, from divorce cases through financial law, taxation law to construction laws. It is now common to use email exchange to support a fact put forth by a party in litigation; however, there appears to be more dispute over digital evidence in some fields than in others. In the US, the common scenario that triggers the use of forensic experts and detailed disputes about digital evidence appears to be misuses of valuable business information of a corporation by a privileged employee. As to European court cases, it can be noted that case studies discussed in academic literature often report questions on digital evidence in the contexts of intellectual-property-related cases and monetary damages in bank card misuse cases.

One can speculate about the reasons of having landmark cases and complex discussions related to digital evidence in the above types of disputes more than in others. The authors believe that the actual availability and relative ease of collection play a great role in that intellectual-property- and business-secret-related disputes heavily rely on digital evidence.

### 4.2.3 Common Law vs Civil Law Systems

Collection of electronic evidence has two main dimensions in civil court litigation: producing evidence in one party's control and securing access to evidence in the other or third party's control. These issues have traditionally been approached very differently by common law and civil law jurisdictions. The sharp contrast between the two legal traditions arise from their historical respect (or lack thereof) for the *nemo tenetur edere instrumenta contra se* principle—that is the principle that no one is bound to produce documents against himself. This concept still has a significant impact on the parties' access to information and evidence, and although it has been gradually abandoned in the interest of justice and fairness of proceedings, civil law courts still take a restrictive approach compared to the permissive US practice.[34]

Common law countries allow active involvement for the litigants in the process and have adversarial systems in place, where collection of evidence takes place through discovery (or disclosure in the UK) procedures, and a party to litigation may directly approach and engage the other party for requesting preservation and production of documents. In civil code countries, the state, through a judge, intermediates and balances between the competing interests of the participants, and parties *offer* evidence to support their case[35] and can get access to evidence that

[34] See Trocker (2014), pp. 12–14.

[35] WP29, Opinion No. 158, p. 4.

they do not possess in restricted and supervised disclosure processes[36] and/or upon requesting the court to collect it for them from other parties.[37] However, it is not only the procedures that differ, but the extent to which common law discovery rules allow seek control and insight into a party's information assets in civil proceedings can turn out as "fishing expeditions"[38] compared to the restrictive approach of civil code jurisdictions, where the burden is on the proponents of evidence to know about the existence thereof and identify it.[39]

The actual problems in cross-border litigations are various and range from jurisdictional questions, through data privacy to state sovereignty.[40] Tensions also arise from the conflicting common law (mainly US) disclosure obligations and data protection regulations in the EU[41] and from the differing notions of privacy,[42] which are discussed separately.

### 4.2.4 Arbitration

Many cross-border business disputes are now seen in arbitral tribunals rather than in courts. International arbitration has been used to resolve an increasing number of intellectual property and technology disputes, and one of the factors in determining choice about governing law and the seat of arbitration can reflect consideration about the locale's readiness and ability to conduct proceedings involving e-discovery (or lack thereof).[43]

Arbitration allows more flexibility and intervention into the process by the parties, unlike litigation at courts.[44] Although the many different views on e-discovery and collection of electronic evidence in arbitration range from "non-issue" to "equally burdensome as in litigation", the main lesson drawn from the overview of practice is that early consideration by the parties is essential.[45]

[36] See, for example, the Spanish and French civil procedures.

[37] See German or Estonian laws on civil procedure.

[38] The term "fishing expedition" denotes the broad scope of US discovery rules that also allow discovery of information that has no direct relevance to the case but could lead to discovery of relevant information.

[39] WP29. Opinion No. 158, pp. 4–5.

[40] See The Sedona Conference (2008).

[41] WP29, Opinion nr 158, p. 3.

[42] See The Sedona Conference (2008), p. 8.

[43] See Nobles (2012), pp. 78–80.

[44] Great example for such flexibility is reflected in the discussion cases relating to the admissibility of Wikileaks cables in international arbitration. There a number of cases where the arbitral tribunal is not setting aside such evidence, but there are only few occasions where this question was expressly addressed. For more, see Ireton (2015), pp. 231–242.

[45] See Howell (2009), pp. 156–162.

Arbitral tribunals can be assisted by national courts in taking evidence.[46] The question whether discovery is covered was also addressed by courts. The English court decided that the Model Law deals with the taking of evidence and not the disclosure process, thereby making clear distinction between evidence in hearing and outside hearing,[47] while a Canadian appellate court found that Article 27 was broad enough to include pre-trial discovery.[48] This difference, however, may be accounted for since the differences between the definitions of evidence in these jurisdictions are not insignificant because they could result in a completely different scope, costs, burden and technique for electronic evidence collection, depending on the jurisdiction again. This leads to the conclusion that early consideration of collection of evidence (or, in other words, the "meet and confer" principle) is a crucial element of international arbitration.[49]

### 4.2.5 Internal Investigations

As the other side of the coin in collection of evidence, it may be located internally to the organisation. There could be a series of reasons for producing evidence from one's own system; the UK's Director's and Corporate Advisor's Guide to Digital Investigations and Evidence names just a few of them, such as disputed transactions, showing compliance with legal and regulatory requirements, support of insurance claim, investigation of suspected fraud, employee problems, complaints of negligence, "smaller" cyber attacks or theft of data.[50] Another author refers to situations when the legal conduct of a company is brought into question that can trigger an investigation by regulatory authorities or be a prelude to litigation.[51]

The common thing in these situations is that digital evidence is practically available (or at least should be); however, it still has to be identified, collected, filtered and analysed before use. Apart from specific cases, where there are special legal considerations not to collect data from own systems (obstacles could arise from privacy, employment law, blocking statutes, limits from surveillance, etc.), for

[46] Article 27 of UNCITRAL Model Law on International Commercial Arbitration states that "[t]he arbitral tribunal or a party with the approval of the arbitral tribunal may request from a competent court of this State assistance in taking evidence. The court may execute the request within its competence and according to its rules on taking evidence."

[47] BNP Paribas and others v. Deloitte and Touche LLP, Commercial Court, England, 28 November 2003, [2003] EWHC 2874 (Comm).

[48] Jardine Lloyd Thompson Canada Inc. v. SJO Catlin, Alberta Court of Appeal, Canada, 18 January 2006, [2006] ABCA 18 (CanLII), available on the Internet at http://canlii.ca/t/1mch7. Accessed 22 May 2015.

[49] In arbitration, it is typically possible for the parties to agree on their own procedural rules, which is different from the default rules of the arbitral tribunal, as well as it is possible to agree in relevant procedures already in the commercial contract that precedes the dispute.

[50] See Sommers (2008), p. 9.

[51] See Attfield and Blandford (2011), p. 39.

the discussion it is presumed that accessing and collecting data do not need intervention by an external authority.

Still one of the most significant practical problems for lawyers is how to filter relevant data from raw data, how to structure it in a way that would enable sensemaking and be presentable in case it is needed in litigation or other proceedings. This question should not be underestimated considering that, firstly, large amount of unstructured raw data cannot satisfy the admissibility requirements in courts; secondly, initial investigations may end up with collections consisting of millions of documents.[52] All authors emphasise the utmost importance of some level of planning, but it is clear that in the absence of appropriate organisational measures much potential evidence will never be collected and/or will become worthless as a result of contamination.[53]

In an article, Attfield and Blandford compare the model of intelligence analysis with the model of sensemaking in legal investigation, where the first model assumes external sources of data and in the latter the sources were internal. This resulted in the internal processes having a separate step to build an initial database that was searched and filtered subsequently, whereas in the intelligence analysis model the collection phase and decision about what to recover was in each case coupled with "issue focusing" (something like investigating a thread).[54] In other words in legal investigations, such as answering to e-discovery request or preparing for litigation, there is an initial step to "collect all we have" from potential sources of evidence, while the intelligence analysis model lacks this step or more precisely is built into the subsequent phases.

The manner of collection will likely have an impact on the reliability, and thus the admissibility, of the evidence; therefore, the decision about how evidence will be acquired, physically and practically, needs to be an informed one. The UK guidance on digital investigations recommends to "produce a written policy for evidence collection and preservation, plus a series of specific guides to cover particular resources".[55] Authors writing about corporate legal investigations emphasise that the retention policy of organisation is important in the process of e-discovery, and this policy may differ in cases of injuries, dismissals and incidents involving management.[56]

It is concluded by Martinez that there is a need for a vision of legal informatics, not only from criminal viewpoint of digital evidence, but one that addresses the appropriate challenges of enterprises regarding their business, corporate and third party relations and is capable of establishing the elements of electronic documents that support them and assist in preparing for an eventual legal process where the electronically stored information is a factor for succeeding or failing.[57]

---

[52] Ibid, p. 45.

[53] See Sommers (2008).

[54] See Attfield and Blandford (2011), p. 49.

[55] See Sommers (2008), p. 31.

[56] See Cano Martínez (2012), p. 4.

[57] Ibid, pp. 12–13.

## *4.3 Specific Evidence Regulations: Common Elements, Unique Features, Good Practices*

A more focused approach deals with the specific features, differences of regulation in different jurisdictions and the incompatibilities between legal systems' evidence regulation, when it comes to collection of digital evidence, especially e-discovery. Authors address regulatory compliance risks and discuss "comity" in the context of blocking statutes (privacy and labour laws, state sovereignty objections)[58] and sometimes deliver targeted tactical advice on how to cope with arising problems discussing cases and hands-on legal issues.

### 4.3.1 Criminal Law Context

It is easy to make fatal errors when collecting digital evidence. Digital evidence is latent, like fingerprints or DNA evidence; crosses jurisdictional borders quickly and easily; is easily altered, damaged or destroyed; and can be time sensitive. The very nature of data and information held in electronic form makes it easier to manipulate than traditional forms of data. This creates specific issues for the justice system and requires that the handling of such data be carried out in a manner that ensures that the continued integrity of the information may be maintained and proved. Decision-makers can rely on the standard to determine the credibility of digital evidence.[59] However, legislation in Europe mostly does not stipulate in their legal codes a specific definition of what electronic evidence is: electronic evidence is equivalent to traditional evidence. Most jurisdictions admit analogue and digital evidence as a form of document, and the meaning of a document invariably extends to anything recorded in any form, which must be right.[60] Countries apply by "analogy" the regulations in the general procedures for traditional evidence.[61]

Since the ultimate goal is the use of acquired and analysed evidence to support a case in court, electronic evidence must be obtained in compliance with existing legislation and best practice procedure to be admissible in a trial. Although the details differ depending on national legislation, the following basic criteria must generally be taken into account:

- Authenticity: it must be possible to positively tie evidentiary material to the investigated incident.
- Completeness: it must tell the whole story and not just a particular perspective.

---

[58] See The Sedona Conference (2011); The Sedona Conference (2008); Perry (2008), p. 231; Yip (2012), p. 595.

[59] See Lazetik and Koshevaliska (2014), p. 70.

[60] See Mason (2008a, b), p. xxxiv.

[61] See Insa (2004), p. 34.

- Reliability: there must be nothing about how the evidence was collected and subsequently handled which causes doubt about its authenticity and veracity.
- Believability: it must be readily believable and understandable to a judge and/or the members of a jury.
- Proportionality: its application to digital forensics establishes that the whole investigative process must be adequate and appropriate: the benefits that are to be gained by using a specific measure must outweigh the harms for the party or parties affected by the measure.[62]

The law should provide for the admission of electronic evidence in court. Procedures need to be put in place on the handling of electronic evidence. Investigators and forensic experts need to adhere to these regulations to make evidence admissible in court proceedings.[63]

There are provisions in Slovenian code of criminal procedure that regulate basic standards (guidelines) for the collection of electronic evidence for criminal proceedings, and are because in the great majority of cases, it is not the electronic device that is crucial, but the data stored on it.[64] In Slovenian code of criminal procedure, it is stipulated that as in the case of the investigation of an electronic device, only a properly qualified person can be instructed to preserve the data.[65] A qualified person is a person designated by the employer who, by possession of a recognised degree, certificate or professional standing or by extensive knowledge, training and experience, has successfully demonstrated ability to identify and solve or resolve problems relating to the subject matter, the work or the project and, when required, is properly licensed in accordance with federal, state or local laws and regulations.[66]

In the Croatian Criminal Procedure Code, it is stipulated that the authority carrying out the search (of electronic devices) may order a professional assistant to undertake such measures. As for the regulation, it is not necessary that an appropriately qualified police expert perform the search of electronic device. The legal term 'professional assistant' is broad enough to allow the police to employ the service of a digital evidence specialist from the private sector as and when they are needed.[67]

Naturally, there are many definitions about qualified persons, and the Slovenian Criminal Procedure Act does not give an answer either—who is qualified enough? This is up to the court to decide whether the investigator is qualified enough or not. However, it is quite likely that the cross-examination will not give enough

---

[62] See Mukasey et al. (2008), p. 13.

[63] See CyberCrime@IPA (2011), p. 43.

[64] See Selinsek (2010), p. 77.

[65] Ibid, p. 79.

[66] See http://www.iadclexicon.org/qualified-person/.

[67] See Skrtic (2013), p. 131.

arguments for the court to decide (due to the fact that parties may not have enough knowledge on the subject either).

The qualifications of digital evidence specialists should be rigorously challenged in court where it is not clear if the person purporting to be an "expert" really is a digital evidence specialist.[68] Law enforcement digital evidence examiners and some private sector service providers try to adhere to a general practice of functioning as evidence specialists to avoid the certain pitfalls associated with declaring themselves to be "technology experts". We do not yet have a generation of forensic investigators, examiners and members of the legal profession who are equally adept at conducting sound objective through investigations and positioning findings in the form of sound litigation in matters involving digital evidence.[69]

### 4.3.2 Civil Cases

In civil cases, the US courts addressed the specific question of digital evidence and e-discovery starting from the 2001 *McPeek v Aschroft*[70] case, followed by the very instructive *Rowe*[71] and *Zubulake* I-III[72] cases. However, in international e-discovery cases, there has been little guidance on how to deal with the unique

[68] See Mason (2008a, b).

[69] See Talleur (2002), p. 2.

[70] 202 F.R.D. 31 (D.D.C. 2001) The court used the marginal utility approach to help determine which party should bear the costs of production and ordered the producing party to restore a limited number of backup tapes containing emails that may have been pertinent to the case. Id. at 34. The court held that there was enough likelihood of finding responsive emails in backup tapes created over a 1-year period to justify imposing the costs of search on the producing party. The court further ordered the producing party to keep a record of its costs so the parties could argue whether the search results would justify further backup tape restoration.

[71] Rowe Entertainment, Inc. v. The William Morris Agency, Inc. 205 F.R.D. 421 (S.D.N.Y. 2002). In this case, the court refused to issue a blanket order. The producing party moved for a blanket protective order precluding discovery of email stored on backup disks and other media. The court held that while there was no justification for a blanket protective order, the costs associated with restoring and producing the emails should be shifted to the requesting party. In doing so, the court created and applied an eight-factor cost-shifting test. The Rowe test considers eight factors: (1) the specificity of the discovery request, (2) the likelihood of discovering critical information, (3) the availability of such information from other sources, (4) the purposes for which the responding party maintains the requested data, (5) the relative benefit to the parties of obtaining the information, (6) the total cost associated with production, (7) the relative ability of each party to control costs and its incentive to do so and (8) the resources available to each party. Id. at 429. The eight factors are equally relevant, and none is given greater weight than the other. Id. at 429.

[72] The Zubulake court revised the Rowe test into seven factors for a court to consider; the factors are as follows: (1) the extent to which the request is specifically tailored to discover relevant information; (2) the availability of such information from other sources; (3) the total cost of production, compared to the amount in controversy; (4) the total cost of production, compared to the resources available to each party; (5) the relative ability of each party to control costs and its incentive to do so; (6) the importance of the issues at stake in the litigation; and (7) the relative benefits to the parties of obtaining the information. Zubulake I, 217 F.R.D. at 322.

problems, such as who should bear the translation, transmission, transportation costs or fines imposed by foreign authorities for infringing blocking statutes.[73] In *Aerospatiale*,[74] the US court established a five-factor test[75] to consider whether the discovery should be allowed despite foreign blocking statutes.[76] In other words, the US courts could put litigants in the situation where they cannot comply with both the US order and the foreign blocking statute, and they must make a choice which one to comply with.

While there appears to be some intolerance towards the intrusive US e-discovery requests in international cases, the UK court took a blunt approach in the case of National Grid Electricity Transmission Plc vs ABB Ltd & Ors international disclosure dispute, where in response to the French party's argument that compliance with the disclosure request would violate the French blocking statute and therefore there is a real risk of prosecution, Justice Roth went on analysing the purpose and history of the French law.[77] He observed that the context of the French legislation was important as it was introduced "because of concern in France at what were seen as abusive discovery requests being made of French companies facing litigation in particular in the United States"; other French companies were not prosecuted for complying with discovery orders, and jurisdiction is exercised over the defendant under EU legislation.[78]

Some authors provided useful comparison of common law and civil law practices in dealing with evidence. Hjort compared the Norwegian and English regulations of electronic disclosure and showed that in Norway the extreme case is when a party presents evidence that is adversely affecting its case—as opposed to UK disclosure, where this is the obligation of the parties. Also, there is no preservation of evidence, and Norway seems to accept the "mysterious disappearance" of evidence to a much larger extent than the UK courts.[79]

---

[73] See Yip (2012), pp. 618–620.

[74] Societe Nationale Industrielle Aerospatiale v. U.S. Dist. Ct. for S. Dist. of Iowa, 482 U.S. 522, *544* n.28 (1987).

[75] These five factors are (1) the importance to the ... litigation of the documents or other information requested, (2) the degree of specificity of the request, (3) whether the information originated in the United States, (4) the availability of alternative means of securing the information and (5) the extent to which noncompliance with the request would undermine important interests of the United States or compliance with the request would undermine important interests of the state where the information is located.

[76] Court generally allowed international e-discovery with some limitations; however, there are a number of states that enacted statutes prohibiting such discoveries in order to protect their citizens from intrusive discovery procedures or in order to protect some state interests, such as banking secrets.

[77] National Grid Electricity Transmission Plc v ABB Ltd & Ors [2013] EWHC 822 (Ch) (11 April 2013). Available at http://www.bailii.org/ew/cases/EWHC/Ch/2013/822.html. Accessed 23.05.2015.

[78] At 44–48.

[79] See Hjort (2011), pp. 76–91.

She concluded that "[i]n legal systems with and without disclosure, there will always be a risk that not all the relevant evidence will be presented. In many ways, ESI [electronically stored information] as evidence challenges legal procedural systems because of the massive amounts of information that is stored with little or no structure. A procedural system can cause problems to the parties, where there is a possibility of drowning in less relevant evidence or failing to obtain relevant evidence. It is not realistic to 'turn every stone'. The aim should be to develop a system where the parties contribute in turning only the necessary stones without significant costs."[80]

## 4.4 Harmonisation

Policy analysis in this category concentrates on harmonisation and working toward effective cross-border legal cooperation in obtaining/taking evidence. Ongoing efforts have strategic focus on how to harmonise and achieve greater compatibility between the different systems.[81]

The issue of digital evidence was discussed already in 1985 in the United Nations, when the UNCITRAL Commission's Recommendation on the Value of Computer Records was endorsed by the General Assembly's Resolution.[82] The preceding report of the Secretary General dealt with the role of electronic documents in international trade and addressed its evidential value.[83] The conclusion at that time was that the recognition of the legal value of computer records was desired and justified, but there were legal obstacles; therefore, review of legal requirements was necessary; however, they did not see the need for harmonisation of the rules of evidence because the differences have caused no harm so far to international trade.[84] Thirty years after the UNCITRAL's opinion that there is no need for harmonised law on electronic evidence and number, authors call for uniform laws in this field pointing out that the challenges to businesses dealing with complex cross-border litigation are uniform when it comes to e-discovery, irrespective of forum or venue, and this will be exacerbated by cloud computing.[85]

When discussing collection of evidence, two important legal instruments must be mentioned: the Hague Convention of 18 March 1970 on the Taking of Evidence Abroad in Civil or Commercial Matters and the Council Regulation (EC) No 1206/

---

[80] Ibid, p. 91.

[81] See ELI-UNIDROIT, Transnational Civil Procedure – Formulation of Regional Rules, Working Group on Access to Information and Evidence, Study LXXVIA – Doc. 2 Corr., First Report November 2014.

[82] A/RES/40/71 of 11. December 1985

[83] A/CN./265.

[84] A/RES/40/71 of 11. December 1985.

[85] See Garrie and Gelb (2012); Trocker (2014).

2001 of 28 May 2001 on Cooperation between the courts of the Member States in the taking of evidence in civil or commercial matters.

The Hague Evidence Convention is the main international instrument that sets forth the rules and procedure for requesting the taking of evidence abroad and for complying with such request. The Convention provides for taking of evidence by means of letters of requests or by diplomatic or consular agents and commissioners, and it creates an important bridge between common law and civil law traditions. However, the Convention does not allow US-style e-discovery in states, which made a reservation that it will not execute a Letter of Request for common law pre-trial discovery of documents. Survey of 2013 by the Permanent Bureau suggests that the Convention is not consistently used for taking digital evidence.[86]

A novel and flexible approach is taken by the EU Evidence Regulation,[87] which created a new system—direct and rapid transmission and execution of requests for the taking of evidence by courts. The Regulation makes it possible for one Member State's court to directly contact another Member State's court with requests for the taking of evidence or to take evidence directly in another Member State.[88] Although the Evidence Regulation has been praised for introducing welcomed improvements for litigants, the fundamental objective of access to justice in the European Union points to the need of eliminating obstacles to the good functioning of civil procedure.[89] Any common code of civil procedure should take into account the impact of modern computer technology on the access and production of evidence, the problems related to the access to information and evidence in the pre-litigation stage and whether the civil law traditions should "compete" with or learn from the common law discovery and disclosure models.[90]

In the criminal law field exist a number of instruments and initiatives that aim at harmonisation or to provide guidance on different aspects of dealing with digital evidence. One of the most cited guidance materials is the UK Association of Chief Police Officers' (ACPO's) Good Practice Guide for Computer-Based Electronic Evidence,[91] which is primarily addressed to law enforcement and first responders

[86] In 2013, there were nearly 20,000 letters of requests issued under the Convention; however, there were only 7 instances of when the Letter of Request expressly requested information stored in digital form. Synopsys of responses to the Questionnaire of November 2013 Relating to the Hague Convention of 18 March 1970 on the Taking of Evidence Abroad in Civil or Commercial Matters. Available at http://www.hcch.net/upload/wop/2014/2014sc_id02.pdf. Accessed 24.05.2015.

[87] Council Regulation (EC) No 1206/2001 of 28 May 2001 on cooperation between the courts of the Member States in the taking of evidence in civil or commercial matters.

[88] The latter is possible if there are no coercive measures required and the taking of evidence can be performed on voluntary basis and it left some key terms, such as 'evidence', undefined for enabling compatibility between different jurisdictions. The Regulation is limited to civil and commercial cases, and it prevails over other agreements, such as the Hague Evidence Convention.

[89] See Trocker (2014), p. 4.

[90] Ibid, p. 5.

[91] Available at http://www.cps.gov.uk/legal/assets/uploads/files/ACPO_guidelines_computer_evidence[1].pdf. Accessed 24.05.2015.

but also laid down a number of general principles that can be very useful in any digital investigation.[92] In addition to this, there are US-based standardisation efforts, such as the guidelines by the Scientific Working Group of Digital Evidence and International Organization on Digital Evidence,[93] and technical guidelines,[94] but certainly the most influential legal instrument is the Council of Europe Cybercrime Convention, which aims to harmonise definitions of cybercrime and procedures for warrants and evidence collection across borders.

The Cybercrime Convention contains provisions on collection of digital evidence, such as expedited preservation of stored computer data and traffic data, production orders, search and seizure of stored computer data, real-time collection of traffic data and interception of content data, and other important procedural rules relating to international cooperation. However, one of the main criticisms of the Convention that many of these rules and possibilities provided here remain theoretical and are not implemented in practice.[95]

## 4.5 *Privacy and Data Protection*

A distinctly discussed major problem area is privacy and data protection,[96] and these authors tend to have operational level focus and advise on how to prepare for potential challenges on organisation level in civil cases but focus on policy choices in the context of criminal law.

In 2008, the Council of Europe has prepared a study on how to make cybercrime investigations compatible with data protection and privacy standards, in particular when implementing the procedural provisions of the Cybercrime Convention. The study observed that "[i]n the equilibrium between security and privacy, the weight seems to be shifting towards security protection by giving up on human rights, including the protection of privacy".[97] The study concluded already in 2008 that

[92] Principle 1: No action taken by law enforcement agencies or their agents should change data held on a computer or storage media which may subsequently be relied upon in court. Principle 2: In circumstances where a person finds it necessary to access original data held on a computer or on storage media, that person must be competent to do so and be able to give evidence explaining the relevance and the implications of their actions. Principle 3: An audit trail or other record of all processes applied to computer-based electronic evidence should be created and preserved. An independent third party should be able to examine those processes and achieve the same result. Principle 4: The person in charge of the investigation (the case officer) has overall responsibility for ensuring that the law and these principles are adhered to.

[93] See at http://www.fbi.gov/about-us/lab/forensic-science-communications/fsc/april2000/swgde.htm/#International (Last accessed 24.05.2015).

[94] Internet RFC 3227 "Guidelines for Evidence Collection and Archiving", available at http://www.ietf.org/rfc/rfc3227.txt (Last accessed 24.05.2015).

[95] See Pradillo (2011), pp. 363–395; Ramalho (2014), pp. 55–75.

[96] See Patzak et al. (2011), pp. 127–139; Chorvat and Pelanek (2013), pp. 255–262.

[97] See van Genderen (2008), p. 9.

considering the field of cybercrime, computer-supported crime, national security and the instruments for investigation, the personal data of a clear criminal suspect is practically treated in the same way in criminal proceedings as the personal data of non-suspect in data mining and judicial "fishing expeditions". Therefore, the need for respecting the fundamental principles in the process of surveillance and criminal procedures was emphasised, and a minimum standard of protection was proposed.[98] This minimum standard is defined by the principles of fair collection, proportionality (minimality), clear description, purpose specification, information of the data subject, general prohibition on processing sensitive data and distinction between categories of data, distinction between the categories of data subjects, and accountability.[99]

Although there are a number of regional and international legal instruments regulating or relevant to the processing of personal data in criminal proceedings,[100] one of the most significant developments on this field can be expected in the framework of the EU data protection reform. The proposed 'police' Directive will apply general data protection principles and rules to the data used by police and judicial authorities to cooperate in criminal matters. The Directive will apply to all data processing by the law enforcement authorities, including those which are processed domestically.[101]

In the context of private dispute resolution, the fundamentally different approaches between the US and the EU toward privacy and data protection lead to a great number of conflicts when it comes to collection of evidence in cases with international dimension. The Sedona Conference in its guidance material on data protection pointed out that the concept of "personal data" in the United States is restricted to specific types of personal and sensitive information, such as personal medical information, social security information, and banking information[while i] n the EU, this would be considered "personal sensitive data," which commands an even greater degree of protection. Processing also defined much more broadly in the EU, as it refers to "any operation or set of operations", which approach is in contrast with US view where processing relates to a technical action. "In this sense, while

---

[98] Ibid, pp. 48–50.

[99] Ibid, p. 50.

[100] For example, ETS 108 and Rec R(87)15 on the use of personal data in the police sector; OECD Guidelines Governing the Protection of Privacy and Transborder Flows of Personal Data (Paris: OECD, 1980), adopted 23.9.1980; UN Guidelines Concerning Computerized Personal Data Files (Doc E/CN.4/1990/72, 20.2.1990), adopted by the UN General Assembly on 4.12.1990; Council of Europe Convention for the Protection of Individuals with regard to Automatic Processing of Personal Data (ETS 108); Directive 95/46/EC of the European Parliament and of the Council of 24 October 1995 on the protection of individuals with regard to the processing of personal data and on the free movement of such data; Council Framework Decision 2008/977/JHA of 27 November 2008 on the protection of personal data processed in the framework of police and judicial cooperation in criminal matters; Council Decision 2008/615/JHA of 23 June 2008 on the stepping up of cross-border cooperation, particularly in combating terrorism and cross-border crime (Prüm Decision).

[101] See at http://europa.eu/rapid/press-release_MEMO-15-3802_en.htm. Accessed 24.05.2015.

the European Union and other countries take a global approach to protection of personal data, the United States takes a very segmented approach as to both the scope of personal data and processing of such data."[102]

Several authors discussed the incompatibility between US e-discovery and European data protection rules.[103] The EU Data Protection Directive prohibits the disclosure of personal data to a party outside the EU without the data subject's specific consent, and therefore it can be considered as a blocking statute preventing discovery throughout the European Union. However, despite the harmonised regulation of data protection in the EU, there are different applications of Directive 95/46, which also resulted in a variety of approaches in civil litigation. This issue was addressed by Article 29 Data Protection Working Party in 2009 in Working Document 1/2009 on pre-trial discovery for cross-border civil litigation.[104] Despite these guidelines, there are no guarantees or clear rules on what conduct will be compliant with the data protection rules. EU data protection regulation and reform is expected to create a clear and coherent but flexible framework, which may somewhat ease the conflicts but most likely result in new issues in cross-border dispute resolutions.

## 4.6 Governance and Management

The last category of problem areas relates to governance and practical management of cases and incidents. Authors discuss technical and technological[105] issues and financial and business risks[106] related to capabilities of dealing with digital evidence, and many emphasise the importance of training, education and capability development.[107] Growing attention is paid to organisational issues and digital forensic readiness.[108]

Cybercrime is a growth industry.[109] Taking into account how many more opportunities cybercriminals have in comparison with cyber units that are budget-wise, it is clear that states are in a difficult position when combating cybercrime. Lack of budget for training is a great weakness of cyber units.[110] Lack of funding

---

[102] See The Sedona Conference (2008).

[103] See Perry (2008), pp. 231–234; Patzak et al. (2011), pp. 127–139; Forster and Almughrabi (2013), pp. 111–144.

[104] 00339/09/EN WP 158.

[105] For example, Taylor et al., "Digital Evidence in Cloud Computing Systems." (2010) Computer Law and Security Review; Cohen, Bilby and Caronni, "Distributed Forensics and Incident Response in the Enterprise." (2011) Digital Investigation.

[106] See Atkinson (2014), pp. 245–261; Nearon (2005), pp. 32–33; Sipior et al. (2014), pp. 328–339.

[107] See Capps (2013), pp. 23–28; Wong (2013), pp. 16–22; Greenstein (2014), p. 40.

[108] See Mouhtaropoulos et al. (2014), pp. 173–179; Mouhtaropoulos et al. (2011), pp. 191–196; Sommers (2008); Hibbard (2014), pp. 313–393.

[109] See Center for Strategic and International Studies (2014), p. 2.

[110] See Cybercrime@IPA (2011), p. 54.

means that there are fewer opportunities to fight cybercrime, and also serious problems may arise in court—it is easy to debate the admissibility of evidence, and therefore it is much harder to get convictions. Because of the complexity of the digital domain, prosecution cases often fail during trial where incompetency is apparent in reconstructing the case and where validation issues are raised.[111] The questions about the expertise of investigators and used software will inevitably occur. Investigators should realise that they are now living in a world dominated by digital evidence and that digital evidence is now the major form of evidence.[112] The same applies to prosecutors and judges also. The validation of the evidence, however, is largely dependent on the skill and knowledge of investigators.[113]

Every time an investigator looks at a working computer at the search and seizure site, the situation is different. The procedure is different and the technique is different. The investigator has to have enough knowledge to decide what actions should be taken. However, it is possible to follow set guidelines about small parts of processes: how to make an image, for instance.

It is difficult to overestimate the importance of this procedure. There are two fundamental principles in relation to copying digital evidence that a digital evidence specialist should be aware of:

(a) The process of making the image should not alter the original evidence. This means the appropriate steps should be taken to ensure that the process used to take the image should not write any data to the original medium.
(b) The process of copying data should produce an exact copy of the original. Such a reproduction should allow the specialist to investigate the files in the way they existed on the original medium.[114]

The International Standardization Organization is in the process of working out a line of standards on digital evidence.[115] The already valid ISO/IEC standard 27037:2012 lists the principles and general requirements to digital evidence, and it is applicable to any digital investigation regardless of context. According to the standard, the fundamental principles of relevance, reliability and sufficiency are important in all investigations, be it a criminal case, a civil case or an internal investigation. Satisfaction of the fundamental principles can be demonstrated by following technical requirements of auditability, repeatability, reproducibility and justifiability. In any case, these principles and technical requirements determine the quality of evidence and therefore play an important role in maximising the evidentiary value and use of digital information and minimising the costs associated with it, which has a direct impact on the choice of tools and methods for collection.

---

[111] See Boddington et al. (2008), p. 4.
[112] See Mason (2008a, b), p. xxxviii.
[113] See Boddington et al. (2008), p. 4.
[114] See Mason (2008a, b), p. xlvii.
[115] See Hibbard (2014), pp. 313–393.

The standard suggests that the proportionality and reasonableness of actions should be assessed depending on the priorities of an organisation in a given case, but it does not provide any further guidance. It can be argued that conducting proportionality and reasonableness analysis are relative but objective ways to measure certain qualities of technologies and procedures, and therefore to address the transnationality aspect of collecting digital evidence, it is possible and necessary to provide overall guidance on these issues in an international document.[116] ISO/IEC standard nr 27050 on e-discovery will hopefully address this shortcoming to some extent, but it is still in the draft phase at the time of writing this article. The latter standard will draw heavily on the Electronic Discovery Reference Model, which is based on the US practice,[117] and it is unclear whether parties in continental legal systems can benefit sufficiently from it.

For digital evidence collection in cross-border dispute resolution, the legal obstacles are certainly one of the most significant problem, and without reflecting on it, the technical and management questions, as described for example in the ISO/IEC standard nr 27037,[118] may become entirely irrelevant.

## 5 Synthesis

Based on the literature analysis, the critical legal components of the Digital Forensic Readiness Model and their interrelations are summarised in Fig. 1 (Modelling the general legal requirements for digital forensic readiness). The model in Fig. 1. contains four main modules (1—Overall quality standards, 2—Accessibility, 3—Availability, 4—Practicalities and discretion) as an integrated framework for analysis, and four gaps (Lack of expertise and knowledge, Lack of enforcement and cooperation, Privacy and blocking statutes, Continuity and review) identify the most common areas where challenges and obstacles arise from related to collection and management of digital evidence. Between the modules, the connecting processes and influencing connections are indicated (planning, implementing, choices on case management strategies, choices on relevance and reliable technology, proportionality).

The modules are each critical components of the system of legal requirements—removal of any of them most likely results in impossibility to collect/use data as digital evidence. The interrelations and connecting processes are important components, but failure to take them into account probably leads to some degree of

---

[116] Addressing the reliability question in electronic transactions in commercial and civil context, see Alba (2014), pp. 387–422.

[117] See at http://www.edrm.net/. Accessed 30.05.2015.

[118] IEC/ISO International Standard nr 27037, Information technology – Security techniques – Guidelines for identification, collection, acquisition, and preservation of digital evidence. First edition 2012.

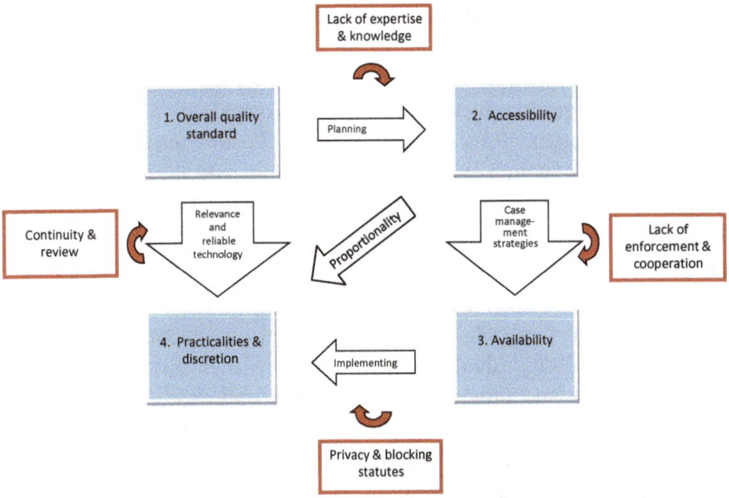


**Fig. 1** Modelling the general legal requirements for digital forensic readiness

divergence from optimal solution. Gaps are external factors that limit the collection and use of digital evidence, and addressing those is the real challenge in practice.

## *5.1 Overall Quality Standard and Substantive Legal Context*

Substantive legal context and nature of the case (such as criminal, civil, administrative, alternative dispute resolution or internal investigation) determine the overall quality (in terms of reliability) requirements to digital evidence due to different standards of burden of proof and degree of flexibility of procedural rules. This certainly affects the choice and method of digital evidence collection. Also depending on what legal tradition the jurisdiction may belong to, the question of what data is relevant can be decided. For instance, in the US, e-discovery process data that is irrelevant to the legal issue but relevant for the collection can be identified. In continental legal systems, relevance typically means the relevance to the legal issue at hand.

Standards of minimum quality (or reliability) of digital evidence should increase proportionally with the "seriousness" of the case and rigidity of procedural rules in each conflict resolution context. As a general rule, the burden of proof on the prosecution to succeed with a criminal case is considerably higher than the standard that is required in a civil dispute.

For example, the International Criminal Court has developed a set of standards that digital evidence must conform to before it is submitted: metadata to be attached, including the chain of custody in chronological order, the identity of the source, the original author and recipient information, and the author and recipient's respective organisations.[119] This rule itself limits the choice of method of collection to those where metadata is acquired, as opposed to making a simple copy of the original file, where metadata is excluded. On the other hand, making a forensic copy of an entire device would be overkill for a civil proceeding, where practically there is a presumption that the information collected is authentic and belongs to the producing party from which it was collected, and using, for example, "export" features of a software will suffice, not talking about the print-outs of documents (for example emails) that are routinely accepted by many courts, although metadata might be completely lacking.

In other words, the more flexible is the procedure of conflict resolution or incident investigation process, the lower the quality standards *may* be sufficient for digital information of evidential value.[120] Following criminal standard forensics may be unreasonable and unnecessarily complex and costly in civil courts or in internal disciplinary proceedings. Also, the "meet and confer" principle is a powerful tool for courts and arbitral tribunals to find the best suitable standards for each particular case, since it requires that the parties agree on the procedures to be followed, which may include reasonably tailored rules as to the quality and other aspects of digital evidence.

Transparency plays a great role in the form of "meet and confer" requirement in civil proceedings, since open discussion and cooperation in setting the rules based on the common interest of the parties makes it possible to address questions of proportionality on subtle levels. Without cooperation between the parties, only extremely disproportionate requests can be tackled.[121] Transparency seems to be working in the civil context. Indeed it is a precondition for finding proportional solutions for many issues concerning collection of digital evidence, such as scope, technique, extent of document production. In criminal context, transparency is a controversial issue, especially in the light of recent surveillance scandals in the US, the UK and elsewhere.

## 5.2 *Accessibility*

Source and type of digital evidence determines accessibility to digital evidence. However, it was demonstrated by the literature review that it has many aspects. Source can be external or internal to an organisation, and the question that who is in

[119] See Ashouri et al. (2014), p. 117.

[120] However, there are exceptions. For example, the restorative justice approaches in juvenile criminal cases can allow relatively great procedural flexibility, but which does not mean that the quality of digital evidence can be allowed to decrease.

[121] In Al-Sweady, R (on the application of) v Secretary of State for the Defence [2009] EWHC 2387 (Admin), the court criticised the Ministry of Defence for failing to carry out a sufficient search for documents and emphasised the importance of an adequate document retrieval system, to avoid the waste of much public money and court time.

control of the evidence (me, opponent, third party) is an important factor. The question of storage and therefore accessibility from technical perspective was addressed by the US courts in *Zubulake* (readily accessible or non-readily accessible). In addition, digital evidence can be system, forensic or user generated, which is an important factor in determining whether there is a need for expert to identify, access, collect or even generate the evidence or whether it is readily recognisable and manageable by the user without technical savvy.

Accessibility as understood here has been an underlying element when courts have addressed questions of proportionality. The difficulty to access data or, in other words, the burden placed on the producing party has been expressed in technical, temporal and monetary terms, and also in terms of interfering with civil and human rights.[122]

The classic elements of proportionality review, which is in essence an optimisation exercise between the factual and legal possibilities, are suitability (or effectiveness), necessity and a reasonable balance between the interests concerned or proportionality in the strict sense.[123] Digital forensic readiness planning, which is itself an optimisation activity on the organisational level, should therefore include legal optimisation and take the above principles into account when identifying and assessing potential evidence and planning collection thereof. The first two elements are concerned with the relationship between the aims of collection and the means or instruments of collection: will the collection of that data further the aims of the investigation, and if yes, can that effect be achieved by less burdensome means? The third element is concerned with balancing the interest between the interests served and interests harmed.

Therefore, considering the factors of accessibility and proportionality in conjunction will determine a number of choices in the practical case management, such as considering sampling techniques instead of collection of all data or application of certain cost-cutting and effectiveness-boosting technologies, such as artificial intelligence and predictive coding.

## 5.3 *Availability*

Compatibility between legal systems and regimes and building bridges between jurisdictions is an underlying element for international investigations and dispute resolution. Harmonisation instruments and common rules exist, such as the Cybercrime Convention, EU evidence regulation, Hague Evidence Convention,

[122] For instance, the European Court of Justice in its decision of 8 April 2014, for example, invalidated the Data Retention Directive and held that the retention of data prescribed in the scale prescribed by the directive went too far in interfering with the right of privacy, although the retention of data was suitable and necessary for achieving the general aim, namely the fight against serious crime. ECJ Judgment in Joined Cases C-293/12 and C-594/12.

[123] See Alexy (2014), pp. 51–57.

bilateral agreements, comity principle, and they provide for the necessary mechanisms for collecting digital evidence across borders. In other words, the actual availability of digital evidence depends on these established or ad hoc mechanisms.

The existence of mechanisms for cooperation in taking evidence does not, however, mean that the collection will take place on the requesting party's terms. It should be noted that the above-mentioned instruments do not establish new procedures for collecting evidence internationally and across borders but typically are limited to linking the apparatus of states parties; they may determine the form, minimum content and communication channels for delivering the requests, etc., but leave the execution regulated by local procedures. Therefore, the legal systems' compatibility may be a determining factor in the scope, form, manner of digital evidence collection. Requesting a US-style e-discovery may have greater success in another common law country than in a legal tradition, where the concept of discovery is not known. Similarly, a case of electronic search in one country may fall into the category of interception in another, depending on the definition of delivery of documents.[124]

## 5.4 Practicalities and Discretion

The process of case management, such as issues of identification, collection, preservation, retention of digital evidence, determines the practical possibilities (like choice of technique, integrity requirement) and reasonableness of using the digital evidence. Case management includes all the potential choices that are given within the limits of laws. This element encompasses the discretion given to a case manager (lawyer, advocate, investigator, prosecutor, etc.). The choices made within this discretion are affected by and depend on the previous elements, and it is hardly possible to prescribe strict rules, since each case is different. However, being aware of the suggestions of guidelines such as the ACPO or the ISO/IEC 27037 is useful, since these documents list the possible choices in common situations.

It is common that the investigator is obliged to decide on-site whether to collect immediately such digital evidence that is in danger of being destroyed; otherwise, it will not be reachable for investigators later. For instance, when during a search the investigator notices that data or storage media could be encrypted[125] or in the case of a running computer, there is a need to collect volatile data.

---

[124] For example, unread emails on one's inbox may be considered as delivered in one place but would qualify as communication in transit elsewhere; therefore, different legal rules would apply.

[125] Andy Spruill explains that if a hard drive is fully encrypted, experts have no easy access to the stored data and their investigative options become limited. The first thing an investigator must do is to determine the level and extent of the encryption. Weak passwords can be cracked, but if the user has implemented a strong password it becomes almost impossible to access via brute force methods. It could be that just a few files are encrypted and there could be unencrypted copies elsewhere on the device. The user could also be a creature of habit and use the same set of

One of the more recent shifts in evidence handling has been the shift away from simply "pulling the plug" as a first step in evidence collection to the adoption of methodologies to acquire evidence "Live" from a suspect computer.[126] Volatile data[127] may also be lost because of other actions performed on the system. In many cases, acquiring volatile data should be given priority over non-volatile data. However, non-volatile data may also be somewhat dynamic in nature (e.g., log files that are overwritten as new events occur).[128] Volatile data involving an event can be collected only from a live system that has not been rebooted or shut down since the event occurred. Every action performed on the system, whether initiated by a person or by the operating system itself, will almost certainly alter the volatile data in some way. Therefore, analysts should decide as quickly as possible whether the volatile data should be preserved. Ideally, the criteria for making this decision should have been documented in advance so that the analyst can make the best decision immediately.

The importance of this decision cannot be stressed enough because powering off the system or even disconnecting it from a network can eliminate the opportunity to collect potentially important information. For example, if a user recently ran encryption tools to secure data, the computer's RAM might contain password hashes, which could be used to determine the passwords.[129] Simply put, in all likelihood perhaps the most important evidence to be gathered in digital evidence collection today and for the near future exists only in the form of the volatile data contained within the computer's RAM.[130] There is no doubt that cybercrime units will always require a capability to collect and deal with evidence that emanates from their investigations. This is particularly so in cases where volatile or other vulnerable evidence is present at the scene of an investigation and which needs dealing with to prevent compromise or destruction of potential evidence.[131]

The above-mentioned situations may require that the investigator do an image of the hard drive (in the case of encryption) or would collect volatile data (live acquisition). The tool used for doing an image of a hard drive by the digital evidence specialist should be appropriate for the task. It is essential that the product that is used is capable of making a sector-by-sector or bit-stream duplicate copy of the hard drive in a way that preserves its integrity. It is also recommended that the hard disk is copied using more than one tool. Such tools can be the subject of cross-

---

passwords. These passwords can be quickly located in easily decipherable formats throughout the system. Available at http://www.evidencemagazine.com/index.php?option=com_content&task=view&id=656. Accessed 30.05.2015.

[126] See Best practices in digital evidence collection available at http://digital-forensics.sans.org/blog/2009/09/12/best-practices-in-digital-evidence-collection/. Accessed 30.05.2015.

[127] Volatile data refers to data on a live system that is lost after a computer is powered down or due to the passage of time.

[128] See Kent et al. (2006), p. 27.

[129] Ibid, p. 53.

[130] See 129.

[131] See CyberCrime@IPA (2011), p. 33.

examination as to the underlying scientific methodology used by the tool, and consideration ought to be given by lawyers to this aspect of the evidence-gathering process.[132]

In addition, the investigator should consider that it has been debated if the evidence gathered from a live computer is reliable. However, collecting evidence from a live computer is no different from collecting physical evidence. The physical crime scene will be modified when the investigator walks around just as the digital crime scene will be modified when the investigator runs digital evidence collection software. The challenge is to minimise the changes, understand the effect of the changes and minimise the trust that is placed on the operating system of the live system.[133]

If the data has not already been acquired by security tools, analysis tools or other means, the general process for acquiring data involves using forensic tools to collect volatile data, duplicating non-volatile data sources to collect their data and securing the original non-volatile data sources. Data acquisition can be performed either locally or over a network. Although it is generally preferable to acquire data locally because there is greater control over the system and data, local data collection is not always feasible (e.g., system in locked room, system in another location). When acquiring data over a network, decisions should be made regarding the type of data to be collected and the amount of effort to use. For instance, it might be necessary to acquire data from several systems through different network connections, or it might be sufficient to copy a logical volume from just one system.[134]

## 5.5 *Gaps in Expertise and Knowledge: The Individual Level*

Lack of expertise and knowledge, lack of capacities and capabilities on personal level, on the legal professional's side can prevent considering the use of digital evidence at all or can lead to misunderstandings as to its value. It may be of little use to know all the substantial and procedural laws related to a legal issue if the case manager is unaware that some digital evidence may exist, what its basic technical features are and how they can influence the case at hand. Therefore, the importance of training and use of experts cannot be overemphasised. Two basic approaches exist, training and use of experts; however, most likely the combination of these would yield the most results.

The US Seventh Circuit pilot program includes in its resulting principles the use of "e-discovery liaison", whose task is to assist the parties in the meet and confer process and must "(a) be prepared to participate in e-discovery dispute resolution;

[132] See Mason (2008a, b), p. xlviii.

[133] See Carrier et al. (2003), p. 14.

[134] See Kent et al. (2006), p. 28.

(b) be knowledgeable about the party's e-discovery efforts; (c) be, or have reasonable access to those who are, familiar with the party's electronic systems and capabilities in order to explain those systems and answer relevant questions; and (d) be, or have reasonable access to those who are, knowledgeable about the technical aspects of e-discovery, including electronic document storage, organisation and format issues and relevant information retrieval technology, including search methodology."[135] There has been numerous positive feedback on this rule to the pilot program, and attorneys often find this the most useful innovation in e-discovery. Similar solutions can be used in other jurisdictions and contexts, supporting the parties and the court.

However, the use of external assistance does not replace own understanding and assessment of a case. What kind of qualifications should the investigator have to be able to perform such tasks in a sound way?

Investigators follow different Good Practice Guides for Digital Evidence. One of such guides is Association of Chief Police Officers Guide (ACPO).[136] Many countries have their internal guidelines that are based on the principles stipulated in ACPO. It should be noted that these guidelines are not mandatory. It is stated in the guide developed by the US Department of Justice for first responders that This guide is intended to assist State and local law enforcement and other first responders who may be responsible for preserving an electronic crime scene and for recognizing, collecting, and safeguarding digital evidence. It is not all-inclusive but addresses situations encountered with electronic crime scenes and digital evidence. All crime scenes are unique and the judgment of the first responder, agency protocols, and prevailing technology should all be considered when implementing the information in this guide. The competence of an investigator is assumed.[137] However, assuming that the investigator is competent enough, in the situation where almost any investigator could find himself, that is, where digital evidence should be collected, he is naïve.

A good practice study on specialised cybercrime units included 21 states. It was brought out that the investigators in cybercrime units have not gone through trainings for digital evidence collecting. Many countries have informed that their

---

[135] Principle 2.02.

[136] See 129.

[137] PRINCIPLES

Principle 1: No action taken by law enforcement agencies, persons employed within those agencies or their agents should change data which may subsequently be relied upon in court.

Principle 2: In circumstances where a person finds it necessary to access original data, that person must be competent to do so and be able to give evidence explaining the relevance and the implications of their actions.

Principle 3: An audit trail or other record of all processes applied to digital evidence should be created and preserved. An independent third party should be able to examine those processes and achieve the same result.

Principle 4: The person in charge of the investigation has overall responsibility for ensuring that the law and these principles are adhered to.

investigators do not have proper preparation in forensics and that their skills are only of investigative value.[138]

Considering that digital evidence can be easily destroyed, altered or damaged, utmost care when collecting it should be applied. Due to the nature of digital evidence, therefore it is necessary to have as clear regulations as possible to ensure the admissibility of digital evidence in court. The officers working in the cybercrime unit will need to be carefully selected and included in ongoing training programmes. The officers need to have knowledge of computers, the Internet, police investigations, legislation governing cybercrime and foreign languages. Depending on their function, they have specific qualifications, mostly in criminal investigation and ICT.[139] This is a reason to keep selecting new officers, preferably young ones who are computer passionate, and to provide them with ongoing training courses. For staff dealing with computer forensic, different selection criteria apply. They must be specialised in this work, but they do not necessarily have to be police officers.[140]

An organisation's forensic guidelines should include general methodologies for investigating an incident using forensic techniques, since it is not feasible to develop comprehensive procedures tailored to every possible situation. However, organisations also should consider developing step-by-step procedures for performing routine tasks, such as imaging a hard disk, capturing and recording volatile information from systems or securing physical evidence (e.g., removable media). The goal for the guidelines and procedures is to facilitate consistent, effective and accurate forensic actions, which is particularly important for incidents that may lead to prosecution or internal disciplinary actions. Because electronic logs and other records can be altered or otherwise manipulated, organisations should be prepared, through their policies, guidelines and procedures, to demonstrate the integrity of such records.[141]

The guidelines should include general methodologies for investigating an incident using forensic techniques, and step-by-step procedures should explain how to perform routine tasks. The guidelines and procedures should support the admissibility of evidence into legal proceedings. Because electronic logs and other records can be altered or otherwise manipulated, organisations should be prepared, through their policies, guidelines and procedures, to demonstrate the reliability and integrity of such records.

The guidelines and procedures should also be reviewed regularly and maintained so that they are accurate.[142] It should be possible for the findings of the investigator to be replicated by a third party, whether it is another police specialist or an independent examiner. It is for this reason that the original investigator should

---

[138] See CyberCrime@IPA (2011), pp. 20–21.

[139] Ibid, p. 44.

[140] Ibid.

[141] See Kent et al. (2006), p. 21.

[142] Ibid, p. 23.

provide a full report of the actions they took and only work on a copy of the original hard drive.[143] At the scene, the best judgment of the investigator (based on training, experience and available resources) will dictate the investigative approach. In some cases, a forensic examination of the computer will be needed. The investigator should be aware that any action taken on the computer system might affect the integrity of the evidence. Only in exigent circumstances (e.g., imminent threat of loss of life or serious physical injury) should an investigator attempt to gain information directly from a computer on the scene. Any action taken should be well documented.[144]

Since forensic efforts are likely to expose information that may deny or corroborate various claims of both the prosecution and the defence, it is the responsibility of investigators and expert witnesses to analyse and report on evidence data in an unbiased fashion. Techniques must be rigorous and repeatable, using accepted scientific methods.[145]

## 5.6 *Gaps in Enforcement and Cooperation: The Institutional Level*

Lack of enforcement and/or cooperation and lack of capacity on institutional level may account for effectively blocking collection of digital evidence that otherwise could be available. Standardisation; the effective enforcement of procedural rules (enactment of compelling sanctions); improvement of organisational capabilities, competences, capacities; and reduction of delays are important factors in enhancing international cooperation and legal harmonisation, as well as trust promotion.

It is important that evidence collected in one state would be admissible in another state's court. There is a distinct need to establish standards for the collection and analysis of digital computer evidence and to create uniform standards for the certification of examiners. In addition, it is needed to establish standards or certifications for high-tech crime investigators. There are standards and accredited methods in the field of forensic expertise; however, this is not the case with first responders.

Although guidelines for investigations are often drawn up at the local level, the transnational nature of cybercrime and traditional crimes in which digital evidence is involved means that it is important that guidelines incorporate plans that will enable evidence to be exchanged between jurisdictions with no impact on their admissibility. For this reason, it is necessary for guidelines to be developed at the national level for the conduct of investigations.[146]

[143] Ibid, p. xlviii.

[144] See Mukasey (2008), p. 11.

[145] See Mercuri (2010), p. 1.

[146] See CyberCrime@IPA (2011), p. 26.

Software development firms, sensing a profitable market, deploy "one-size-fits-all" digital forensic products for use by anyone able to afford the cost of the software, along with 1- and 2-week commercial software certification courses—an approach that has had some appeal with members of the legal, audit, network security and other disciplinary communities seeking to "cross over" into the digital evidence field. These conditions raise a host of standards, independence and related issues implying the potential for mistakes in judgment, error and even wilful misbehaviour on the part of examiners or others in the process and raises frightening possibilities.[147] However, the lack of a leading edge tool and decreasing budgets for acquiring the tools are an ongoing problem. Since no single tool comes highly recommended by the forensics community, it is often desirable to use a range of software tools to acquire the data, thus increasing the budget needed to acquire the appropriate tools. The software tools available are expensive, and law enforcement agencies are operating under restricted budgets and fixed resources.[148] Forensic evidence is only as valuable as the integrity of the method that the evidence was obtained. The methods applied to obtain evidence are best represented if standards are known and readily established by the digital forensics community.[149] In criminal investigations, only forensic tools should be used, since a user might have replaced system commands with malicious programs, such as one to format a hard disk or return false information. However, use of forensic tools is no guarantee that the data retrieved will be accurate. If a system has been fully compromised, it is possible that rootkits and other malicious utilities have been installed that alter the system's functionality at the kernel level. This can cause false data to be returned to user-level tools.[150] The analyst should know how each tool affects or alters the system before collecting the volatile data. The message digest of each tool should be computed and stored safely to verify file integrity. Licensing and version information also should be documented for each forensic tool. In addition, the exact commands that were used to run each forensic tool should be documented (i.e., command line arguments and switches).[151]

Incorporation of digital forensics into mainstream forensic structures, introducing standards and accreditation of providers are something that should be considered while recognising that cybercrime units need to retain a capability to deal with the capture and analysis of vulnerable data during investigations.[152]

The success of any specialised unit that is created will depend on the knowledge, skills, education and the hard work of the people who will staff the unit. In the area of cybercrime, the level of training required to become an effective operative is

---

[147] See Talleur (2002), pp. 2–3.

[148] See Bennett (2011).

[149] Ibid.

[150] See Kent et al. (2006), p. 53.

[151] Ibid.

[152] See CyberCrime@IPA (2011), p. 5.

lengthy, continuing and sometimes expensive.[153] Personnel, equipment and training will remain challenges that cybercrime units of all countries have to face.[154]

## 5.7 *Gaps Due to Privacy and Blocking Statutes*

Privacy, data protection and blocking statutes raise obstacles to collecting digital evidence in civil cases due to fundamental differences in policy between jurisdictions. Privacy, along with some other civil and human rights, is a concern in criminal proceedings also, although these issues differ qualitatively. While in civil cases it is possible to implement preventive measures on a case-by-case basis that will help to ensure and demonstrate compliance with data protection and data privacy rules should the need arise, in criminal context the requirements are different and guarantees are (hopefully) built into the system. In other words, in civil cases a party either respects the data protection rules or not, but there is no room for assessment as to what degree of interference with privacy is allowed taking into account all the circumstances of the case.

Solutions therefore focused on preventing such conflicts between e-discovery and data protection laws and suggest avoidance strategies, such as store private information separately, cull and anonymise data, get consent from data subject, limit data request, establish and use EU-compatible data protection policy and register with the Safe Harbor Framework, request opinion of the supervisory authority, etc.

On the other hand, the European data protection rules can also be used as tool and weapon by private persons in certain legal issues, such as a potential discrimination litigation, which makes it somewhat parallel to the US e-discovery practice in that both allow for requests to disclose all personal data held about a natural person in an organisation (under certain conditions).[155] Data Protection Directive (with its proposed amendments on accessibility, data portability, right to be forgotten, etc.) therefore can be turned into an evidence-gathering tool.

Data protection rules are often used as a blocking statute on the face of e-discovery. For foreign enterprises, more complex solutions, mainly preventive strategies, are available if their assessment indicates that there might be a need for cross-border collection of digital evidence, such as the use of Binding Corporate Rules and model contracts or requesting the explicit consent of the data subject to use and transfer personal data overseas. Other conflicts can be found in trade secret regulation and labour laws; also, access to electronically stored information can be

[153] Ibid, p. 45.

[154] Ibid, p. 55.

[155] In Zubulake v. UBS Warburg e-discovery phase, the plaintiff requested the production of all email exchanges between employees in UBS mentioning her name. The same kind of request can, in theory, be made under the European Data Protection Directive in European jurisdictions.

subject to trade secret regulation and be illegal in one country while allowed in another. Therefore, geographical spread of multinational corporations and use of technology may not be optimal when it comes to the question of collection of digital evidence. For these reasons, many authors call for initiating uniformity in business litigation and a convention on electronic evidence. Convergence in technology should be followed by convergence of laws.

### 5.8 *Gaps in Continuity*

Review is an essential part of planning. Reassessment of needs, identification of new scenarios and risks, updates that reflect the changes in the regulative environment and policies, analysis of failures, incorporating lessons learned into the plan and organisation's policies are activities that keep a plan useful and alive, since whatever measures are adopted, they become rapidly obsolete.

Some authors suggest adopting a three-level plan of action for corporations, including anticipatory measures, incident management measures and long-term measures, whereas the first group focuses, among other issues, on preparing specific guides and policies for collection, preservation and retention of data. It has been shown that regulation relevant to data has been changing, and also there are a number of initiatives in the European Union that will seriously affect the way data is or can be handled.[156] This will change the "playbook" for both businesses and to some extent for law enforcement organisations on how to collect digital evidence.

In the incident management measures group the first responder and incident management team procedures can be pointed out, which should provide guidance for collection of evidence during the response to incidents, when there may not be time for long assessments.[157] But most importantly, such plans, policies, guidelines, etc., should be tested and subjected to periodic review in order to ensure that they are up to date and reflect the needs of an organisation to collect digital evidence while using the resources optimally in order to meet those needs.

## 6 Conclusions and Recommendations

This chapter showed that management and collection of digital evidence has very complex legal aspects in international investigations, be it a criminal case, civil case, arbitration or internal investigation within an organisation. The legal aspect is one of the elements of digital forensic readiness, which focuses on how to be prepared for dealing with digital evidence should the need arise. Technical and

---

[156] For example, the Draft Network and Information Security Directive, COM(2013) 48 final.

[157] See Sommers (2008), pp. 31–34.

organisational aspects of digital forensic readiness have been abundantly addressed by academia and practitioners; however, the legal discussion on related issues has been extremely fragmented. For cross-border digital evidence collection, the legal obstacles are certainly one of the most significant problem, and without reflecting on it, the technical and management questions, as described for example in the ISO/IEC standard nr 27037:2012, may become entirely irrelevant.

In this chapter, we identified and analysed the main legal discussion areas relating to digital evidence, whereas we paid special attention to collection of evidence, as perhaps the most critical moment of the management process. Then the common elements found across jurisdictions and branches of laws were consolidated into a model that provides an integrated framework to assess the modules of legal requirements and the most common obstacles that arise in collecting digital evidence. This framework is not aimed at replacing detailed expert opinion, but it rather gives overall guidance in the process of planning and achieving digital forensic readiness in organisations. For these reasons, it can be used as a legal compass in conducting risk analysis and impact assessment on organisational and project/case level for digital forensic readiness. It may perhaps be most useful to integrate the legal requirements model with the existing and upcoming ISO standards on digital forensics.

It should be noted that although the ISO standards dealing with digital evidence and forensics make a good attempt to cover most aspects of digital evidence from a technical/managerial perspective, this cannot replace harmonisation in the legal field relating to criminal and civil court matters. Therefore, the legal requirements model also indicates the weakest links in digital evidence collection and management on the international level. Solutions to these areas can be provided in an individual pace and can be integrated as consensus (and political will) gradually develops.

## References

Alba M (2014) Order out of chaos: technology, intermediation, trust, and reliability as the basis for the recognition of legal effects in electronic transactions. Creighton Law Rev 47:387–521

Alexy R (2014) Constitutional rights and proportionality. Revus 51–65. doi:10.4000/revus.2783

Ashouri A, Bowers C, Warden C (2014) The 2013 Salzburg Workshop on Cyber Investigations: an overview of the use of digital evidence in international criminal courts. Digit Evid Electron Signature Law Rev 11:115–126

Atkinson JS (2014) Proof is not binary: the pace and complexity of computer systems and the challenges digital evidence poses to the legal system. Birkbeck Law Rev 2:245–261

Attfield S, Blandford A (2011) Making sense of digital footprints in team-based legal investigations: the acquisition of focus. Hum Comput Interact 26:38–71

Bennett DW (2011) The challenges facing computer forensics investigators in obtaining information from mobile devices for use in criminal investigations. In: Forensic Focus – Articles. http://articles.forensicfocus.com/2011/08/22/the-challenges-facing-computer-forensics-investigators-in-obtaining-information-from-mobile-devices-for-use-in-criminal-investigations/. Accessed 31 May 2015

Bennett SC (2013) E-discovery: reasonable search, proportionality, cooperation, and advancing technology. John Marshall J Inf Technol Privacy Law 30:433
Boddington R, Hobbs VJ, Mann G (2008) Validating digital evidence for legal argument
Bolt JW, Wheatley JK (2006) Private rules for international discovery in US District Court: the US-German example. UCLA J Int Law Foreign Aff 11:1
Cano Martínez JJ (2012) Documento Gecti nro. 14 Descubrimiento electrónico: evidencia digital en el contexto empresarial. (Spanish). Revista de Derecho Comunicaciones y Nuevas Tecnologías 3–13
Capps D (2013) Fitting a quart into a pint pot: the legal curriculum and meeting the requirements of practice. Digit Evid Electron Signature Law Rev 10:23–28
Carrier B, Spafford EH et al (2003) Getting physical with the digital investigation process. Int J Digit Evid 2:1–20
Center for Strategic and International Studies (2014) Net losses: estimating the global costs of cybercrime
Chasse K (2012) Why a legal opinion is necessary for electronic records management systems. Digit Evid Electron Signature Law Rev 9:17–30
Chorvat TJ, Pelanek LE (2013) Electronically stored information in litigation. Bus Lawyer 69:255–262
CyberCrime@IPA EU/COE Joint Project on Regional Cooperation against Cybercrime (2011) Specialized cybercrime units – good practice study
Democko BM (2012) Social media and the rules on authentication. Univ Toledo Law Rev 43:367–405
Dodson S, Klebba J (2011) Global civil procedure trends in the twenty-first century. Boston Coll Int Comp Law Rev 35:09–68
Duranti L, Rogers C (2012) Trust in digital records: an increasingly cloudy legal area. Comput Law Secur Rev 28:522–531
Forster O, Almughrabi O (2013) Managing the conflict between US E-Discovery and the German Data Protection Act. Hastings Int Comp Law Rev 36:111–144
Garrie DB, Gelb DK (2012) An argument for uniform E-discovery practice in cross-border civil litigation. J Bus Technol Law 7:341–359
Goode S (2009) The admissibility of electronic evidence. Rev Litig 29:1–64
Greenstein MN (2014) Judges must keep up with technology: it's not just for lawyers. Judges' J 53:40
Grimm PW, Bergstrom LY, O'Toole-Loureiro MM (2012) Authentication of social media evidence. Am J Trial Advoc 36:433
Grobler M with Mouhtaropoulos A, Chang-Tsun Li (2014) Digital forensic readiness: are we there yet? J Int Commer Technol 9:173–179
Hannon MJ (2014) An increasingly important requirement: authentication of digital evidence. J Missouri Bar 70:314–323
Hibbard E (2014) Electronic discovery standardization. Ave Maria Law Rev 12:313–393
Hjort MA (2011) Electronic evidence in control of and adversely affecting the opposing party: a comparative study of English and Norwegian Law. Digit Evid Electron Signature Law Rev 8:76–91
Howell D (2009) Developments in electronic disclosure in international arbitration. Disp Resol Int 3:151
Ireton JO (2015) The admissibility of evidence in ICSID arbitration: considering the validity of WikiLeaks cables as evidence. ICSID Rev 30:231–242. doi:10.1093/icsidreview/siu029
Kent K, Chevalier S, Grance T, Dang H (2006) Guide to integrating forensic techniques into incident response
Kerr OS (2005a) Digital evidence and the new criminal procedure. Columbia Law Rev 105:279–318
Kerr OS (2005b) Searches and seizures in a digital world. Harv Law Rev 119:532–585

Lazetik GB, Koshevaliska O (2014) Digital evidence in criminal procedures-a comparative approach. 63–83

Mason S (2008a) Rethinking concepts in virtual evidence. ICFAI J Cyber Law 7:48–54

Mason S (ed) (2008b) International electronic evidence. British Institute of International and Comparative Law, London

Mason S (2012) Vehicle remote keyless entry systems and engine immobilisers: do not believe the insurer that this technology is perfect. Comput Law Secur Rev 28:195–200

McDonald SA (2014) Authenticating digital evidence from the cloud. Army Lawyer 40–50

Mercuri R (2010) Criminal defense challenges in computer forensics. In: Digital forensics and cyber crime. Springer, pp 132–138

Mouhtaropoulos A, Grobler M, Li C-T (2011) Digital forensic readiness: an insight into governmental and academic initiatives. IEEE, pp 191–196

Nearon BH (2005) Foundations in auditing and digital evidence. CPA J 75:32–33

Nobles KC (2012) Emerging issues and trends in international arbitration. Calf W Int Law J 43:77

O'Toole LC (2008) Admitting that we're litigating in the digital age: a practical overview of issues of admissibility in the technological courtroom. FDCC Q 59:3–17

Patzak A, Hilgard MC, Wybitul T (2011) European and German privacy laws and cross-border data transfer in US discovery procedures. Disp Resol Int 5:127–139

Perry DW (2008) EU data protection directive and major factors relied upon by US courts in transborder discovery requests. Digit Evid Electron Signature Law Rev 5:231–234

Pradillo JCO (2011) Fighting against cybercrime in Europe: the admissibility of remote searches in Spain. Eur J Crime Crim Law Crim Just 19:363–395

Ramalho DS (2014) The use of malware as a means of obtaining evidence in Portuguese criminal proceedings. Digit Evid Electron Signature Law Rev 11:55–75

Rowlingson R (2004) A ten step process for forensic readiness. Int J Digit Evid 2:1–28

Selinsek L (2010) Electronic evidence in the Slovene Criminal Procedure Act. Digit Evid Electron Signature Law Rev 7:77

Seventh Circuit Electronic Discovery Pilot Program – Interim Report of Phase Three (2013)

Sipior JC, Ward BT, Volonino L (2014) Benefits and risks of social business: are companies considering E-discovery? Inf Syst Manage 31:328–339. doi:10.1080/10580530.2014.958031

Skrtic D (2013) Electronic evidence and the Croatian Criminal Procedure Act. Digit Evid Electron Signature Law Rev 10:128–135

Sommers P (2008) Directors' and corporate advisors' guide to digital investigations and evidence

Talleur T (2002) Digital evidence: the moral challenge

The Sedona Conference (2008) Framework for analysis of cross-border discovery conflicts: a practical guide to navigating the competing currents of international data privacy and e-discovery

The Sedona Conference (2010) The Sedona Conference commentary on proportionality in electronic discovery

The Sedona Conference (2011) The Sedona Conference international principles on discovery, disclosure and data protection – best practices, recommendations and principles for addressing the preservation discovery of protected data in U.S. litigation

Trocker N (2014) From ALI-UNIDROIT Principles to common European rules on access to information and evidence? A preliminary outlook and some suggestions. Uniform Law Rev – Revue de droit uniforme 19:239–291. doi:10.1093/ulr/unu016

Turner V, Reinsel D, Gantz JF, Minton S (2014) The digital universe of opportunities: rich data and the increasing value of the internet of things. Report

Van Genderen R van den H (2008) Cybercrime investigation and the protection of personal data and privacy – discussion paper

Wong DH (2013) Educating for the future: teaching evidence in the technological age. Digit Evid Electron Signature Law Rev 10:16–22

Yip JT (2012) Addressing the costs and comity concerns on international E-discovery. Wash Law Rev 87:595

FSC
www.fsc.org
MIX
Papier | Fördert gute Waldnutzung
FSC® C083411

Kolibri 360 GmbH
Ferdinand-Jühlke-Straße 7
99095 Erfurt, Deutschland
produktsicherheit@kolibri360.de